# FOREWORD

One of the best kept secrets in the field of topical stamp collecting will no longer be secret with the publication of this *Orchids on Stamps Handbook*. Peg Alrich has compiled the most comprehensive listing of orchid philatelic material ever put together. This promises to be the bible for orchid philatelists for years to come, as it contains the most common as well as the most obscure material with the orchid theme.

Peg is to be commended for the years of research necessary to compile such a thorough study in her chosen area of philatelic endeavors

Andy Lanier
Lake Worth, Florida

# PREFACE

When I began gathering the informatin that would form this handbook, I had no idea where I would get the help that I needed. The ideas came from many pepole who were very generous with their time and expertise. Their contributions range  from the correct classification of the Orchidaceae to the number identification systems used.

So, I must say a very big thank you to Frank Brunone, Evair de Soares, Sam Flagler, Andy Lanier, Eiji Miyoshi and Rainer Schurbohm.

I feel it's necessary to give a brief explanation of the information I have included, so all stamp collectors — be they beginners or long-time enthusiasts — can jump right in and get the most from this handbook.

In the first column at the far left is listed the stamp's date of issue. The second column lists U.S. *Scott* numbers. A note here: If there is an "M" in front of the number in the second column, then the number is from the German *Michel* catalog. Great Britian's *Stan Gibbons* numbers are in the third column. The face value of each stamp is noted in the fourth column.

The fifth column is a bit tricky. The species names designated are correct with current Taxonomic works. However, this may be different from the name that appears on a stamp. The truth is, sometimes, albeit infrequently,  orchids are identified incorrectly on stamps.

In the very last column, I have provided  a brief description or additional comment, to help with your identification of each stamp.

In compiling this handbook, I have realized no matter how hard you work, there are always errors or stamps that should have been included. This handbook works only because of the information exchanged between collectors. I invite you to write and I will exchange ideas and information regarding this orchid list with you.

Peggy Alrich • 42 South Dean Road • Orlando, Florida 32825 USA

| DATE ISSUE | SCOTT/ MICHEL | GIBBON NUMBER | FACE VALUE | SPECIES NAME | BRIEF DESCRIPTION |
|---|---|---|---|---|---|
| **AITUTAKI** | | | | | |
| 1972/11/20 | 52 | | $0.15 | Cattleya | Bridal Bouquet QE2 {Silver Jubilee} Sheetlet/ 5 stamps |
| 1982/06/24 | 262a | | $0.70 | Odontoglossum | Sheetlet/ Bridal Bouquet Di's {Birthday} )GOLD( |
| | 263a | | $1.00 | Odontoglossum | Sheetlet/ Bridal Bouquet Di's {Birthday} )GOLD( |
| | 264b | | $2.00 | Odontoglossum | Sheetlet/ Bridal Bouquet Di's {Birthday} )GOLD( |
| 1982/08/05 | 268a | | $0.70 | Odontoglossum | Sheetlet/ #262a OP "Royal Birth William of Wales" )SILVER( |
| | 269a | | $1.00 | Odontoglossum | Sheetlet/ #263a OP "Royal Birth William of Wales" )SILVER( |
| | 270a | | $2.00 | Odontoglossum | Sheetlet/ #264a OP "Royal Birth William of Wales" )SILVER( |
| **AJMAN** | | | | | |
| 1972 | M429A | --- | 2 riyals | Cattleya | SS/ 1 stamp, selvage design |
| | M430A | --- | 1 riyal | Cattleya | SS/ 1 stamp, selvage design |
| | M431A | --- | 1.25 riy | Odontoglossum | SS/ 1 stamp, selvage design |
| **ALAND** | | | | | |
| 1989/04/10 | 40 | | $1.50 | Dactylorhiza sambucina | |
| | 44 | | $2.50 | Cephalanthera longifolia | |
| | 56 | | $14.00 | Cypripedium calceolus | |
| **ALBANIA** | | | | | |
| 1968/05/10 | 1150 | | 25 quind | Cattleya dowiana v. aurea | |
| | 2284 | | 90 quind | Orchis paparisti | |
| | 2285 | | 2.10 lek | Orchis albanica | |
| **ANGUILLA** | | | | | |
| 1969/06/10 | 73 | | $0.50 | Cattleya chocoensis | |
| 1978/02/20 | 282 | | $0.15 | Tetramicra canaliculata | |
| 1980/12/18 | 404 | | $0.05 | Tetramicra canaliculata | #282 SC & OP "Separation 1980" |
| | 410 | | $0.15 | Tetramicra canaliculata | #282 OP "Separation 1980" |
| | 414 | | $0.25 | Tetramicra canaliculata | #282 SC & OP "Separation 1980" |
| **ANTIGUA** | | | | | |
| 1982/07/01 | 664 | | $1.00 | Odontoglossum | Bridal Bouquet Di's {Birthday}      Sheetlet/ 5 stamps |
| 1982/08/30 | 673 | | $1.00 | Odontoglossum | #664 OP "Royal Baby"      Sheetlet/ 5 stamps |
| 1984/06/01 | 799 | | $2.00 | Odontoglossum | #664 SC in either )GOLD or SILVER( Sheetlet/ 5 stamps |
| | 800 | | $2.00 | Odontoglossum | #673 SC in either )GOLD or SILVER( Sheetlet/ 5 stamps |
| 1985/07/10 | 867 | | $1.00 | Phalaenopsis | Bouquet Queen Mother's {Birthday} |
| 1985/07/15 | 866A | | $0.90 | Phalaenopsis | Bouquet Queen Mother's {Birthday}  Sheetlet/ 5 stamps |
| 1986/04/21 | 925 | | $0.60 | Cattleya | Bridal Bouquet QE2 {60th Birthday} |
| 1988/02/08 | 1068 | | $0.25 | Cattleya | Bridal Bouquet QE2 {40th Wedding Anniversary} |
| 1990/04/17 | 1285 | | $0.15 | Vanilla mexicana | |
| | 1286 | | $0.45 | Epidendrum ibaguense | |
| | 1287 | | $0.50 | Epidendrum secundum | |
| | 1288 | | $0.60 | Maxillaria conferta | |
| | 1289 | | $1.00 | Oncidium altissimum | |
| | 1290 | | $2.00 | Spiranthes lanceolata | |
| | 1291 | | $3.00 | Ionopsis utricularioides | |
| | 1292 | | $5.00 | Epidendrum nocturnum | |
| | 1293 | | $6.00 | Octomeria graminifolia | SS/ 1 stamp |
| | 1294 | | $6.00 | Rodriguezia lanceolata | SS/ 1 stamp |
| **ARGENTINA** | | | | | |
| 1959/05/23 | 680 | | 1 peso | Cattleya labiata | |
| 1982/12/04 | 1348 | | 800 peso | Oncidium bifolium | |
| 1984/11/09 | 1443 | | 100 aust | Oncidium bifolium | |
| 1985/08/22 | 1517 | | 10 austr | Oncidium bifolium | #1517a Phosophos paper variety |
| **AUSTRALIA** | | | | | |
| 1939 | Telegrm TG42e | --- | | Dendrobium bigibbum | |
| 1942/02/12 | 196 | | 5.5 penc | Thelymitra aristata | |
| 1968/07/10 | 438 | | $0.25 | Dendrobium bigibbum | |

| DATE ISSUE | SCOTT/ MICHEL | GIBBON NUMBER | FACE VALUE | SPECIES NAME | BRIEF DESCRIPTION |
|---|---|---|---|---|---|

## AUSTRALIA {Continued}

| DATE ISSUE | SCOTT/ MICHEL | GIBBON NUMBER | FACE VALUE | SPECIES NAME | BRIEF DESCRIPTION |
|---|---|---|---|---|---|
| 1981/09/28 | Enve | #38 | $0.24 | Dendrobium bigibbum | Envelope/ Stamp has orchid |
| 1982/05/19 | Enve | #49 | $0.27 | Dendrobium bigibbum | Envelope/ Stamp has orchid |
| 1986/09/18 | 997 | | $0.36 | Elythranthera emarginata | |
| | 998 | | $0.55 | Dendrobium nindii | |
| | 999 | | $0.90 | Caleana major | |
| | 1000 | | $1.00 | Thelymitra veriegata | |

## AZORES {Portugal}

| DATE ISSUE | SCOTT/ MICHEL | FACE VALUE | SPECIES NAME | BRIEF DESCRIPTION |
|---|---|---|---|---|
| 1981/09/21 | 327 | 20 escud | Platanthera micrantha | |
| | Booklet 328a | $85.50 | Platanthera micrantha | Booklet/ 1 pane of 4 stamps, 1 is #327 |

## BAHAMAS

| DATE ISSUE | SCOTT/ MICHEL | FACE VALUE | SPECIES NAME | BRIEF DESCRIPTION |
|---|---|---|---|---|
| 1987/10/20 | 636 | $0.10 | Cattleyopsis lindeni | |
| | 637 | $0.40 | Encyclia lucayana | |
| | 638 | $0.45 | Encyclia hodgeana | |
| | 639 | $0.50 | Encyclia lleidae | |
| | 639a | SS | Encyclia | SS/ 4 stamps #636 thru #639 |

## BARBADOS

| DATE ISSUE | SCOTT/ MICHEL | GIBBON NUMBER | FACE VALUE | SPECIES NAME | BRIEF DESCRIPTION |
|---|---|---|---|---|---|
| 1970/08/24 | 350 | | $0.10 | Epidendrum ciliare | |
| | 352a | | SS | Epidendrum ciliare | SS/ 5 stamps, 1 is #350 |
| 1974/09/16 | 396 | | $0.01 | Cattleya gaskelliana v. alba | #396a/543 Wmk 314 and #396b/510 Wmk 373 |
| | 397 | | $0.02 | Renanthera storiei | #397a/544 Wmk 314 and #397b/511 Wmk 373 |
| | 398 | | $0.03 | Dendrobium Rose Marie | #398a/545 Wmk 314 and #398b/512 Wmk 373 |
| | 399 | | $0.04 | Epidendrum ibaguense | #399a/546 Wmk 314 and #399b/513 Wmk 373 |
| | 400 | | $0.05 | Schomburgkia humboldtii | #400b/514 Wmk 373 |
| | 400a | Bookle | $1.12 | Schomburgkia | Booklet/3 panes of #400/4, #401/4 and #404/4 stamps |
| | 401 | | $0.08 | Oncidium ampliatum | |
| | 402 | | $0.10 | Arachnis Maggie Oei | #402a/547 Wmk 314 and #402b/515 Wmk 373 |
| | 403 | | $0.12 | Dendrobium aggregatum | #403b/516 Wmk 373 |
| | 404 | | $0.15 | Paphiopedilum FC Puddle | #404a/548 Wmk 314 and #404b/517 Wmk 373 |
| | 405 | | $0.25 | Epidendrum ciliare | #405a/549 Wmk 314 and #405b/518 Wmk 373 |
| | 406 | | $0.35 | Bletia patula | #406a/550 Wmk 314 |
| | 407 | | $0.50 | Phalaenopsis schilleriana v. Sunset Glow | #407b/520 Wmk 373 |
| | 408 | | $1.00 | Ascocenda Red Gem | #408a/551 Wmk 314 and #408b/521 Wmk 373 |
| | 409 | | $2.50 | Brassolaeliocattleya Nugget | #409b/522 Wmk 373 |
| | 410 | | $5.00 | Caularthron bicornutum | #410b/523 Wmk 373 |
| | 411 | | $10.00 | Vanda Josephine Black | #411b/524 Wmk 373 |
| 1977/02/07 | 454 | | $1.00 | Cattleya | Bridal Bouquet QE2 {Silver Jubilee} |
| 1977/05/03 | 404C | | $0.20 | Spathoglottis aurea v. The Gold | |
| | 406B | | $0.45 | Phalaenopsis schilleriana v. Sunset Glow | #406b/519 Wmk 373 |
| 1977/10/11 | Aero | #K6 | $0.25 | Epidendrum ciliare | Aerogram/ Stamp has two orchids |
| 1977/10/31 | 469 | | $1.00 | Cattleya | Bridal Bouquet QE2 {Royal Visit} |
| 1979/05/29 | B2 | | $0.28+4 | Bletia patula | #406 Surcharged |
| 1979/11/19 | Aero | #K7 | $0.25 | Epidendrum ciliare | Aerogram/ #K6 PR, panels switched |
| 1981/07/22 | 547 | | $0.28 | Cattleya | Charles Wedding Wreath |
| 1982/07/01 | 587 | | $1.20 | Odontoglossum | Bridal Bouquet Di's {Birthday} |

## BARBUDA

| DATE ISSUE | SCOTT/ MICHEL | FACE VALUE | SPECIES NAME | BRIEF DESCRIPTION |
|---|---|---|---|---|
| 1982/08/30 | 8215 | $1.00 | Odontoglossum | Antigua #664 OP "Barbuda Mail" Sheetlet/ 5 stamps, 1 label |
| 1982/10/12 | 8218 | $1.00 | Odontoglossum | Antigua #673 OP "Barbuda Mail" Sheetlet/ 5 stamps, 1 label |
| 1985/11/08 | 8560 | $1.00 | Phalaenopsis | Antigua #867 OP "Barbuda Mail" in >SILVER or BLACK< |
| 1985/12/01 | 8559A | $0.90 | Phalaenopsis | Antigua #886A OP "Barbuda Mail" Sheetlet/ 5 stamps, 1 label |
| 1986/04/21 | 8625 | $1.00 | Laelia species | |
| | 8627 | $2.50 | Cymbidium | |
| | 8628 | $5.00 | Cymbidium | SS/ 1 stamp, on sides |
| 1986/08/12 | 8636 | $0.60 | Cattleya | Antigua #925 OP "Barbuda Mail" |
| 1988/07/04 | 8820 | $0.25 | Cattleya | Antigua #1068 OP "Barbuda Mail" |
| 1990/07/15 | 9032 | $0.15 | Vanilla mexicana | Antigua #1285 OP "Barbuda Mail" |
| | 9033 | $0.45 | Epidendrum ibaguense | Antigua #1286 OP "Barbuda Mail" |
| | 9034 | $0.50 | Epidendrum secundum | Antigua #1287 OP "Barbuda Mail" |
| | 9035 | $0.60 | Maxillaria conferta | Antigua #1288 OP "Barbuda Mail" |

| DATE ISSUE | SCOTT/ MICHEL | GIBBON NUMBER | FACE VALUE | SPECIES NAME | BRIEF DESCRIPTION |
|---|---|---|---|---|---|

## BARBUDA {Continued}

| DATE ISSUE | SCOTT/ MICHEL | GIBBON NUMBER | FACE VALUE | SPECIES NAME | BRIEF DESCRIPTION |
|---|---|---|---|---|---|
| 1990/07/15 | 9036 | | $1.00 | Oncidium altissimum | Antigua #1289 OP "Barbuda Mail" |
| | 9037 | | $2.00 | Spiranthes lanceolata | Antigua #1290 OP "Barbuda Mail" |
| | 9038 | | $3.00 | Ionopsis utricularioides | Antigua #1291 OP "Barbuda Mail" |
| | 9039 | | $5.00 | Epidendrum nocturnum | Antigua #1292 OP "Barbuda Mail" |
| | 9040 | | $6.00 | Octomeria graminifolia | SS/ 1 stamp, Antigua #1293 OP "Barbuda Mail" |
| | 9041 | | $6.00 | **Rodriguezia lanceolata** | SS/ 1 stamp, Antigua #1294 OP "Barbuda Mail" |

## BELGIAN CONGO

| DATE ISSUE | SCOTT/ MICHEL | GIBBON NUMBER | FACE VALUE | SPECIES NAME | BRIEF DESCRIPTION |
|---|---|---|---|---|---|
| 1952/05/20 | 268 | | $0.50 | Eurychone galeandrae | |
| 1952/08/25 | 274 | | 2 francs | Ansellia gigantea | |
| 1953/01/05 | 283 | | 50 franc | Eulophia cucullata | |

## BELGIUM

| DATE ISSUE | SCOTT/ MICHEL | GIBBON NUMBER | FACE VALUE | SPECIES NAME | BRIEF DESCRIPTION |
|---|---|---|---|---|---|
| 1940 | Post | | $0.50 | Vanilla | Advertising Postcard/ Aliante Socri-Vanila )French( |
| | Post | | $0.50 | Vanilla | Advertising Postcard/ Aliante Socri-Vanila )Flemish( |
| 1951/09/22 | B498 | | $0.90 | Miltonia | Corsage )Greenish Grey( |
| | B499 | | 1.75 fra | Miltonia | Corsage )Plum( |
| | B500 | | 3 francs | Miltonia | Corsage )Green( |
| | B501 | | 4 francs | Miltonia | Corsage )Gray Blue( |
| | B502 | | 8 francs | Miltonia | Corsage )Sepia( |
| 1954 | Post | | 1.20 fra | Vanilla | Advertising Postcard/ Letter "Molens Vanille Pudding" |
| | Post | | 1.20 fra | Vanilla | Advertising Postcard/ Box "Molens Vanille Pudding" |
| | Post | | 1.20 fra | Vanilla | Advertising Postcard/ Logo "Molens Vanille Pudding" |
| | Post | | 1.20 fra | Vanilla | Advertising Postcard/ PANA "Sucre Vanilline" |
| 1955/02/15 | 484 | | 4 francs | Paphiopedilum insigne | Ghent International Flower Exhibition |
| | NS | --- | EXHIBIT | Paphiopedilum insigne | Exhibition Sheet/ 3 stamps, 1 is #484 |
| 1985/03/01 | Post | --- | Prepaid | Cattleya | Announcement Postcard/ And other orchid cancels )Flemish( |
| | Post | --- | Prepaid | Cattleya | Announcement Postcard/ And other orchid cancels )French( |
| | Post | --- | Prepaid | Cattleya | Announcement Postcard/ And other orchid cancels )German( |
| 1985/03/18 | 1187 | | 12 franc | Vanda coerulea | |
| | 1188 | | 12 franc | Phalaenopsis Lippstick v. Malibu | |
| | 1189 | | 12 franc | Sophrolaeliocattleya Riffe Burlingame | |
| 1987/03/16 | B1060 | | 9 francs | Ophrys apifera | |
| 1990/02/01 | Post | --- | Prepaid | Cattleya harrisoniana | Announcement Postcard/ Cancels )Flemish( |
| | Post | --- | Prepaid | Cattleya harrisoniana | Announcement Postcard/ Cancels )French( |
| | Post | --- | Prepaid | Cattleya harrisoniana | Announcement Postcard/ Cancels )German( |
| 1990/03/03 | 1334 | | 14 franc | Cattleya harrisoniana | |

## BELIZE

| DATE ISSUE | SCOTT/ MICHEL | GIBBON NUMBER | FACE VALUE | SPECIES NAME | BRIEF DESCRIPTION |
|---|---|---|---|---|---|
| 1977/02/07 | 385 | | $2.00 | Cattleya | Bridal Bouquet QE2 {Silver Jubilee} and #385a Wmk sideways |
| 1980/12/30 | M534 | | $1.00 | Cattleya | Label, in Child's hand |
| 1981/12/18 | M610 | | $0.50 | Encyclia cochleata | |
| 1985/07/25 | 528 | | SS | Cattleya | SS/ 10 stamps, 2 are #528g and #528i |
| | 528g | | $0.50 | Bletia & Brassavola | Br.Honduras #307 RP, stamp on stamp |
| | 528i | | $0.50 | Cattleya | #385 RP, stamp on stamp |
| 1985/10/09 | 549 | | $4.00 | Epidendrum stamfordianum | Sheetlet/ 3 stamps and 3 strips, 1 is #549 |
| 1985/12/20 | 561 | | SS | Cattleya | SS/ 10 stamps, 2 are #561g and #561i |
| | 561g | | $0.50 | Bletia & Brassavola | #528g OP "Pre-World Cup Football, Mexico 1986" |
| | 561i | | $0.50 | Cattleya | #528i OP "Pre-World Cup Football, Mexico 1986" |
| 1987/12/16 | 647 | | $0.01 | Laelia euspatha | 8/1 |
| | 647a | | SH | Stanhopea shuttleworthii | Sheetlet/ 1 Label {35/1}, 2 stamps each #647 thru #653 |
| | 648 | | $0.02 | Encyclia citrina | 20/1 |
| | 649 | | $0.03 | Masdevallia chimaera v. backhousiana | 19/1 |
| | 650 | | $0.04 | Paphiopedilum tautzianum | 65/1 |
| | 651 | | $0.05 | Trichopilia suavis v. alba | 31/1 |
| | 652 | | $0.06 | Odontoglossum hebraicum | 37/1 |
| | 653 | | $0.07 | Cattleya trianae v. schroederiana | 46/1 |
| | 654 | | $0.10 | Rhynchostylis gigantea | 22/1 |
| | 654a | | SH | Oncidium splendidum | Sheetlet/ 1 Label {78/1}, 2 stamps each #654 thru #660 |
| | 655 | | $0.30 | Cattleya warscewiczii | 72/1 |
| | 656 | | $0.50 | Chysis bractescens | 18/1 |

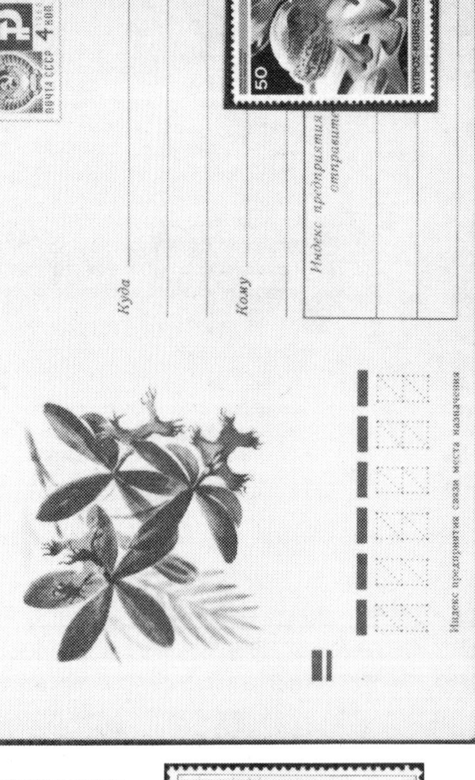
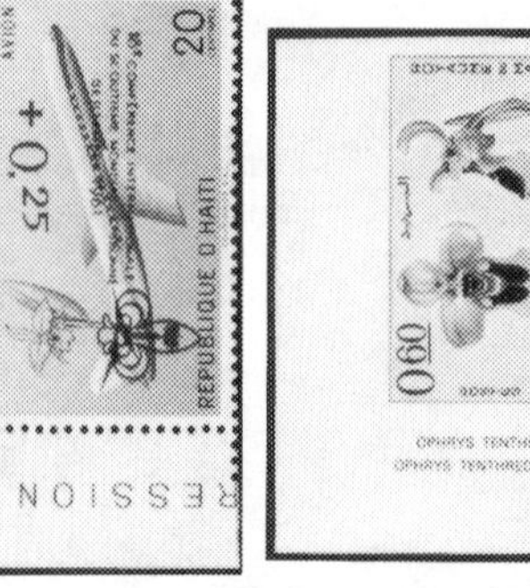

SHARJAH 1972 Unlisted; ZIL ELOIGNE SESEL M397; SAINT KILDA 1970 Unlisted; RUSSIA 1973 Envelope; CYPRUS 566; PANAMA C357; HAITI CB32a ; MOROCCO 131; GUYANA 373 & 610a; SAINT VINCENT 494; BELIZE 657; and BULGARIA 3141.

## BELIZE {Continued}

| DATE ISSUE | SCOTT/MICHEL | GIBBON NUMBER | FACE VALUE | SPECIES NAME | BRIEF DESCRIPTION |
|---|---|---|---|---|---|
| 1987/12/16 | 657 | | $0.70 | Cattleya rochellensis | 85/1 |
| | 658 | | $1.00 | Laeliocattleya elegans | 52/1 |
| | 659 | | $1.50 | Laelia anceps v. percivaliana | 36/1 |
| | 660 | | $3.00 | Laelia gouldiana | 59/1 |
| | 660A | | $3.00 | Miltoniopsis roezlii | SS/ 1 stamp {69/1} |
| | 661 | | $5.00 | Cattleya dowiana v. aurea | SS/ 1 stamp {5/1} |
| 1990/11/01 | 716 | | $0.25 | Cattleya bowringiana | |
| | 717 | | $0.50 | Brassavola digbyana | |
| | 718 | | $0.60 | Sobralia macrantha | |
| | 719 | | $0.75 | Chysis bractescens | |
| | 720 | | $1.00 | Vanilla planifolia | |
| | 721 | | $2.00 | Epidendrum polyanthum | |

## BHUTAN

| DATE ISSUE | SCOTT/MICHEL | GIBBON NUMBER | FACE VALUE | SPECIES NAME | BRIEF DESCRIPTION |
|---|---|---|---|---|---|
| 1967/02/09 | M133 | | 10 chetr | Pleione hookeriana | |
| | M137 | | 4 ngultr | Pleione hookeriana | |
| 1968/05/20 | M216 | | 6 ngultr | Dendrobium nobile | >3D< |
| | MB14 | | SS | Dendrobium nobile | SS/ 4 stamps, 1 is #M216 >3D< |
| 1970/06/01 | M362 | | 20 chetr | Pleione hookeriana | #M137 Surcharged |
| 1976/05/29 | 221 | | 1 chetru | Coelogyne ochracea | |
| | 222 | | 2 chetru | Thunia alba | |
| | 223 | | 3 chetru | Dendrobium parishii | |
| | 229 | | 10 ngult | Dendrobium primulinum & Vanda coerulea | SS/ 1 stamp |
| 1981/07/01 | 333 | | 25 chetr | Odontoglossum | Bridal Bouquet Di's {Birthday} |
| 1982/11/19 | 362 | | 25 chetr | Odontoglossum | #333 OP "Royal Baby" |
| 1984/08/29 | 434 | | 3 ngultr | Pleione hookeriana | Background of car |
| 1984/10/01 | 458 | | 40 ngult | Odontoglossum | #333 Surcharged |
| | 479 | | 40 ngult | Odontoglossum | #362 Surcharged |
| 1990/04/06 | 870 | | 10 chetr | Renanthera monachica | |
| | 871 | | 50 chetr | Vanda coerulea | |
| | 872 | | 1 ngultr | Phalaenopsis violacea | |
| | 873 | | 2 ngultr | Dendrobium nobile | |
| | 874 | | 5 ngultr | Vandopsis lissochiloides | |
| | 875 | | 6 ngultr | Paphiopedilum rothschildianum | |
| | 876 | | 7 ngultr | Phalaenopsis schilleriana | |
| | 877 | | 9 ngultr | Paphiopedilum insigne | |
| | 878 | | 10 ngult | Paphiopedilum bellatulum | |
| | 879 | | 20 ngult | Doritis pulcherrima | |
| | 880 | | 25 ngult | Cymbidium giganteum | |
| | 881 | | 35 ngult | Phalaenopsis mariae | |
| | 882 | | 30 ngult | Vanda coerulescens | SS/ 1 stamp |
| | 883 | | 30 ngult | Vandopsis parishii | SS/ 1 stamp |
| | 884 | | 30 ngult | Dendrobium aphyllum | SS/ 1 stamp |
| | 885 | | 30 ngult | Phalaenopsis amabilis | SS/ 1 stamp |
| | 886 | | 30 ngult | Paphiopedilum haynaldianum | SS/ 1 stamp |
| | 887 | | 30 ngult | Dendrobium loddigesii | SS/ 1 stamp |
| | 888 | | 30 ngult | Vanda alpina | SS/ 1 stamp |
| | 889 | | 30 ngult | Phalaenopsis equestris | SS/ 1 stamp |
| | 890 | | 30 ngult | Vanda cristata | SS/ 1 stamp |
| | 891 | | 30 ngult | Phalaenopsis cornu-cervi | SS/ 1 stamp |
| | 892 | | 30 ngult | Paphiopedilum niveum | SS/ 1 stamp |
| | 893 | | 30 ngult | Dendrobium margaritaceum | SS/ 1 stamp |

## BOLIVIA

| DATE ISSUE | SCOTT/MICHEL | GIBBON NUMBER | FACE VALUE | SPECIES NAME | BRIEF DESCRIPTION |
|---|---|---|---|---|---|
| 1962/06/28 | 460 | | 400 boli | Vanda tricolor v. suavis | |
| 1962/06/28 | 462 | | 1000 bol | Sobralia macrantha | |
| 1974/05/15 | 558 | | $0.20 | Cattleya nobilior | |
| | 559 | | $0.50 | Zygopetalum bolivianum | #559a Black omitted |
| | 560 | | 1 peso | Huntleya meleagris | |
| | C327 | | 2.50 pes | Cattleya luteola | |
| | C328 | | 3.80 pes | Stanhopea grandiflora | |
| | C329 | | 4 pesos | Catasetum saccatum | |

| DATE ISSUE | SCOTT/ MICHEL | GIBBON NUMBER | FACE VALUE | SPECIES NAME | BRIEF DESCRIPTION |
|---|---|---|---|---|---|

## BOLIVIA {Continued}

| DATE ISSUE | SCOTT/ MICHEL | GIBBON NUMBER | FACE VALUE | SPECIES NAME | BRIEF DESCRIPTION |
|---|---|---|---|---|---|
| 1974/05/15 | C330 | | 5 pesos | Maxillaria triloris | |
| 1974/05/20 | MB38 | --- | SS | Stanhopea & Cattleya | SS/ 2 stamps #C328 and #558 "Soccer Champions, Munich 1974" |
| | MB39 | --- | SS | Zygopetalum & Huntleya | SS/ 2 stamps #559 and #560 "Soccer Champions, Munich 1974" |
| 1974/05/31 | MB40 | 943a | 14.90 pe | Maxillaria triloris | SS/ 3 stamps, 1 is #C330 |
| | MB41 | 943b | 15.50 pe | Catasetum saccatum | SS/ 3 stamps, 1 is #C329 |
| | MB42 | 943c | 16.70 pe | Cattleya luteola | SS/ 3 stamps, 1 is #C327 |
| 1974/09/21 | MB44 | --- | 14.90 pe | Maxillaria triloris | SS/ #MB40 OP "Frankfurt, Argentina and UPU" |
| | MB45 | --- | 15.50 pe | Catasetum saccatum | SS/ #MB41 OP "UPU Congress" |
| | MB46 | --- | 16.70 pe | Cattleya luteola | SS/ #MB42 OP "UPU Congress" |
| 1984/06/27 | 704 | | 10,000 b | Stanhopea grandiflora | #C328 SC and #704a Inverted surcharge |
| 1985/12/31 | MB148 | --- | 10,000 b | Stanhopea grandiflora | SS/ 1 stamp #704 RP, along with a Rafael painting |
| 1989/02/17 | 782 | | $0.50 | Paphiopedilum hybrid | |

## BOPHTHATSWANA

| DATE ISSUE | SCOTT/ MICHEL | GIBBON NUMBER | FACE VALUE | SPECIES NAME | BRIEF DESCRIPTION |
|---|---|---|---|---|---|
| 1983 | Telegrm T16b | --- | | Disa uniflora | |

## BOTSWANA

| DATE ISSUE | SCOTT/ MICHEL | GIBBON NUMBER | FACE VALUE | SPECIES NAME | BRIEF DESCRIPTION |
|---|---|---|---|---|---|
| 1978/11/06 | 224 | | 25 thebe | Ansellia gigantea | |
| 1989/10/30 | 464 | | 8 thebe | Eulophia angolensis | |
| | 465 | | 15 thebe | Eulophia hereroensis | |
| | 466 | | 30 thebe | Eulophia speciosa | |
| | 467 | | 60 thebe | Eulophia petersii | |

## BRITISH HONDURAS

| DATE ISSUE | SCOTT/ MICHEL | GIBBON NUMBER | FACE VALUE | SPECIES NAME | BRIEF DESCRIPTION |
|---|---|---|---|---|---|
| 1953/09/01 | 155 | | L5.00 | Cattleya bowringiana | |
| 1968/04/16 | 208 | | $0.05 | Schomburgkia tibicinis | 20th Anniversary of Economic Commission for Latin America |
| | 209 | | $0.10 | Maxillaria tenuifolia | |
| | 210 | | $0.22 | Bletia purpurea | |
| | 211 | | $0.25 | Sobralia macrantha | |
| 1969/04/09 | 226 | | $0.05 | Brassavola digbyana | |
| | 227 | | $0.10 | Cattleya bowringiana | |
| | 228 | | $0.22 | Lycaste cochleata | |
| | 229 | | $0.25 | Coryanthes speciosa | |
| 1970/04/02 | 255 | | $0.05 | Encyclia cochleata | |
| | 256 | | $0.15 | Brassavola nodosa | |
| | 257 | | $0.22 | Cycnoches warscewiczii | |
| | 258 | | $0.25 | Brassia maculata | |
| 1972/11/20 | 306 | | $0.26 | Bletia purpurata & Brassavola nodosa | #306a/341a Wmk inverted  [Bletia left and Brassavola right] |
| | 307 | | $0.50 | Bletia purpurata & Brassavola nodosa | Bletia left and Brassavola right |

## BRITISH INDIAN OCEAN TERRETORIES

| DATE ISSUE | SCOTT/ MICHEL | GIBBON NUMBER | FACE VALUE | SPECIES NAME | BRIEF DESCRIPTION |
|---|---|---|---|---|---|
| 1968/01/17 | 2 | | $0.10 | Vanilla planifolia | Seychelles #199 OP "B.I.O.T." and #2a Some dots missing |

## BRITISH SOLOMON ISLANDS

| DATE ISSUE | SCOTT/ MICHEL | GIBBON NUMBER | FACE VALUE | SPECIES NAME | BRIEF DESCRIPTION |
|---|---|---|---|---|---|
| 1965/05/24 | 129 | | $0.01 | Dendrobium veratrifolium | |
| | 136 | | 1 shilli | Dendrobium macrophyllum | |
| | 137 | | 1/3 shil | Dendrobium spectabile | |
| 1966/02/14 | 150 | | $0.02 | Dendrobium veratrifolium | #129 SC and #150a Wmk sideways |
| | 157 | | $0.10 | Dendrobium macrophyllum | #136 SC and #157a Wmk sideways |
| | 158 | | $0.12 | Dendrobium spectabile | #137 SC and #158a Wmk sideways |
| | 159 | | $0.13 | Dendrobium spectabile | #137 SC and #159a Wmk sideways |
| 1972/07/03 | 241 | | $0.20 | Spathoglottis plicata | |
| | 242 | | $0.25 | Ephemerantha comata | |
| | 243 | | $0.35 | Dendrobium cuthbertsonii | |

## BRITISH VIRGIN ISLANDS

| DATE ISSUE | SCOTT/ MICHEL | GIBBON NUMBER | FACE VALUE | SPECIES NAME | BRIEF DESCRIPTION |
|---|---|---|---|---|---|
| 1981/03/03 | 401 | | $0.05 | Oncidium prionochilum | |
| 1981/07/22 | 406 | | $0.10 | Oncidium prionochilum | Charles Wedding Wreath and #406b Wmk inverted |
| | Booklet 406a | | $3.40 | Oncidium prionochilum | Booklet/ 1 pane of 4 stamps, 1 is #406 |
| 1987/09/20 | 588 | | $1.50 | Epidendrum brittonianum | |

| DATE ISSUE | SCOTT/ MICHEL | GIBBON NUMBER | FACE VALUE | SPECIES NAME | BRIEF DESCRIPTION |
|---|---|---|---|---|---|

# BRAZIL

| DATE ISSUE | SCOTT/ MICHEL | GIBBON NUMBER | FACE VALUE | SPECIES NAME | BRIEF DESCRIPTION |
|---|---|---|---|---|---|
| 1939/08/23 | 477 | | 400 reis | Cattleya bicolor | #477a perf proof |
| 1943/11/13 | 616 | | $0.40 | Cattleya labiata | #616a perf proof |
| 1946/11/08 | 652 | | $0.40 | Laelia purpurata | #652a unwatermark |
| 1959/10/04 | 896 | | 2.50 cru | Cattleya labiata | #896a marble paper |
| 1963/11/05 | 968 | | 8 cruzer | Laelia | |
| 1971/11/16 | 1203 | | 40 cruze | Laelia purpurata v. werkhauserii | |
| 1976/06/04 | 1438 | | 1 cruzer | Acacallis cyanea | |
| 1980/10/03 | 1711 | | 5 reis | Cattleya amethystoglossa | |
| | 1712 | | 5 reis | Laelia cinnabarina | |
| | 1713 | | 24 reis | Zygopetalum citrinum | |
| | 1714 | | 28 reis | Laelia tenebrosa | |
| 1982/04/17 | 1792a | | 75 cruze | Laelia purpurata | |
| | 1792b | | 80 cruze | Oncidium flexuosum | |
| | 1792c | | 85 cruze | Cleistes revoluta | SS/ 3 stamps, #1792a thru #1792c |
| 1983/05/21 | 1860 | | 215 cruz | Cattleya anceps | Background of bird |
| 1987/12/03 | 2121 | | 6 cruzer | Laelia lobata | |
| | 2122 | | 6 cruzer | Cattleya guttata | |
| 1987/12/21 | 2124 | | 7 cruzer | Odontoglossum grande | Lower left |

# BULGARIA

| DATE ISSUE | SCOTT/ MICHEL | GIBBON NUMBER | FACE VALUE | SPECIES NAME | BRIEF DESCRIPTION |
|---|---|---|---|---|---|
| 1960/07/27 | 1111 | | 60 stoti | Cypripedium calceolus | |
| 1986/02/12 | 3140 | | $0.05 | Dactylorhiza romana | |
| | 3141 | | $0.13 | Epipactis palustris | |
| | 3142 | | $0.30 | Ophrys cornuta | |
| | 3143 | | $0.32 | Limodorum abortivum | |
| | 3144 | | $0.42 | Cypripedium calceolus | |
| | 3145 | | $0.60 | Orchis papilionacea | Sheetlet/ 6 stamps, #3140 thru #3145 |
| 1990/01/01 | Enve | --- | $0.05 | Cattleya | Envelope/ Cachet has single >Pink< orchid |
| | Enve | --- | $0.05 | Laelia | Envelope/ Cachet has single orchid |
| 1990/06/01 | Enve | --- | $0.05 | Cattleya | Envelope/ Cachet has single >Blue< orchid |

# BURUNDI

| DATE ISSUE | SCOTT/ MICHEL | GIBBON NUMBER | FACE VALUE | SPECIES NAME | BRIEF DESCRIPTION |
|---|---|---|---|---|---|
| 1966/04/30 | 143 | | 1.50 fra | Ansellia gigantea v. nilotica | |
| 1966/05/18 | 149 | | 6.50 fra | Ansellia gigantea v. nilotica | |
| | MB-- | --- | SS | Ansellia gigantea v. nilotica | SS/ #MB17 "Royaume du Burundi" without >GOLD< Overprint |
| | MB-- | --- | SS | Ansellia gigantea v. nilotica | SS/ #MB18 "Royaume du Burundi" without >GOLD< Overprint |
| | MB-- | --- | SS | Ansellia gigantea v. nilotica | SS/ #MB19 "Royaume du Burundi" without >GOLD< Overprint |
| | MB-- | --- | SS | Ansellia gigantea v. nilotica | SS/ #MB20 "Royaume du Burundi" without >GOLD< Overprint |
| 1966/10/10 | C19 | | 10 franc | Ansellia gigantea v. nilotica | GOLD background |
| 1967/02/06 | 161 | | 1.50 fra | Ansellia gigantea v. nilotica | #143 OP "Republic du Burundi" |
| | 167 | | 6.50 fra | Ansellia gigantea v. nilotica | #149 OP "Republic du Burundi" |
| | C29 | | 10 franc | Ansellia gigantea v. nilotica | #C19 OP "Republic du Burundi" >GOLD< background |
| | MB17 | | SS | Ansellia gigantea v. nilotica | SS/ 8 stamps, 1 is orchid >Coat of Arms in center frame< |
| | MB18 | | SS | Ansellia gigantea v. nilotica | SS/ 8 stamps, 1 is orchid >Flag of Country in center frame< |
| | MB19 | | SS | Ansellia gigantea v. nilotica | SS/ 8 stamps, 1 is orchid >Map of Country in center frame< |
| | MB20 | | SS | Ansellia gigantea v. nilotica | SS/ 8 stamps, 1 is orchid >Gazania Flower in center frame< |
| 1970/11/28 | C140 | | 6 francs | Cattleya | Bouquet Queen Fabiola of Belgium |
| | C142a | | SS | Cattleya | SS/ 3 stamps, 1 is #C140 |
| 1972/02/06 | 411 | | $0.50 | Platycoryne crocea | |
| | 412 | | 1 franc | Cattleya trianae | |
| | 413 | | 2 francs | Eulophia cucullata | |
| | 414 | | 3 francs | Cymbidium Hamsey | |
| | 415 | | 4 francs | Thelymitra pauciflora | |
| | 416 | | 5 francs | Miltassia hybrid | |
| | 417 | | 6 francs | Miltonia hybrid | |
| 1972/11/29 | 418 | | 7 francs | Platycoryne crocea | |
| | 419 | | 8 francs | Cattleya trianae | |
| | 420 | | 9 francs | Eulophia cucullata | |
| | 421 | | 10 franc | Cymbidium Hamsey | |
| 1973/01/18 | C168 | | 13 franc | Thelymitra pauciflora | |
| | C169 | | 14 franc | Miltassia hybrid | |

## BURUNDI {Continued}

| DATE ISSUE | SCOTT/ MICHEL | GIBBON NUMBER | FACE VALUE | SPECIES NAME | BRIEF DESCRIPTION |
|---|---|---|---|---|---|
| 1973/01/18 | C170 | | 15 franc | Miltonia hybrid | |
| | C171 | | 18 franc | Platycoryne crocea | |
| | C172 | | 20 franc | Cattleya trianae | |
| | C173 | | 27 franc | Eulophia cucullata | |
| | C174 | | 36 franc | Cymbidium Hamsey | |

## CANADA

| DATE ISSUE | SCOTT/ MICHEL | GIBBON NUMBER | FACE VALUE | SPECIES NAME | BRIEF DESCRIPTION |
|---|---|---|---|---|---|
| 1965/07/21 | 424 | | $0.05 | Cypripedium acaule | |
| 1973/10/17 | Aero | A43 | $0.15 | Cypripedium acaule | Aerogram/ Stamp and cachet has single orchid |
| | Aero | LS14 | $0.08 | Cypripedium acaule | Domesogram/ Stamp and cachet has single orchid |
| 1974/03/04 | Aero | LS26 | $0.08 | Cypripedium acaule | Domesogram/ #LS14 RP, revised spelling "Postes" |
| 1974/11/19 | Aero | A55 | $0.15 | Cypripedium acaule | Aerogram/ #A43 RP, revised spelling "Postes" |
| 1977/04/22 | 711 | | $0.10 | Cypripedium passerinum | Descriptive tabs, No. 1 >Perf 12x12.5< #711b Precancelled |
| 1977/11/01 | Booklet BK77 | | $0.50 | Cypripedium passerinum | Booklet/ Cover design >Sepia< |
| 1978/04/01 | Booklet BK78 | | $0.50 | Cypripedium passerinum | Booklet/ Cover design >Green< |
| 1978/10/03 | 711a | | $0.10 | Cypripedium passerinum | Descriptive tabs, No.2 >Perf 13< |
| 1979/04/28 | Booklet BK80 | | $0.50 | Cypripedium passerinum | Booklet/ Cover design >Blue< |
| 1979/10/04 | 786 | | $0.10 | Cypripedium passerinum | Descriptive tabs, No. 3 >Perf 13x13.5< |

## CAYMAN ISLANDS

| DATE ISSUE | SCOTT/ MICHEL | GIBBON NUMBER | FACE VALUE | SPECIES NAME | BRIEF DESCRIPTION |
|---|---|---|---|---|---|
| 1962/11/28 | 155 | | 1.5 penn | Schomburgkia thomsoniana | |
| 1971/04/07 | 287 | | 1/4 penn | Dendrophylax fawcettii | |
| | 288 | | $0.02 | Schomburgkia thomsoniana | |
| | 289 | | $0.10 | Vanilla claviculata | |
| | 290 | | $0.40 | Oncidium variegatum | |
| 1981/07/22 | 471 | | $0.20 | Schomburgkia thomsoniana | Charles Wedding Wreath |
| 1982/07/01 | 488 | | $0.40 | Odontoglossum | Bridal Bouquet Di's {Birthday} |
| 1985/03/13 | 535 | | $0.05 | Schomburgkia thomsoniana v. minor | |
| | 536 | | $0.10 | Schomburgkia thomsoniana | |
| | 537 | | $0.25 | Encyclia plicata | |
| | 538 | | $0.50 | Dendrophylax fawcettii | |

## CENTRAL AFRICA

| DATE ISSUE | SCOTT/ MICHEL | GIBBON NUMBER | FACE VALUE | SPECIES NAME | BRIEF DESCRIPTION |
|---|---|---|---|---|---|
| 1966/05/16 | 67 | | 2 francs | Eulophia cucullata | |
| | 68 | | 5 francs | Eulophia horsfallii | |
| | 69 | | 10 franc | Tridactyle bicaudata | |
| | 70 | | 15 franc | Polystachya affinis | |
| | 71 | | 20 franc | Eulophia alta | |
| | 72 | | 25 franc | Microcoelia macrorhynchium | |
| 1967/05/08 | 78 | | 10 franc | Microcoelia macrorhynchium | #72 Surcharged |
| 1981/09/21 | C253 | | 500 fran | Odontoglossum | Bridal Bouquet Di's {Wedding} |
| | C253a | | 500 fran | Odontoglossum | MS/ 1 stamp, Bridal Bouquet Di's {Wedding} |
| 1982/07/01 | MB191 | | 1500 fra | Odontoglossum | MS/ 1 stamp, Bridal Bouquet Di's {Birthday} >GOLD< |
| 1982/07/20 | C274 | | 600 fran | Odontoglossum | SS/ 1 stamp, Bridal Bouquet Di's {Birthday} |
| 1982/09/01 | 8203_ | | 1500 fra | Odontoglossum | MS/ 1 stamp, Bridal Bouquet Di's {Wedding} >GOLD< |
| | 8203a | | 10 franc | Odontoglossum | MS/ #8203 Surcharged |
| 1984/02/25 | 648 | | 500 fran | Odontoglossum | Bridal Bouquet Di's {Wedding} |
| | 648a | | SS | Odontoglossum | SS/ 6 stamps, 1 is #648 |
| 1986/05/30 | 828 | | 400 fran | Eulophia erthoplata | |
| | 828a | | 400 fran | Eulophia erthoplata & Cyrtorchis arcuata | MS/ 1 stamp |
| | 830 | | 600 fran | Eulophia cucullata | SS/ 1 stamp |

## CEYLON

| DATE ISSUE | SCOTT/ MICHEL | GIBBON NUMBER | FACE VALUE | SPECIES NAME | BRIEF DESCRIPTION |
|---|---|---|---|---|---|
| 1949/02/04 | 301 | | $0.05 | Arachnis moschifera | Corsage |
| 1949/04/05 | 303 | | $0.25 | Arachnis moschifera | Corsage |
| 1950/02/04 | 309 | | $0.15 | Dendrobium macarthiae | |
| 1952/02/01 | 314 | | $0.35 | Phaius tankervilleae | |
| 1954/06/01 | 314a | | $0.35 | Phaius tankervilleae | #314 RP, with dot added |
| 1958/07/15 | 351 | | $0.35 | Phaius tankervilleae | #314 RP, with name in Tamil language |
| 1958/10/01 | 342 | | $0.15 | Dendrobium macarthiae | #309 RP, with name in Tamil language |

## CHAD

| DATE ISSUE | SCOTT/ MICHEL | GIBBON NUMBER | FACE VALUE | SPECIES NAME | BRIEF DESCRIPTION |
|---|---|---|---|---|---|
| 1984/02/01 | 515b | | 600 fran | Odontoglossum | SS/ 1 stamp, Bridal Bouquet Di's {Wedding} |

| --- | --- | --- | --- | --- | --- |

## CHILE

| DATE ISSUE | SCOTT/ MICHEL | GIBBON NUMBER | FACE VALUE | SPECIES NAME | BRIEF DESCRIPTION |
| --- | --- | --- | --- | --- | --- |
| 1988/08/23 | 795 | | $30.00 | Chloraea chrysantha | SS/ 16 stamps, 1 is #795a |

## CHINA

| DATE ISSUE | SCOTT/ MICHEL | GIBBON NUMBER | FACE VALUE | SPECIES NAME | BRIEF DESCRIPTION |
| --- | --- | --- | --- | --- | --- |
| 1981/12/20 | Post | NC1 | 4 fen | Cymbidium | Postcard/ Eight orchids stylized on left side |
| 1982/03/01 | Enve | --- | 8 fen | Cymbidium species | Envelope/ Stamp has orchid |
| 1983/05/01 | NS | --- | EXHIBIT | Cymbidium | Exhibition Sheet/ 1 stamp {Anhui/Hefei Stamp Show} |
| 1988/12/25 | 2184 | | 8 fen | Cymbidium goeringii v. Lungzi | |
| | 2185 | | 10 fen | Cymbidium faberi v. Dayipin | |
| | 2186 | | 20 fen | Cymbidium sinense v. margicoloratum | |
| | 2187 | | 50 fen | Cymbidium ensifolium v. Dafengwei | |
| | 2188 | | 2 yuan | Cymbidium faberi v. honglianban | SS/ 1 stamp |

## CHINA {Taiwan}

| DATE ISSUE | SCOTT/ MICHEL | GIBBON NUMBER | FACE VALUE | SPECIES NAME | BRIEF DESCRIPTION |
| --- | --- | --- | --- | --- | --- |
| 1954/01/28 | 1092 | | $0.40 | Phaius sinensis | In top frame |
| | 1095a | | SS | Phaius sinensis | SS/ 4 stamps, 1 is #1092 |
| 1954/10/21 | 1100 | | $0.40 | Cymbidium species | Frame design |
| | 1101 | | $5.00 | Cymbidium species | Frame design |
| 1958/03/20 | 1189 | | $0.20 | Phalaenopsis aphrodite | |
| | 1190 | | $0.40 | Laeliocattleya Mme. Chiang Kai-Shek | |
| | 1191 | | $1.40 | Cycnoches chlorochilon | |
| | 1192 | | $3.00 | Dendrobium phalaenopsis | |
| 1963/12/17 | 1381 | | $0.40 | Cymbidium ensifolium | |
| 1974/05/15 | 1881 | | $5.00 | Words | Island/ Named Lan-yu "Orchid" |
| 1978/09/20 | Aero | --- | $7.50 | Words | Aerogram/ Cachet has island named Lan-yu "Orchid" |
| 1986/02/20 | 2520 | | $10.00 | Dendrobium bigibbum | Flower arrangement |
| 1989/06/07 | 2686 | | $3.00 | Words | Poetry/ "I once attended 9 fields of orchids ..." |

## CHRISTMAS ISLANDS

| DATE ISSUE | SCOTT/ MICHEL | GIBBON NUMBER | FACE VALUE | SPECIES NAME | BRIEF DESCRIPTION |
| --- | --- | --- | --- | --- | --- |
| 1977/04/30 | 77 | | $0.09 | Saccolabium archytas v. ridley | |
| 1986/06/30 | 183 | | $0.33 | Brachypeza archytas | |
| 1990/07/11 | 275 | | $0.41 | Saccolabium archytas v. ridley | #77 RP, stamp on stamp |
| | 276 | | $0.75 | Saccolabium archytas | Background design |
| 1990/10/03 | 294 | | $0.38 | Corymborchis veratrifolia | |

## CISKEI

| DATE ISSUE | SCOTT/ MICHEL | GIBBON NUMBER | FACE VALUE | SPECIES NAME | BRIEF DESCRIPTION |
| --- | --- | --- | --- | --- | --- |
| 1983 | Telegrm T16c | --- | | Disa uniflora | |

## COLOMBIA

| DATE ISSUE | SCOTT/ MICHEL | GIBBON NUMBER | FACE VALUE | SPECIES NAME | BRIEF DESCRIPTION |
| --- | --- | --- | --- | --- | --- |
| 1947/02/07 | 546 | | $0.01 | Masdevallia nycterina | |
| | 547 | | $0.02 | Miltoniopsis vexillaria | |
| | 548 | | $0.05 | Cattleya chocoensis | |
| | 549 | | $0.05 | Odontoglossum crispum | |
| | 550 | | $0.05 | Cattleya dowiana v. aurea | |
| | 551 | | $0.10 | Cattleya labiata v. trianae | |
| 1947/11/08 | 555 | | $0.25 | Vanilla vine | Botanist Triana >Olive Green< |
| 1948/03/20 | 567 | | $0.15 | Vanilla vine | #555 RP, unwatermarked >Green< |
| 1948/05/01 | RA37 | | $0.01 | Vanilla species | Upper right/ Stamp surcharged with new value |
| 1950/08/22 | 580 | | $0.01 | Masdevallia chimaera | |
| | 581 | | $0.02 | Odontoglossum crispum | |
| | 582 | | $0.03 | Cattleya labiata v. trianae | |
| | 583 | | $0.04 | Masdevallia nycterina | |
| | 584 | | $0.05 | Cattleya dowiana v. aurea | |
| | 585 | | $0.11 | Miltoniopsis vexillaria | |
| 1952/10/30 | 610 | | $0.15 | Vanilla vine | #567 SC & OP "Latin American Sidergica Conference" |
| 1953/09/01 | C232 | | $0.05 | Miltoniopsis vexillaria | #585 Surcharged |
| 1959/06/26 | 697 | | $0.10 | Cattleya gigas v. warscewiczii | |
| | C317 | | 1.20 pes | Cattleya gigas v. warscewiczii | |
| | C318 | | 5 pesos | Cattleya gigas v. warscewiczii | |
| 1959/12/01 | C342 | | 1.20 pes | Cattleya gigas v. warscewiczii | #C317 OP "Unificado and airplane shape" |
| 1960/05/10 | C361 | | $0.35 | Odontoglossum luteo-purpureum | |
| | C364 | | $0.05 | Odontoglossum luteo-purpureum | |
| | C365 | | $0.10 | Stanhopea tigrina v. wardii | |

## COLOMBIA {Continued}

| DATE ISSUE | SCOTT/ MICHEL | GIBBON NUMBER | FACE VALUE | SPECIES NAME | BRIEF DESCRIPTION |
|---|---|---|---|---|---|
| 1960/05/10 | C367 | | 1 peso | Odontoglossum luteo-purpureum | |
| | C370 | | 1 peso | Stanhopea tigrina v. wardii | |
| 1962/01/30 | C422 | | $0.20 | Odontoglossum luteo-purpureum | |
| | C423 | | $0.25 | Stanhopea tigrina v. wardii | |
| | C425 | | 2 pesos | Odontoglossum luteo-purpureum | |
| 1965/10/31 | C468 | | $0.20 | Cattleya trianae | |
| 1967/05/23 | C489 | | 1 peso | Cattleya dowiana v. aurea | |
| | C490 | | 1.20 pes | Masdevallia coccinea | |
| | C491 | | 5 pesos | Catasetum macrocarpum | |
| | C491a | | SS | Catasetum | SS/ 3 stamps, #C489 thru #C491 |
| 1970/09/24 | 791 | | 2 pesos | Cattleya trianae | #C468 RP, stamp on stamp |
| 1972/04/20 | 807 | | 20 pesos | Maxillaria triloris | Descriptive tabs |
| | C572 | | 1.30 pes | Mormodes rolfeanum | |
| 1974/11/14 | C611 | | 1 peso | Sophronitis grandiflora | Tree limb |
| 1977/06/06 | C635 | | 25 pesos | Odontioda Itaque, Odontoglossum Moselle & Vuylsteckeara Rutilant    SS/ 1 stamp | |
| 1978/04/18 | 862 | | 2.50 pes | Cattleya trianae | |
| 1979/05/10 | 863 | | 3 pesos | Cattleya trianae | |
| 1980/05/27 | C690 | | 12 pesos | Cattleya | Tree limb |
| 1982/07/28 | 900j | | 7 pesos | Odontoglossum | Flower arragement |
| 1989/06/29 | C805 | | 110 peso | Phragmipedium | SS/ 7 stamps, 1 is #C805b |

## COMOROS

| DATE ISSUE | SCOTT/ MICHEL | GIBBON NUMBER | FACE VALUE | SPECIES NAME | BRIEF DESCRIPTION |
|---|---|---|---|---|---|
| 1969/03/20 | 80 | | 10 franc | Vanilla planifolia | |
| 1969/03/28 | C28 | | 200 fran | Angraecum eburneum | |
| 1977/11/19 | J11 | | 20 franc | Acampe pachyglossa | |
| | J16 | | 200 fran | Vanilla planifolia | |

## COMOROS-STATE

| DATE ISSUE | SCOTT/ MICHEL | GIBBON NUMBER | FACE VALUE | SPECIES NAME | BRIEF DESCRIPTION |
|---|---|---|---|---|---|
| 1976/12/30 | MB69 | --- | 500 fran | Vanilla planifolia | SS/ Background |
| 1977/04/14 | MB76 | --- | 500 fran | Cypripedium calceolus | SS/ Background |

## CONGO

| DATE ISSUE | SCOTT/ MICHEL | GIBBON NUMBER | FACE VALUE | SPECIES NAME | BRIEF DESCRIPTION |
|---|---|---|---|---|---|
| 1960/06/30 | 331 | | 2 francs | Ansellia gigantea | Belgian Congo #274 OP "Congo" & #331a OP inverted |
| | 339 | | 50 franc | Eulophia cucullata | Belgian Congo #283 OP "Congo" |

## COOK ISLANDS

| DATE ISSUE | SCOTT/ MICHEL | GIBBON NUMBER | FACE VALUE | SPECIES NAME | BRIEF DESCRIPTION |
|---|---|---|---|---|---|
| 1969/10/08 | 266 | | $0.25 | Vanda teres | Sheetlet/ 8 stamps |
| 1972/11/20 | 336 | | $0.10 | Cattleya | Bridal Bouquet QE2 {Silver Jubilee} Sheetlet/ 8 stamps |
| | 337 | | $0.15 | Cattleya | Bridal Bouquet QE2 {Silver Jubilee} Sheetlet/ 8 stamps |
| | 338 | | $0.30 | Cattleya | Bridal Bouquet QE2 {Silver Jubilee} Sheetlet/ 8 stamps |
| 1982/06/21 | 677A | | $1.25 | Odontoglossum | SS/ 4 stamps, Bridal Bouquet Di's {Birthday} |
| | 678A | | $2.50 | Odontoglossum | SS/ 4 stamps, Bridal Bouquet Di's {Birthday} |
| 1982/08/03 | 681A | | $1.25 | Odontoglossum | SS/ #677A OP "Birth of Prince William" >SILVER< |
| | 682A | | $2.50 | Odontoglossum | SS/ #678A OP "Birth of Prince William" >SILVER< |
| 1984/10/15 | 834 | | $1.25 | Odontoglossum | SS/ #667A OP "Birth HRH Prince Henry" >GOLD< |
| | 836 | | $2.50 | Odontoglossum | SS/ #678A OP "Birth HRH Prince Henry" >GOLD< |
| 1987/02/12 | 983 | | $9.40 | Odontoglossum | SS/ #678A SC & OP "Revalued Jan. 1987..." >GOLD< |

## COSTA RICA

| DATE ISSUE | SCOTT/ MICHEL | GIBBON NUMBER | FACE VALUE | SPECIES NAME | BRIEF DESCRIPTION |
|---|---|---|---|---|---|
| 1938/01/11 | 184 | | $0.01 | Cattleya skinneri | |
| 1967/06/15 | C443 | | $0.05 | Chondrorhyncha aromatica | |
| | C444 | | $0.10 | Miltonia endresii | |
| | C445 | | $0.15 | Stanhopea cirrhata | |
| | C446 | | $0.25 | Trichopilia suavis | |
| | C447 | | $0.35 | Odontoglossum schlieperianum | |
| | C448 | | $0.50 | Cattleya skinneri | |
| | C449 | | 1 colon | Cattleya dowiana | |
| | C450 | | 2 colon | Odontoglossum chiriquense | |
| 1975/03/07 | C613 | | $0.25 | Mormodes buccinator | >Perf 13.5< Dull paper and >Perf 10.5< Shiny paper |
| | C614 | | $0.25 | Gongora claviodora | >Perf 13.5< Dull paper and >Perf 10.5< Shiny paper |
| | C615 | | $0.25 | Masdevallia ephippium | >Perf 13.5< Dull paper and >Perf 10.5< Shiny paper |
| | C616 | | $0.25 | Encyclia spondiadum | >Perf 13.5< Dull paper and >Perf 10.5< Shiny paper |

| DATE ISSUE | SCOTT/ MICHEL | GIBBON NUMBER | FACE VALUE | SPECIES NAME | BRIEF DESCRIPTION |
|---|---|---|---|---|---|

## COSTA RICA {Continued}

| DATE ISSUE | SCOTT/ MICHEL | GIBBON NUMBER | FACE VALUE | SPECIES NAME | BRIEF DESCRIPTION |
|---|---|---|---|---|---|
| 1975/03/07 | C617 | | $0.65 | Lycaste skinneri v. alba | >Perf 13.5< Dull paper and >Perf 10.5< Shiny paper |
| | C618 | | $0.65 | Peristeria elata | >Perf 13.5< Dull paper and >Perf 10.5< Shiny paper |
| | C619 | | $0.65 | Miltoniopsis roezlii | >Perf 13.5< Dull paper and >Perf 10.5< Shiny paper |
| | C620 | | $0.65 | Brassavola digbyana | >Perf 13.5< Dull paper and >Perf 10.5< Shiny paper |
| | C621 | | $0.80 | Epidendrum mirabile | >Perf 13.5< Dull paper and >Perf 10.5< Shiny paper |
| | C622 | | $0.80 | Barkeria lindleyana | >Perf 13.5< Dull paper and >Perf 10.5< Shiny paper |
| | C623 | | $0.80 | Cattleya skinneri | >Perf 13.5< Dull paper and >Perf 10.5< Shiny paper |
| | C624 | | $0.80 | Sobralia macrantha v. splendens | >Perf 13.5< Dull paper and >Perf 10.5< Shiny paper |
| | C625 | | 1.40 col | Lycaste cruenta | >Perf 13.5< Dull paper and >Perf 10.5< Shiny paper |
| | C626 | | 1.40 col | Oncidium obryzatum | >Perf 13.5< Dull paper and >Perf 10.5< Shiny paper |
| | C627 | | 1.40 col | Gongora armeniaca | >Perf 13.5< Dull paper and >Perf 10.5< Shiny paper |
| | C628 | | 1.40 col | Sievekingia suavis | >Perf 13.5< Dull paper and >Perf 10.5< Shiny paper |
| | C629 | | 1.75 col | Hexisea bidentata | |
| | C630 | | 2.15 col | Chondrorhyncha discolor | |
| | C631 | | 2.50 col | Oncidium kramerianum | |
| | C632 | | 3.25 col | Cattleya dowiana | |
| 1976/03/01 | C654 | | $0.30 | Maxillaria albertii | #C654a Brown omitted |
| | C656 | | 2 colon | Pleurothallis johnsoni | |
| 1978/11/01 | C715 | | 1.75 col | Hexisea bidentata | #C629 OP "50th Aniverario del primer de PAM AM" |
| | C716 | | 2.15 col | Chondrorhyncha discolor | #C630 OP "50th Aniverario del primer de PAM AM" |
| | C717 | | 2.50 col | Oncidium kramerianum | #C631 OP "50th Aniverario del primer de PAM AM" |
| | C718 | | 1.75 col | Hexisea bidentata | #C629 OP "50th Aniverario de vistia de Lindbergh" |
| | C719 | | 2.15 col | Chondrorhyncha discolor | #C630 OP "50th Aniverario de vistia de Lindbergh" |
| | C720 | | 2.50 col | Oncidium kramerianum | #C631 OP "50th Aniverario de vistia de Lindbergh" |
| 1978/11/13 | C723 | | $0.50 | Lycaste skinneri v. alba | #C617 SC >Perf 13.5< Dull paper >Perf 10.5< Shiny paper |
| | C724 | | $0.50 | Peristeria elata | #C618 SC >Perf 13.5< Dull paper >Perf 10.5< Shiny paper |
| | C725 | | $0.50 | Miltoniopsis roezlii | #C619 SC >Perf 13.5< Dull paper >Perf 10.5< Shiny paper |
| | C726 | | $0.50 | Brassavola digbyana | #C620 SC >Perf 13.5< Dull paper >Perf 10.5< Shiny paper |
| | C727 | | 1.20 col | Chondrorhyncha discolor | #630 Surcharged |
| | C728 | | 2 colon | Oncidium kramerianum | #631 Surcharged |
| 1980 | Aero | --- | $0.02 | Sobralia amabilis | Aerogram/ Cachet has single orchid |
| 1980/09/24 | C801 | | 3.40 col | Cattleya skinneri v. alba & Oncidium isthmi | |
| 1983/04/25 | Aero | --- | 8.40 col | Sobralia amabilis | Aerogram/ Cachet has single orchid |
| 1985/12/03 | 332 | | $0.06 | Brassia arcuigera | Sheetlet/ 3 stamps and 5 strips, #332 thru #334 |
| | 333 | | $0.06 | Epidendrum peraltensis | |
| | 334 | | $0.06 | Maxillaria species | |
| | 335 | | $0.13 | Oncidium turialbae | Sheetlet/ 3 stamps and 5 strips, #335 thru #337 |
| | 336 | | $0.13 | Trichopilia marginata | |
| | 337 | | $0.13 | Stanhopea ecornuta | |
| 1989/10/23 | 420 | | 10 colon | Cattleya skinneri | |

## CUBA

| DATE ISSUE | SCOTT/ MICHEL | GIBBON NUMBER | FACE VALUE | SPECIES NAME | BRIEF DESCRIPTION |
|---|---|---|---|---|---|
| 1958/12/16 | 611 | | $0.02 | Cattleyopsis lindeni | |
| | 612 | | $0.04 | Oncidium guibertianum | |
| 1960/02/03 | 633 | | $0.01 | Oncidium guibertianum | #612 Surcharged |
| 1965/07/20 | 977 | | $0.05 | Cattleya labiata | |
| 1966/12/20 | 1179 | | $0.01 | Paphiopedilum Eurylochus | |
| | 1180 | | $0.01 | Cattleya speciosissima | |
| | 1181 | | $0.01 | Cattleya mendelii v. majestica | |
| | 1182 | | $0.01 | Cattleya trianae v. amesiana | |
| | 1183 | | $0.01 | Cattleya labiata v. macfarlanei | |
| | 1183a | | SS | Cattleya | SS/ 5 stamps, #1179 thru #1183, plus 1 label |
| | 1184 | | $0.03 | Paphiopedilum Morganiae v. Burfordiense | |
| | 1185 | | $0.03 | Cattleya Countess of Derby | |
| | 1186 | | $0.03 | Paphiopedilum hookerae v. volonteanum | |
| | 1187 | | $0.03 | Cattleya gigas v. Regina Burfordinse | |
| | 1188 | | $0.03 | Paphiopedilum stonei v. cannartae | |
| | 1188a | | SS | Paphiopedilum | SS/ 5 stamps, #1184 thru #1188, plus 1 label |
| | 1189 | | $0.13 | Cattleya mendelii v. Duchess of Montrose | |
| | 1190 | | $0.13 | Oncidium macranthum | |
| | 1191 | | $0.13 | Paphiopedilum stonei v. platytaenium | |
| | 1192 | | $0.13 | Cattleya dowiana v. aurea | |

## CUBA {Continued}

| DATE ISSUE | SCOTT/ MICHEL | GIBBON NUMBER | FACE VALUE | SPECIES NAME | BRIEF DESCRIPTION |
|---|---|---|---|---|---|
| 1966/12/20 | 1193 | | $0.13 | Laelia anceps | |
| | 1193a | | SS | Laelia | SS/ 5 stamps, #1189 thru #1193, plus 1 label |
| 1971/05/15 | 1620 | | $0.01 | Cattleya skinneri | |
| | 1621 | | $0.02 | Vanda hybrid | |
| | 1622 | | $0.03 | Paphiopedilum venustum | |
| | 1623 | | $0.04 | Paphiopedilum glaucophyllum | |
| | 1624 | | $0.05 | Vanda tricolor | |
| | 1625 | | $0.13 | Paphiopedilum Mowgli | |
| | 1626 | | $0.30 | Paphiopedilum Solum | |
| 1972/02/25 | 1677 | | $0.01 | Brassocattleya Sindrossiana | |
| | 1678 | | $0.02 | Paphiopedilum Doraeus | |
| | 1679 | | $0.03 | Paphiopedilum exul | |
| | 1680 | | $0.04 | Paphiopedilum Rosy Dawn | |
| | 1681 | | $0.05 | Paphiopedilum Champollion | |
| | 1682 | | $0.13 | Paphiopedilum Bucolique | |
| | 1683 | | $0.30 | Paphiopedilum Sullanum | |
| 1973/03/26 | 1780 | | $0.01 | Dendrobium hybrid | |
| | 1781 | | $0.02 | Paphiopedilum exul v. O'Brien | |
| | 1782 | | $0.03 | Vanda Miss Joaquim v. Rose Marie | |
| | 1783 | | $0.04 | Phalaenopsis schilleriana | |
| | 1784 | | $0.05 | Vanda Gilbert Tribulet | |
| | 1785 | | $0.13 | Dendrobium hybrid | |
| | 1786 | | $0.30 | Arachnis Catherine | |
| 1977/05/01 | Post | --- | $0.13 | Cattleya | Postcard/ Picture side, two orchids in red flower arrangement |
| 1978/05/01 | Post | --- | $0.13 | Vanda tricolor | Postcard/ Picture side has orchid |
| 1980/05/20 | 2328 | | $0.01 | Bletia purpurea | |
| | 2329 | | $0.04 | Oncidium leiboldii | |
| | 2330 | | $0.06 | Encyclia cochleata | |
| | 2331 | | $0.10 | Cattleyopsis lindeni | |
| | 2332 | | $0.13 | Encyclia fucata | |
| | 2333 | | $0.30 | Encyclia phoenicea | |
| 1981/05/01 | Post | --- | $0.13 | Cattleya | Postcard/ Picture side has two orchids |
| 1982/05/01 | Post | --- | $0.13 | Cattleya | Postcard/ Four small white cattleyas and other flowers |
| | Post | --- | $0.13 | Cattleya | Postcard/ Picture side has two orchids |
| | Post | --- | $0.13 | Dendrobium | Postcard/ Picture side has two orchids |
| 1983/05/01 | Post | --- | $0.20 | Cattleya | Postcard/ Picture side has single orchid |
| 1983/12/20 | 2631 | | $0.05 | Epidendrum cubincola | #2633a Strip of 5, 1 is #2631 |
| | 2662 | | $0.90 | Encyclia fucata | |
| 1984/05/01 | Post | --- | $0.20 | Dendrobium | Postcard/ Picture side has orchid spray |
| 1984/05/13 | Post | --- | $0.20 | Cattleya | Postcard/ Picture side has single orchid |
| 1986/02/25 | 2839 | | $0.08 | Dendrobium phalaenopsis | |
| 1986/09/15 | 2881 | | $0.01 | Cattleya hardyana | |
| | 2882 | | $0.04 | Brassolaeliocattleya Horizon v. Flight | |
| | 2883 | | $0.05 | Phalaenopsis margil v. Moses | |
| | 2884 | | $0.10 | Laeliocattleya prism v. palette | |
| | 2885 | | $0.30 | Phalaenopsis violacea | |
| | 2886 | | $0.50 | Disa uniflora | |
| 1987/05/01 | Aero | --- | $0.05 | Dendrobium phalaenopsis | Aerogram/ #__ RP, with "Felicidades Mama" added to design |
| | Aero | --- | $0.05 | Dendrobium phalaenopsis | Aerogram/ Stamp has orchid |
| 1989/10/27 | 3151 | | $0.01 | Govenia utriculata | |
| | 3152 | | $0.01 | Laelia grandis | |
| | 3154 | | $0.01 | Cattleya trianae | |
| | 3155 | | $0.01 | Cochleanthes discolor | |
| | 3155a | --- | $0.01 | Govenia | Strip/ 5 stamps, #3151, #3152, #3154 and #3155 |
| | 3157 | | $0.05 | Epidendrum fragrans | |
| | 3159 | | $0.05 | Miltoniopsis vexillaria | |
| | 3160 | | $0.05 | Odontoglossum rossii | |
| | 3160a | --- | $0.05 | Epidendrum | Strip/ 5 stamps, #3157, #3159 and #3160 |
| | 3161 | | $0.10 | Laelia anceps | |
| | 3162 | | $0.10 | Laelia anceps v. alba | |
| | 3164 | | $0.10 | Brassavola acaulis | |
| | 3165 | | $0.10 | Pescatoria cerina | |

| DATE ISSUE | SCOTT/ MICHEL | GIBBON NUMBER | FACE VALUE | SPECIES NAME | BRIEF DESCRIPTION |
|---|---|---|---|---|---|
| **CUBA {Continued}** | | | | | |
| 1989/10/27 | 3165a | | $0.10 | Laelia | Strip/ 5 stamps, #3161, #3162, #3164 and #3165 |
| | 3166 | | $0.20 | Coryanthes leucocorys | |
| | 3170 | | $0.20 | Cattleya mossiae | |
| | 3170a | | $0.20 | Coryanthes | Strip/ 5 stamps, #3166 and #3170 |
| **CYPRUS** | | | | | |
| 1981/07/06 | 565 | | 25 milli | Ophrys kotschyi | |
| | 566 | | 50 milli | Orchis punctulata | |
| | 567 | | 75 milli | Ophrys argolica | |
| | 568 | | 150 mill | Epipactis veratrifolia | Sheetlet/ 4 stamps and 4 blocks, #565 thru #568 |
| **CZECHOSLOVAKIA** | | | | | |
| 1959/03/23 | 905 | | 60 haler | Paphiopedilum | Right, in hair |
| 1961/11/27 | 1082 | | 15 haler | Cypripedium calceolus | |
| 1967/08/30 | 1490 | | 20 haler | Miltonia spectabilis | |
| | 1492 | | 40 haler | Lycaste deppei | |
| | 1496 | | 1.40koru | Dendrobium phalaenopsis | |
| 1973/03/26 | 1895 | | 3.60 kor | Cypripedium Clunatec | |
| 1980/08/13 | 2322 | | 4 koruna | Paphiopedilum Maudiae | Sheetlet/ 10 stamps |
| **DENMARK** | | | | | |
| 1953 | Booklet --- | | 25 ore | Vanilla | Advertising Booklet/ Toms Bonzo Chokolade med "Vanillecreme" |
| 1974/08/01 | Post | | Prepaid | Dactylorhiza purpurella | Announcement Postcard/ Cachet has single orchid plant |
| 1974/09/19 | 561 | | 120 ore | Dactylorhiza purpurella | |
| 1990/06/14 | 921 | | 3.50 kro | Cephalanthera rubra | |
| | 922 | | 3.75 kro | Orchis purpurea | |
| | 923 | | 4.75 kro | Cypripedium calceolus | |
| | Booklet 921a | | 35 krona | Cephalanthera rubra | Booklet/ 1 pane of 10 stamps and Cover design |
| **DOMINICA** | | | | | |
| 1951/07/01 | 129 | | $0.08 | Vanilla Beans Drying | Edward VI |
| 1951/10/15 | 139 | | $0.08 | Vanilla Beans Drying | #129 OP "New Constitution 1951" |
| 1954/10/01 | 149 | | $0.08 | Vanilla Beans Drying | QE2 |
| 1972/06/05 | 339 | | $0.60 | Oncidium papilio | |
| | 340a | | SS | Oncidium papilio | SS/ 4 stamps, 1 is #339 |
| 1981/04/30 | 700 | | $3.00 | Epidendrum | SS/ 1 stamp, background on tree limb |
| 1982/07/01 | 775 | | $4.00 | Odontoglossum | Bridal Bouquet Di's {Birthday} Sheetlet/ 5 stamps, 1 label |
| 1982/09/01 | 784 | | $4.00 | Odontoglossum | #775 OP "Royal Baby" |
| 1985/07/15 | 906 | | $0.60 | Phalaenopsis | Bouquet Queen Mother's {Birthday} |
| 1986/05/05 | 950 | | $0.02 | Cattleya | Bridal Bouquet QE2 {60th Birthday} |
| 1988/02/15 | 1064 | | $0.45 | Cattleya | Bridal Bouquet QE2 {40th Wedding Anniversary} |
| 1988/07/25 | 1085 | | $0.45 | Polystachya luteola | SS/ 20 stamps, 1 is #1085n |
| 1989/09/06 | 1186 | | $0.10 | Oncidium pusillum | |
| 1989/09/28 | 1187 | | $0.35 | Encyclia cochleata | |
| | 1188 | | $0.45 | Epidendrum ciliare | |
| | 1189 | | $0.60 | Cyrtopodium andersoni | |
| | 1190 | | $1.00 | Habenaria pauciflora | |
| | 1191 | | $2.00 | Maxillaria alba | |
| | 1192 | | $3.00 | Selenipedium palmifolium | |
| | 1193 | | $4.00 | Brassavola cucullata | |
| | 1194 | | $5.00 | Oncidium lanceanum | SS/ 1 stamp |
| | 1195 | | $5.00 | Comparettia falcata | SS/ 1 stamp |
| **DOMINICAN REPUBLIC** | | | | | |
| 1967/04/01 | RA37 | | $0.01 | Domingoa nodosa | |
| 1970/04/30 | RA49 | | $0.01 | Elleanthus capitatus | |
| 1972/04/02 | RA55 | | $0.01 | Oncidium tuerckheimii | |
| 1975/04/01 | RA71 | | $0.01 | Cattleyopsis rosea | |
| 1976/04/06 | RA75 | | $0.01 | Oncidium calochilum | |
| 1977/04/22 | RA80 | | $0.01 | Oncidium variegatum | |
| 1977/08/19 | 788 | | $0.04 | Broughtonia domingensis | |
| 1981/12/14 | C349 | | $0.07 | Encyclia cochleata | |
| | C350 | | $0.10 | Broughtonia domingensis | |

SAMOA 465; TURKS & CACIOS ISLANDS 532; ANTIGUA 664; INDONESIA 1012a; SAINT HELENA 374; LESOTHO 374; GUERNSEY 70; NEW ZEALAND 703; TRINIDAD & TOBAGO 286; PENRHYN 220; SABAH 7; ZAMBIA 280; BRAZIL 652; GERMANY DDR 1059; FRANCE 1192; BARBADOS 398 & 408; LAOS 231; SWEDEN 1763; MONTSERRAT 660; BHUTAN M362; ECUADOR C508; ZAIRE 1148; and VIETNAM M1059.

## DOMINICAN REPUBLIC {Continued}

| | | | | | |
|---|---|---|---|---|---|
| 1981/12/14 | C351 | | $0.25 | Encyclia truncata | |
| | C352 | | $0.75 | Elleanthus capitatus | |

## ECUADOR

| | | | | | |
|---|---|---|---|---|---|
| 1956/12/29 | 602 | | $0.80 | Oncidium macranthum | Deep Violet |
| 1957/12/16 | 627 | | $0.90 | Oncidium macranthum | Bright Blue |
| 1960/08/20 | 670 | --- | SS | Oncidium macranthum | SS/ 2 stamps, also without >SILVER< inscription |
| 1960/08/27 | 670a | --- | $0.80 | Oncidium macranthum | Deep Violet on Ivory |
| | 670b | --- | $0.90 | Oncidium macranthum | Deep Green on Ivory |
| 1972/07/21 | C508 | | 4 sucre | Epidendrum secundum | |
| | C509 | | 6 sucre | Maxillaria striata | |
| | C510a | | SS | Epidendrum | SS/ 3 stamps, 2 are #C508 and #C509 |
| 1975/11/18 | 930 | | $0.20 | Phragmipedium caudatum v. lindenii | |
| | 933 | | $0.50 | Cochlioda vulcanica | |
| | 934 | | $0.60 | Odontoglossum hallii | |
| | 936 | | $1.00 | Odontoglossum cirrhosum | |
| 1980/11/24 | 1003 | | 1.20 suc | Cattleya maxima | |
| | 1004 | | 3 sucre | Comparettia speciosa | |
| | 1005 | | 3.40 suc | Cattleya iricolor | |
| | 1006 | | 20 sucre | Cattleya | SS/ 3 vignettes of #1003 thru #1005 |
| | C709 | | 7.60 suc | Anguloa uniflora | |
| | C710 | | 10.60 su | Scuticaria salesiana | |
| | C711 | | $0.50 | Helcia sanguinolenta | |
| | C712 | | 100 sucr | Anguloa uniflora | |
| | C713 | | 20 sucre | Anguloa | SS/ 2 vignettes of #C709 and #C711 |
| | C714 | | 20 sucre | Scuticaria | SS/ 2 vignettes of #C710 and #C712 |
| 1990/12/01 | 1254 | | 100 sucr | Sobralia species | |
| | 1256 | | 100 sucr | Cattleya species | |

## EQUATORIAL GUINEA

| | | | | | |
|---|---|---|---|---|---|
| 1974/08/20 | M426 | --- | 1 peseta | Cypripedium calceolus | |
| | M427 | --- | 3 peseta | Laelia gouldiana | |
| | M428 | --- | 5 peseta | Catasetum atratum | |
| | M429 | --- | 8 peseta | Angraecum sesquipedale | |
| | M430 | --- | 10 peset | Vanda teres | |
| | M432 | --- | 15 peset | Cattleya dowiana | |
| | M433 | --- | 25 peset | Paphiopedilum praestans | |
| | MB436 | --- | 200 pese | Laeliocattleya callistoglossa | SS/ 1 stamp |
| | MB437 | --- | 250 pese | Maxillaria sanderiana | SS/ 1 stamp |

## FALKLAND ISLANDS

| | | | | | |
|---|---|---|---|---|---|
| 1968/10/09 | 169 | | 3 pence | Codonorchis lessonii | |
| | 179 | | 1 pound | Gavillea macroptera | |
| 1971/02/15 | --- | | 1 pound | Gavillea macroptera | #179 RP, Type II |
| | 200 | | 2 pence | Codonorchis lessonii | #169 Surcharged |
| 1972/06/01 | 213 | | 2 pence | Codonorchis lessonii | #213a/294 Wmk |
| 1982/08/16 | 350 | | 37 pence | Odontoglossum | Bridal Bouquet Di's {Birthday} |
| 1991 | | | 31 pence | Chloraea gaudichaudi | |
| | | | 26 pence | Codonorchis lessonii | |
| | | | 12 pence | Gavillea australis | |
| | | | 62 pence | Gavillea littoralis | |

## FALKLAND DEPENDIENCIES

| | | | | | |
|---|---|---|---|---|---|
| 1982/09/07 | 1L74 | | 37 pence | Odontoglossum | Bridal Bouquet Di's {Birthday} |

## FAROES

| | | | | | |
|---|---|---|---|---|---|
| 1988/02/08 | 170 | | 3 krone | Dactylorhiza maculata | |

## FIJI

| | | | | | |
|---|---|---|---|---|---|
| 1962/12/03 | 184 | | 2 shilli | Dendrobium prasinum | #184a/319a Wmk sideways |
| 1968/07/15 | 254 | | 5 shilli | Arundina graminifolia | |
| 1969/01/13 | 274 | | $0.50 | Arundina graminifolia | |

<table>
<tr><td>DATE<br>ISSUE</td><td>SCOTT/<br>MICHEL</td><td>GIBBON<br>NUMBER</td><td>FACE<br>VALUE</td><td>SPECIES NAME</td><td>BRIEF DESCRIPTION</td></tr>
</table>

## FIJI {Continued}

| DATE ISSUE | SCOTT/ MICHEL | GIBBON NUMBER | FACE VALUE | SPECIES NAME | BRIEF DESCRIPTION |
|---|---|---|---|---|---|
| 1972/01/04 | 305 | | $0.01 | Cirrhopetalum umbellatum | #305b/505 Wmk sideways |
| | 305a | Bookle | $0.20 | Cirrhopetalum umbellatum | Booklet/ 2 panes, 1 is #305/8 stamps |
| | 307 | | $0.03 | Calanthe triplicata | #307a/460 Wmk to left and #307b/507a Wmk 373 |
| | 308 | | $0.04 | Bulbophyllum species | #308a/461 Wmk sideways and #308b/508a Wmk 373 |
| | 310 | | $0.06 | Phaius tankervilleae | #310a/463 Wmk sideways and #310b/510a Wmk 373 |
| | 312 | | $0.10 | Acanthephippium vitiense | #312b/512 Wmk 373 |
| | 313 | | $0.15 | Dendrobium tokai | #313a/466 Wmk sideways and #313b/513 Wmk 373 |
| | 316 | | $0.30 | Dendrobium gordonii | #316b/516 Wmk 373 |
| | 320 | | $2.00 | Dendrobium platygastrium | #320a/473 Wmk sideways and #320b/520 Wmk 373 |
| 1972/11/20 | 328 | | $0.10 | Dendrobium prasinum | QE2 {25th Wedding Anniversary} |
| | 329 | | $0.25 | Dendrobium prasinum | QE2 {25th Wedding Anniversary} |
| 1977/02/07 | 371 | | $0.10 | Dendrobium | Bouquet QE2 {Royal Visit} |
| 1981/07/22 | 442 | | $0.06 | Dendrobium macranthum, Aeridachnis Apple Blossom & Cattleya/ Charles Wedding Wreath | |
| 1988/11/07 | 595 | | $0.09 | Dendrobium mohlianum | |
| | 596 | | $0.30 | Dendrobium cattilare | |

## FRANCE

| DATE ISSUE | SCOTT/ MICHEL | GIBBON NUMBER | FACE VALUE | SPECIES NAME | BRIEF DESCRIPTION |
|---|---|---|---|---|---|
| 1888/03/18 | Letcd | HG | $0.15 | Vanilla | Advertising Lettercard/ Dethes and "Vanilles" T/S10 |
| 1888/04/30 | Letcd | HG | $0.15 | Vanilla | Advertising Lettercard/ "Import of The's et Vanilles" |
| 1920 | Booklet | Y/0041 | 5 francs | Vanilla | Advertising Booklet/ "Vanille" >1'Ovomaltine< T/S24 |
| 1921 | Booklet | Y/0042 | 2 francs | Vanilla | Advertising Booklet/ "Vanille" >Ric-Ka< |
| 1922 | Booklet | Y/0047 | 2 francs | Vanilla | Advertising Booklet/ "Vanillee" >Reglisse Florent< T/S44 |
| 1967/07/29 | 1192 | | $0.40 | Sobralia sessilis | |

## FRENCH POLYNESIA

| DATE ISSUE | SCOTT/ MICHEL | GIBBON NUMBER | FACE VALUE | SPECIES NAME | BRIEF DESCRIPTION |
|---|---|---|---|---|---|
| 1975/10/15 | C120 | | 44 franc | Cattleya | |
| 1979/01/25 | 300 | | 10 franc | Vanda species | |
| 1983/10/19 | 388 | | 45 franc | Dendrobium | Headress |
| 1984/10/24 | 402 | | 53 franc | Dendrobium | Headress |
| 1990/01/11 | 530 | | 34 franc | Vanilla tahitiensis | |
| | 531 | | 35 franc | Vanilla tahitiensis | Bean Pods |

## FUJERIA

| DATE ISSUE | SCOTT/ MICHEL | GIBBON NUMBER | FACE VALUE | SPECIES NAME | BRIEF DESCRIPTION |
|---|---|---|---|---|---|
| 1971 | M785 | --- | 15 riyal | Epidendrum | SS/ 1 stamp, background of butterfly |
| | M857 | --- | 10 riyal | Laelia | SS/ 1 stamp, on sides with birds |
| 1972 | M1333 | --- | 70 dinar | Odontoglossum | |
| | M1334 | --- | 1 riyal | Cattleya | |

## GABON

| DATE ISSUE | SCOTT/ MICHEL | GIBBON NUMBER | FACE VALUE | SPECIES NAME | BRIEF DESCRIPTION |
|---|---|---|---|---|---|
| 1964/11/16 | 178 | | 15 franc | Eulophia horsfallii | |
| 1971/05/07 | C110 | | 75 franc | Cymbidium | |
| | C111a | | SS | Cymbidium | SS/ 2 stamps, 1 is #C110 |
| | C111b | | SS | Cymbidium | SS/ 2 stamps, 1 is #C110 with >GOLD< border and numbered |

## GAMBIA

| DATE ISSUE | SCOTT/ MICHEL | GIBBON NUMBER | FACE VALUE | SPECIES NAME | BRIEF DESCRIPTION |
|---|---|---|---|---|---|
| 1977/07/01 | 358 | | 10 butut | Eulophia guineensis | |
| 1987/05/25 | 689A | | 2.25 dal | Eulophia guineensis | |
| 1988/03/15 | 729 | | 75 butut | Cattleya | Bridal Bouquet QE2 {40th Wedding Anniversary} |
| | 731 | | 3 dalasy | Cattleya | Bridal Bouquet QE2 {40th Wedding Anniversary} |
| 1989/12/18 | 918 | | 20 butut | Bulbophyllum lepidum | |
| | 919 | | 75 butut | Tridactyle tridactylites | |
| | 920 | | 1 dalasy | Vanilla imperialis | |
| | 921 | | 1.25 dal | Oeceoclades maculata | |
| | 922 | | 2 dalasy | Polystachya affinis | |
| | 923 | | 4 dalasy | Ancistrochilus rothschildianus | |
| | 924 | | 5 dalasy | Angraecum distichum | |
| | 925 | | 10 dalas | Liparis guineensis | |
| | 926 | | 15 dalas | Plectrelminthus caudatus | SS/ 1 stamp |
| | 927 | | 15 dalas | Eulophia guineensis | SS/ 1 stamp |
| 1990/06/14 | 999 | | 15 dalas | Ansellia africana | |

## GERMANY

| DATE ISSUE | SCOTT/ MICHEL | GIBBON NUMBER | FACE VALUE | SPECIES NAME | BRIEF DESCRIPTION |
|---|---|---|---|---|---|
| 1920 | Letcd | HG65 | 40 pfenn | Vanilla | Advertising Lettercard/ Words "Vanillestangen, Vanillinzucker" |

| DATE ISSUE | SCOTT/ MICHEL | GIBBON NUMBER | FACE VALUE | SPECIES NAME | BRIEF DESCRIPTION |
|---|---|---|---|---|---|

## GERMANY {Continued}

| DATE ISSUE | SCOTT/ MICHEL | GIBBON NUMBER | FACE VALUE | SPECIES NAME | BRIEF DESCRIPTION |
|---|---|---|---|---|---|
| 1963/04/26 | 858 | | 15 pfenn | Cypripedium calceolus | |
| 1984/10/18 | B623 | | 50 pfenn | Aceras anthropophora | |
| | B624 | | 60 pfenn | Orchis ustulata | |
| | B625 | | 80 pfenn | Limodorum abortivum | |
| | B626 | | 120 pfen | Dactylorhiza sambucina | |
| | Booklet --- | | 6 marks | Limodorum | Private Booklet/ 1 pane of 5 stamps #B625 |
| | Booklet --- | | 7.20 mar | Limodorum | Private Booklet/ 1 pane of 6 stamps #B625 |

## GERMANY {Bayern}

| DATE ISSUE | SCOTT/ MICHEL | GIBBON NUMBER | FACE VALUE | SPECIES NAME | BRIEF DESCRIPTION |
|---|---|---|---|---|---|
| 1900 | Post | HG40 | 5 pfenni | Vanilla | Advertising Lettercard/ Word "Vanillin" >Fabrikate< |
| 1901/09/10 | Post | HG46 | 5 pfenni | Vanilla | Advertising Postcard/ Double Reply with "Vanillinzucher" |

## GERMANY {Berlin}

| DATE ISSUE | SCOTT/ MICHEL | GIBBON NUMBER | FACE VALUE | SPECIES NAME | BRIEF DESCRIPTION |
|---|---|---|---|---|---|
| 1978/10/12 | 9NB150 | | 50 pfenn | Cephalanthera rubra | |
| 1979/08/09 | 9N434 | | 50 pfenn | Paphiopedilum Aureum | #9N434 Fluorescent missing |
| 1984/10/18 | 9NB216 | | 50 pfenn | Listera cordata | |
| | 9NB217 | | 60 pfenn | Ophrys insectifera | |
| | 9NB218 | | 80 pfenn | Epipactis palustris | |
| | 9NB219 | | 120 pfen | Orchis coriophora | |
| | Booklet --- | | 4.50 mar | Ophrys | Private Booklet/ 1 pane of 5 stamps #9NB217 |
| | Booklet --- | | 5.40 mar | Ophrys | Private Booklet/ 1 pane of 6 stamps #9NB217 |

## GERMANY {Berlin-Hasna}

| DATE ISSUE | SCOTT/ MICHEL | GIBBON NUMBER | FACE VALUE | SPECIES NAME | BRIEF DESCRIPTION |
|---|---|---|---|---|---|
| 1900 | Post | --- | 2 pfenni | Vanilla | Advertising Postcard/ Word "Vanille" >L. Jaeckel's< |

## GERMANY DDR

| DATE ISSUE | SCOTT/ MICHEL | GIBBON NUMBER | FACE VALUE | SPECIES NAME | BRIEF DESCRIPTION |
|---|---|---|---|---|---|
| 1957/04/12 | 327 | | 20 pfenn | Cypripedium calceolus | |
| 1966/12/08 | 880 | | 20 pfenn | Cephalanthera rubra | |
| 1968/11/12 | 1057 | | 5 pfenni | Laeliocattleya Maggie Raphaela v. alba | |
| | 1058 | | 10 pfenn | Paphiopedilum Albertianum | |
| | 1059 | | 15 pfenn | Cattleya fabria | |
| | 1060 | | 20 pfenn | Cattleya aclandiae | |
| | 1061 | | 40 pfenn | Sobralia macrantha | |
| | 1062 | | 50 pfenn | Dendrobium Alpha | |
| 1969/04/04 | 1098 | | 30 pfenn | Dactylorchis latifolia | |
| 1970/04/28 | 1197 | | 30 pfenn | Orchis militaris | |
| 1976/06/15 | 1729 | | 10 pfenn | Himantoglossum hircinum | |
| | 1730 | | 20 pfenn | Dactylorhiza incarnata | |
| | 1731 | | 25 pfenn | Anacamptis pyramidalis | |
| | 1732 | | 35 pfenn | Dactylorhiza sambucina | |
| | 1733 | | 40 pfenn | Orchis coriophora | |
| | 1734 | | 50 pfenn | Cypripedium calceolus | |

## GHANA

| DATE ISSUE | SCOTT/ MICHEL | GIBBON NUMBER | FACE VALUE | SPECIES NAME | BRIEF DESCRIPTION |
|---|---|---|---|---|---|
| 1959/10/05 | 59 | | 5 shilli | Odontoglossum grande | |
| 1965/07/19 | 224 | | 60 pesew | Odontoglossum grande | #59 SC & OP "19th July 1965" and #224a Double surcharge |
| 1970/11/02 | 404 | | 20 pesew | Ansellia africana | |
| 1982/04/27 | 790 | | 65 pesew | Ansellia africana | |
| | 793b | | 50 peswe | Ansellia africana | SS/ 4 stamps, 1 is #790 with new value |
| 1984/04/01 | 923 | | 2.30 ced | Eulophia cucullata | |
| 1984/07/01 | 926 | | 60 cedi | Eulophia cucullata | SS/ 1 stamp |
| 1990/11/01 | 1224 | | 40 cedi | Aerangis luteo-alba | SS/ 20 stamps, 1 is #1224s |
| 1991/01/01 | | | 4 cedi | Ancistrochilus rothachildianus | Sheetlet 10 stamps |
| | | | 6 cedi | Bolusiella imbricata | SS/ 1 stamp |
| | | | 60 pesew | Bulbophyllum barbigerum | Sheetlet/ 10 stamps |
| | | | 2 cedi | Diaphananthe kamerunensis | Sheetlet/ 10 stamps |
| | | | 6 cedi | Diaphananthe rutila | SS/ 1 stamp |
| | | | 20 pesew | Eulophia guineensis | Sheetlet 10 stamps |
| | | | 40 pesew | Eurychone rothschildiana | Sheetlet/ 10 stamps |
| | | | 3 cedi | Podangis dactyloceras | Sheetlet 10 stamps |
| | | | 80 pesew | Polystachya galeata | Sheetlet 10 stamps |
| | | | 5 cedi | Rangaeris musicola | Sheetlet/ 10 stamps |

| DATE ISSUE | SCOTT/ MICHEL | GIBBON NUMBER | FACE VALUE | SPECIES NAME | BRIEF DESCRIPTION |
|---|---|---|---|---|---|
| **GIBRALTAR** | | | | | |
| 1977/04/01 | 340 | | 1/2 penn | Orchis tridentata | |
| 1982/02/22 | 340a | --- | 1/2 penn | Orchis tridentata | #340 RP, with "1982" changed in selvage |
| **GREAT BRITIAN** | | | | | |
| 1939/07/17 | Telegrm T20 | | --- | Paphiopedilum | |
| 1984/09/03 | Booklet FB27 | | 50 pence | Dendrobium nobile & Miltonia hybrid | Booklet/ Cover design >Lavendar< |
| 1985/01/15 | Booklet FB28 | | 50 pence | Cypripedium calceolus & Ophrys apifera | Booklet/ Cover design >Lavendar< |
| 1985/04/23 | Booklet FB29 | | 50 pence | Bifrenaria speciosa & Vanda tricolor | Booklet/ Cover design >Lavendar< |
| 1985/07/23 | Booklet FB30 | | 50 pence | Cymbidium speciosa & Arpophyllum jamaicense | Booklet/ Cover design >Lavendar< |
| 1991/02/15 | Booklet | | 1 st | Ophrys | Booklet/ Pane of 10 stamps, 1 is #   ; Lower right |
| **GRENADA** | | | | | |
| 1975/09/22 | 665 | | $0.75 | Vanilla planifolia | |
| | 666 | | $2.00 | Maxillaria species | |
| 1986/11/17 | 1428 | | $4.00 | Cattleya | |
| 1988/02/15 | 1577 | | $0.15 | Cattleya | Bridal Bouquet QE2 {40th Wedding Anniversary} |
| 1988/10/05 | 1681a | | SS | Cymbidium | SS/ 4 stamps, selvage design {Yoko Minamino, singer} |
| 1990/03/06 | 1795 | | $0.01 | Odontoglossum triumphans | |
| | 1796 | | $0.25 | Oncidium splendidum | |
| | 1797 | | $0.60 | Laelia anceps | |
| | 1798 | | $0.75 | Cattleya trianae | |
| | 1799 | | $1.00 | Odontoglossum rossii | |
| | 1800 | | $2.00 | Brassia gireoudiana | |
| | 1801 | | $3.00 | Cattleya dowiana | |
| | 1802 | | $4.00 | Sobralia macrantha | |
| | 1803 | | $6.00 | Laelia rubescens | SS/ 1 stamp |
| | 1804 | | $6.00 | Oncidium lanceanum | SS/ 1 stamp |
| **GRENADA-GRENADINES** | | | | | |
| 1984/04/09 | 8427 | | $4.00 | Selenipedium palmifolium | |
| | 8430 | | $4.00 | Selenipedium palmifolium | #8427 OP "19th UPU Congress" |
| 1988/02/15 | 8802 | | $0.30 | Cattleya | Bridal Bouquet QE2 {40th Wedding Anniversary} |
| 1990/03/06 | 9020 | | $0.15 | Brassocattleya Thalie | |
| | 9021 | | $0.20 | Odontocidium Tigersum | |
| | 9022 | | $0.50 | Odontioda Hambuhren | |
| | 9023 | | $0.75 | Paphiopedilum Delrosi | |
| | 9024 | | $1.00 | Vuylstekeara Yokara | |
| | 9025 | | $2.00 | Paphiopedilum Geelong | |
| | 9026 | | $3.00 | Wilsonara Tigerwood | |
| | 9027 | | $4.00 | Cymbidium Ormoulu | |
| | 9028 | | $6.00 | Odontonia Sappho | SS/ 1 stamp |
| | 9029 | | $6.00 | Cymbidium Vieux Rose | SS/ 1 stamp |
| **GUADELOUPE** | | | | | |
| 1905 | 54 | | $0.01 | Vanilla planifolia | Bluish black |
| | 55 | | $0.02 | Vanilla planifolia | Violet Brown |
| | 56 | | $0.04 | Vanilla planifolia | Bistre Brown |
| | 57 | | $0.05 | Vanilla planifolia | Green |
| | 59 | | $0.10 | Vanilla planifolia | Rose |
| | 62 | | $0.15 | Vanilla planifolia | Violet |
| 1906 | Letcd | HG7 | $0.10 | Vanilla planifolia | Lettercard/ Stamp has five bean sprays >Red on Buff< |
| | Letcd | HG8 | $0.15 | Vanilla planifolia | Lettercard/ Stamp has five bean sprays >Violet on Buff< |
| | Post | HG12 | $0.05 | Vanilla planifolia | Postcard/ Stamp has five bean sprays >Green on Greenish< |
| | Post | HG13 | $0.10 | Vanilla planifolia | Postcard/ Stamp has five bean sprays >Red on Greenish< |
| 1915 | B1 | | $0.10 | Vanilla planifolia | #59 Surcharged |
| 1917 | B2 | | $0.15 | Vanilla planifolia | #62 Surcharged and #B2a Double surcharged |
| 1922 | 58 | | $0.05 | Vanilla planifolia | Deep Blue |
| | 60 | | $0.10 | Vanilla planifolia | Green |
| 1925 | 61 | | $0.10 | Vanilla planifolia | Red on Bluish |
| **GUATEMALA** | | | | | |
| 1897/01/01 | Post | HG9 | $0.03 | Oncidium | Postcard/ In the four corners >Light Blue and Black< |
| 1939/09/07 | 293 | | $0.02 | Lycaste skinneri v. alba | |

## GUATEMALA {Continued}

| DATE ISSUE | SCOTT/ MICHEL | GIBBON NUMBER | FACE VALUE | SPECIES NAME | BRIEF DESCRIPTION |
|---|---|---|---|---|---|
| 1953/10/23 | C189 | | $0.04 | Lycaste skinneri v. alba | |
| | C190 | | $0.05 | Lycaste skinneri v. alba | In Girl's hand |
| 1967/01/12 | C354 | | $0.10 | Lycaste skinneri v. alba | |
| 1968/08/23 | C418 | | $0.10 | Lycaste skinneri v. alba | Claret and Green |
| | C419 | | $0.20 | Lycaste skinneri v. alba | Orange and Black |
| | C420 | | $0.50 | Lycaste skinneri v. alba | Ultramarine and Claret |
| 1975/05/10 | C559 | | $0.09 | Lycaste skinneri v. alba | >Perf 12.5< and #C559a >Perf 12.5x13.5< |
| 1975/12/12 | C572 | | $0.08 | Lycaste skinneri v. alba | Yellow |
| 1975/12/19 | C571 | | $0.01 | Lycaste skinneri v. alba | Green |
| 1976/05/10 | C573 | | $0.26 | Lycaste skinneri v. alba | Rose |
| 1978/12/07 | C652 | | $0.01 | Cattleya pachecoi | |
| | C653 | | $0.01 | Sobralia xantholeuca | |
| | C654 | | $0.01 | Cypripedium irapeanum | |
| | C655 | | $0.01 | Oncidium splendidum | |
| | C656 | | $0.03 | Cattleya bowringiana | |
| | C657 | | $0.03 | Encyclia cordigera | |
| | C658 | | $0.03 | Epidendrum imatophyllum | |
| | C659 | | $0.03 | Barkeria skinneri | |
| | C660 | | $0.08 | Spiranthes speciosa | |
| | C661 | | $0.20 | Lycaste skinneri v. alba | |
| | Enve | --- | $0.08 | Cattleya guatemalensis | Envelope/ Cachet has single orchid |
| 1985/07/01 | C794 | | $0.08 | Lycaste skinneri v. alba | Upper left |

## GUERNSEY

| DATE ISSUE | SCOTT/ MICHEL | GIBBON NUMBER | FACE VALUE | SPECIES NAME | BRIEF DESCRIPTION |
|---|---|---|---|---|---|
| 1972/05/24 | 70 | | 2.5 penc | Dactylorhiza maculata | |
| 1986/05/22 | 332 | | 14 pence | Orchis laxiflora | |

## GUINEA

| DATE ISSUE | SCOTT/ MICHEL | GIBBON NUMBER | FACE VALUE | SPECIES NAME | BRIEF DESCRIPTION |
|---|---|---|---|---|---|
| 1985/09/23 | 937 | | 35 syli | Odontoglossum | Bridal Bouquet Di's {Wedding} |

## GUYANA

| DATE ISSUE | SCOTT/ MICHEL | GIBBON NUMBER | FACE VALUE | SPECIES NAME | BRIEF DESCRIPTION |
|---|---|---|---|---|---|
| 1972/09/18 | 138 | | $0.10 | Cattleya violacea | >Perf 13.5<; #138b/547a >Perf 13< and #138a Wmk |
| | 139 | | $0.15 | Oncidium lanceanum | >Perf 13.5<; #139a/548a >Perf 13< and #139b Wmk |
| | 140 | | $0.20 | Paphinia cristata | >Perf 13.5<; #140b/549a >Perf 13< and #140a Wmk |
| | 141 | | $0.25 | Gongora quinquenervis >value center< | #141a Wmk |
| | 142 | | $0.40 | Scuticaria steelii | #142a Wmk |
| 1973/08/20 | 141A | | $0.25 | Gongora quinquenervis >value right< | #141 >Perf 13.5<RP, flower corrected, #141Aa/550ab >Perf 13< |
| 1975/12/01 | --- | F4 | $0.25 | Gongora quinquenervis >value center< | #550 OP "Revenue Only" |
| | --- | F4a | $0.25 | Gongora quinquenervis >value right< | #550a OP "Revenue Only" |
| | --- | F5 | $0.40 | Scuticaria steelii | #551 OP "Revenue Only" |
| 1981/03/20 | 329 | | $0.30 | Sophronitis species | SS/ 12 stamps, 1 is #329d >Beside sloth< |
| 1981/06/08 | --- | 013 | $0.10 | Gongora quinquenervis >value center< | #F4 OP "OPS, 10 and 3 vertical bars" |
| 1981/07/07 | --- | 809 | $0.15 | Oncidium lanceanum | #548 OP "1981" >Black< |
| | --- | 811a | $0.40 | Scuticaria steelii | #F5 OP "1981" >Black< |
| | --- | 839 | $6.25 | Scuticaria steelii | #F5 Surcharged |
| | --- | 023 | $0.15 | Oncidium lanceanum | #548 OP "OPS" and some of the Zeros in "OPS" different |
| 1981/11/14 | --- | 864 | $0.15 | Oncidium lanceanum | #548 OP "1981" >Red< and #864a >Perf 13< |
| | --- | 869a | $1.10 | Gongora quinquenervis >value center< | #013 OP "110" and some of the Zeros in "10" different |
| 1982/02/08 | --- | 887 | $0.20 | Paphinia cristata | #549 OP "1982" >Blue< and #887a >Perf 13< |
| | --- | 889 | $0.25 | Gongora quinquenervis >value right< | #550a OP "1982" >Blue< and #889b >Perf 13< |
| | --- | 889a | $0.25 | Gongora quinquenervis >value center< | #550 OP "1982" >Blue< |
| | --- | 919 | $1.80 | Scuticaria steelii | #F5 OP "1982" and "180" >Blue< |
| 1982/06/07 | --- | 977 | $0.15 | Oncidium lanceanum | #548 OP "1982" >Blue< and #977a >Perf 13< |
| 1982/10/01 | --- | 1009 | $0.15 | Oncidium lanceanum | #023 OP "POSTAGE" and some of the Zeros in "OPS" different |
| 1983/04/01 | --- | 1083 | $0.50 | Gongora quinquenervis >value center< | #013 OP "FIFTY CENTS" some of the Zeros in "OPS" different |
| 1983/05/02 | --- | 1090 | $2.50 | Scuticaria steelii | #551 SC and some of the Zeros in "2.50" different |
| 1984/05/04 | --- | 1241 | $0.25 | Gongora quinquenervis >value right< | #550a OP "Protecting Our Heritage and #1241a >Perf 13< |
| | --- | 1242 | $0.30 | Oncidium lanceanum | #548 SC & OP "Protecting Our Heritage" |
| | --- | 1247 | $0.90 | Scuticaria steelii | #551 SC & OP "Protecting Our Heritage" |
| | --- | 1247a | $0.90 | Scuticaria steelii | #F5 SC & OP "Protecting Our Heritage" |
| | --- | 1248 | $1.80 | Scuticaria steelii | #919 SC & OP "Protecting Our Heritage" |
| | --- | 1252 | $3.20 | Scuticaria steelii | #551 SC & OP "Protecting Our Heritage" |

## GUYANA {Continued}

| DATE ISSUE | SCOTT/ MICHEL | GIBBON NUMBER | FACE VALUE | SPECIES NAME | BRIEF DESCRIPTION |
|---|---|---|---|---|---|
| 1984/05/04 | --- | 1253 | $3.50 | Scuticaria steelii | #551 SC & OP "Protecting Our Heritage" |
| 1984/09/15 | --- | 1390 | $0.30 | Sophronitis species | SS/ 12 stamps, 1 is #329d OP "1984" >Black< |
| 1984/10/01 | --- | 1341 | $0.25 | Cattleya violacea | #548 OP "bar and small 25" and #1341a >Perf 13< |
| | --- | 1342 | $0.25 | Oncidium lanceanum | #864a OP "bar amd small 25" |
| | --- | 1343 | $0.25 | Oncidium lanceanum | #548 OP "one Fleur-de-lis and small 25" |
| | --- | 1344 | $0.25 | Oncidium lanceanum | #809 OP "one Fleur-de-lis and small 25" |
| | --- | 1345 | $0.25 | Oncidium lanceanum | #864 OP "one Fleur-de-lis and small 25" |
| | --- | 1346 | $0.25 | Oncidium lanceanum | #977 OP "one Fleur-de-lis and small 25" and #1346a >Perf 13< |
| | --- | 1347 | $0.25 | Oncidium lanceanum | #1009 OP "one Fleur-de-lis and small 25" |
| | --- | 1348 | $0.25 | Oncidium lanceanum | #023 OP "one Fleur-de-lis and small 25" |
| | --- | 1352 | $0.20 | Paphinia cristata | #549 OP "two Fleur-de-lis and small 1984" and #1352a >Perf 13< |
| | --- | 1357 | $0.20 | Paphinia cristata | #549 OP "small 1984" and #1357a >Perf 13< |
| | --- | 1357b | $0.20 | Paphinia cristata | #887 OP "two Fleur-de-lis" |
| | --- | 1358 | $0.25 | Gongora quinquenervis >value center< | #550 OP "two Fleur-de-lis and small 1984" |
| | --- | 1358a | $0.25 | Gongora quinquenervis >value center< | #889 OP "two Fleur-de-lis" and #1358d >Perf13< |
| | --- | 1359 | $0.25 | Gongora quinquenervis >value right< | #F4 OP "two Fleur-de-lis and small 1984" |
| | --- | 1359a | $0.25 | Gongora quinquenervis >value center< | #F4a OP "two Fleur-de-lis and small 1984" & #1359b OP inverted |
| 1985/06/03 | --- | 1513 | $6.00 | Scuticaria steelii | #F5 SC in condensed type and 12 thin lines |
| 1985/07/02 | 373 | | $0.25 | Cattleya lawrenceana | 12/1 |
| | 374 | | $0.25 | Laeliocattleya elegans | 52/1 |
| | 375 | | $0.25 | Cattleya warscewiczii | 72/1 |
| | 376 | | $0.25 | Paphiopedilum Io | 23/1 |
| | 377 | | $0.25 | Laelia euspatha | 8/1 |
| | 378 | | $0.25 | Paphiopedilum rothschildianum | 61/1 |
| | 379 | | $0.25 | Phalaenopsis speciosa | 51/1 |
| | 380 | | $0.25 | Oncidium ampliatum v. majus | 70/1 |
| | 381 | | $0.25 | Dendrobium heterocarpum | 63/1 |
| | 382 | | $0.25 | Laelia gouldiana | 59/1 and #382a Wmk "Dark Red Flowers" |
| | 383 | | $0.25 | Dimorphorchis lowii | 71/1 |
| | 384 | | $0.30 | Chondrorhyncha aromatica | 53/1 and #384a/1849 Wmk >Blue< |
| | 385 | | $0.30 | Odontoglossum triumphans | 86/1 |
| | 386 | | $0.40 | Cattleya guttata v. leopoldii | 77/1 |
| | 387 | | $0.40 | Odontoglossum reichenheimii | 96/1 and #409a Wmk |
| | 388 | | $0.45 | Paphiopedilum selligerum v. majus | 54/1 |
| | 389 | | $0.45 | Cattleya trianae v. alba | 81/1 |
| | 390 | | $0.50 | Dendrobium brymerianum | 92/1 |
| | 391 | | $0.55 | Rhynchostylis gigantea | 22/1 and #391a/1777 Wmk |
| | 392 | | $0.55 | Dendrobium wardianum | 9/1 and #392a/1776 Wmk |
| | 393 | | $0.55 | Odontoglossum harryanum | 49/1 and #393a/1778 Wmk |
| | 394 | | $0.55 | Oncidium macranthum | 64/1 and #394a/1779 Wmk |
| | 395 | | $0.55 | Gastorchis humblotii | 17/1 |
| | 396 | | $0.60 | Odontoglossum insleayi v. splendens | 7/1 |
| | 397 | | $0.60 | Laelia autumnalis v. xanthotropis | 10/1 |
| | 398 | | $0.60 | Cattleya percivaliana | 2/1 |
| | 399 | | $0.60 | Trichopilia suavis v. alba | 31/1 |
| | 400 | | $0.60 | Masdevallia chimaera v. backhousiana | 19/1 |
| | 401 | | $0.60 | Sobralia xantholeuca | 44/1 |
| | 402 | | $0.60 | Encyclia vitellina | 47/1 |
| | 403 | | $0.60 | Aerangis articulata | #409 {55/1} RP, with new value >Black< |
| | 404 | | $0.60 | Vanda coerulea | 57/1 |
| | 405 | | $0.60 | Oncidium lanceanum | 73/1 |
| | 406 | | $0.60 | Cattleya labiata v. gaskelliana | 75/1 |
| | 407 | | $0.60 | Cattleya labiata v. warneri | 95/1 |
| | 408 | | $0.60 | Cattleya eldorado v. crocata | 93/1 |
| | 409 | | $0.75 | Aerangis articulata | 55/1 and #409a Wmk >Blue< |
| | 410 | | $0.75 | Cattleya dowiana v. aurea | 5/1 |
| | 411 | | $0.90 | Odontoglossum luteo-purpureum v. prionopetalum | 84/1 |
| | 412 | | $0.90 | Paphiopedilum lemoinierianum | 89/1 |
| | 413 | | $1.00 | Paphiopedilum tautzianum | 65/1 and #413a/1854 Wmk >Blue< |
| | 414 | | $1.00 | Laelia albida | 68/1 |
| | 415 | | $1.00 | Oncidium tigrinum | 88/1 |
| | 416 | | $1.20 | Vanda teres | 27/1 |

## GUYANA {Continued}

| DATE ISSUE | SCOTT/ MICHEL | GIBBON NUMBER | FACE VALUE | SPECIES NAME | BRIEF DESCRIPTION |
|---|---|---|---|---|---|
| 1985/07/02 | 417 | | $1.20 | Laelia anceps v. percivaliana | 36/1 |
| | 418 | | $1.20 | Odontoglossum hallii v. xanthoglossum | 28/1 |
| | 419 | | $1.20 | Phalaenopsis amabilis | 11/1 |
| | 420 | | $1.20 | Odontoglossum crispum | 1/1 |
| | 421 | | $1.20 | Cattleya trianae v. schroederiana | 46/1 |
| | 422 | | $1.20 | Odontoglossum hebraicum | 37/1 |
| | 423 | | $1.20 | Plectrelminthus caudatus | 67/1 |
| | 424 | | $1.20 | Laelia anceps v. sanderiana | 56/1 |
| | 425 | | $1.20 | Dendrobium nobile v. sanderiana | 58/1 |
| | 426 | | $1.20 | Miltoniopsis roezlii | 69/1 |
| | 427 | | $1.30 | Paphiopedilum sanderianum | 3/1 |
| | 428 | | $1.30 | Chysis bractescens | 18/1 |
| | 429 | | $1.30 | Oncidium concolor | 30/1 |
| | 430 | | $1.30 | Odontoglossum crispum v. hrubyanum | 29/1 |
| | 431 | | $1.30 | Coelogyne cristata v. maxima | 6/1 and #431a/1767 Wmk |
| | 432 | | $1.30 | Maxillaria sanderiana | 25/1 and #432a/1771 Wmk |
| | 433 | | $1.30 | Masdevallia caudata & v. xanthocorys | 13/1 and #433a/1768 Wmk |
| | 434 | | $1.30 | Encyclia citrina | 20/1 and #434a/1770 Wmk |
| | 435 | | $1.30 | Zygopetalum intermedium | 16/1 |
| | 436 | | $1.30 | Paphiopedilum oenanthum v. superbum | 38/1 |
| | 437 | | $1.30 | Cymbidium mastersii | 66/1 |
| | 438 | | $1.30 | Cattleya ballantineana | 91/1 |
| | 439 | | $1.50 | Vanda sanderiana | 62/1 |
| | 440 | | $1.50 | Cattleya violacea | 32/1 |
| | 441 | | $1.50 | Stanhopea shuttleworthii | 35/1 |
| | 442 | | $1.50 | Paphiopedilum niveum | 34/1 |
| | 443 | | $1.50 | Laelia anceps v. stella & v. barkeriana | 48/1 |
| | 444 | | $1.50 | Lycaste skinneri & v. alba | 41/1 |
| | 445 | | $1.50 | Odontoglossum crispum v. kinlesideanum | 45/1 and #445a/1803 Wmk |
| | 446 | | $1.50 | Phalaenopsis stuartiana | 42/1 and #446a/1802 Wmk |
| | 447 | | $1.50 | Laelia harpophylla | 40/1 and #447a/1801 Wmk |
| | 448 | | $1.50 | Odontoglossum edwardii | 26/1 |
| | 449 | | $1.50 | Oncidium splendidum | 78/1 |
| | 450 | | $1.50 | Phalaenopsis leuchorrhoda | 87/1 |
| | 451 | | $1.50 | Epidendrum prismatocarpum | 76/1 |
| | 452 | | $1.80 | Cattleya mendelii v. Duke of Marlborough | 15/1 |
| | 453 | | $2.00 | Odontoglossum rossii | 4/1 |
| | 454 | | $2.00 | Angraecum sesquipedale | 14/1 |
| | 455 | | $2.00 | Cattleya trianae v. ernesti | 43/1 and #455a/1806 Wmk |
| | 456 | | $2.00 | Oncidium jonesianum & v. phaeanthum | 21/1 |
| | 457 | | $2.00 | Odontoglossum luteo-purpureum | 33/1 |
| | 458 | | $2.00 | Odontoglossum hebraicum v. aspersum | 79/1 |
| | 459 | | $2.25 | Odontoglossum blandum | 24/1 and #459a/1863 Wmk >Blue< |
| | 460 | | $2.25 | Odontoglossum grande | 60/1 |
| | 461 | | $2.50 | Vanda hookeriana | 74/1 |
| | 462 | | $2.60 | Dendrobium superbiens | 39/1 |
| | 463 | | $3.00 | Paphiopedilum argus | 83/1 |
| | 464 | | $3.20 | Dendrobium leechanum | 50/1 |
| | 465 | | $3.20 | Odontoglossum humeanum | 82/1 |
| | 466 | | $3.30 | Cattleya dowiana v. chrysotoxa | 80/1 |
| | 467 | | $3.50 | Odontoglossum constictum | 94/1 |
| | 468 | | $3.60 | Cattleya rochellensis | 85/1 |
| | 469 | | $3.75 | Catasetum pileatum | 90/1 and #469a Wmk |
| 1985/07/06 | --- | 1536 | $1.30 | Chysis bractescens | #428 {18/1} OP "Queen Mother 1900-1985" |
| | --- | 1537 | $1.30 | Odontoglossum crispum v. hrubyanum | #430 {29/1} OP "Queen Mother 1900-1985" |
| | --- | 1538 | $1.30 | Oncidium concolor | #429 {30/1} OP "Queen Mother 1900-1985" |
| | --- | 1539a | $2.00 | Odontoglossum rossii | #453 {4/1} OP "Lady Bowes-Lyon 1900-1923" |
| | --- | 1539b | $2.00 | Odontoglossum rossii | #453 {4/1} OP "Duchess of York 1923-1937" |
| | --- | 1539c | $2.00 | Odontoglossum rossii | #453 {4/1} OP "Queen Elizabeth 1937-1952" |
| | --- | 1539d | $2.00 | Odontoglossum rossii | #453 {4/1} OP "Queen Mother 1952-1985" |
| 1985/09/12 | --- | 1570a | $2.00 | Encyclia citrina | #434 {20/1} SC & OP "Lady Bowes-Lyon 1900-1923" |
| | --- | 1570b | $2.00 | Encyclia citrina | #434 {20/1} SC & OP "Duchess of York 1923-1937" |

| DATE ISSUE | SCOTT/ MICHEL | GIBBON NUMBER | FACE VALUE | SPECIES NAME | BRIEF DESCRIPTION |
|---|---|---|---|---|---|

## GUYANA {Continued}

| DATE ISSUE | SCOTT/ MICHEL | GIBBON NUMBER | FACE VALUE | SPECIES NAME | BRIEF DESCRIPTION |
|---|---|---|---|---|---|
| 1985/09/12 | --- | 1570c | $2.00 | Encyclia citrina | #434 {20/1} SC & OP "Queen Elizabeth 1937-1952" |
|  | --- | 1570d | $2.00 | Encyclia citrina | #434 {20/1} SC & OP "Queen Mother 1952-1985" |
| 1985/10/12 | --- | 1598 | $3.50 | Paphiopedilum tautzianum | #413 {65/1} SC & OP "Cristobal Colon 1492-1992" |
| 1985/10/29 | --- | 1608 | $0.40 | Scuticaria steelii | #551 OP "POSTAGE" |
| 1985/11/03 | --- | 1619a | $0.55 | Rhynchostylis gigantea | #391 {22/1} OP "Christmas 1985" >Red< |
|  | --- | 1619b | $0.55 | Rhynchostylis gigantea | #391 {22/1} OP "Happy New Year" >Red< |
|  | --- | 1619c | $0.55 | Rhynchostylis gigantea | #391 {22/1} OP "Merry Christmas" >Red< |
|  | --- | 1619d | $0.55 | Rhynchostylis gigantea | #391 {22/1} OP "Happy Holidays" >Red< |
| 1985/11/15 | --- | 1646 | $0.30 | Sophronitis species | SS/ 12 stamps, 1 is #329d OP "1985" >Red< |
| 1986/01/13 | --- | 1657 | $1.50 | Phalaenopsis stuartiana | #446 {42/1} OP "Reichenbachia 1886-1986" |
|  | --- | 1658 | $2.00 | Cattleya trianae v. ernesti | #455 {43/1} OP "Reichenbachia 1886-1986" |
| 1986/04/21 | --- | 1684 | $1.30 | Masdevallia caudata & v. xanthocorys | #433 {13/1} OP "1926-1986 Queen Elizabeth" |
|  | --- | 1685a | $1.30 | Coelogyne cristata v. maxima | #431 {6/1} SC & OP "Queen Elizabeth 1926-1986" |
|  | --- | 1685b | $2.00 | Coelogyne cristata v. maxima | #431 {6/1} SC & OP "Queen Elizabeth 1926-1986" |
|  | --- | 1685c | $2.60 | Coelogyne cristata v. maxima | #431 {6/1} SC & OP "Queen Elizabeth 1926-1986" |
|  | --- | 1685d | $3.30 | Coelogyne cristata v. maxima | #431 {6/1} SC & OP "Queen Elizabeth 1926-1986" |
| 1986/08/20 | 470 |  | $0.30 | Rhynchostylis coelestis | 30/2 |
|  | 471 |  | $0.40 | Cattleya ballantineana | #438 {91/1} RP, with new value |
|  | 472 |  | $0.45 | Odontoglossum coradinei | 21/2 |
|  | 473 |  | $0.45 | Cattleya schroederae v. alba | 17/2 |
|  | 474 |  | $0.50 | Laelia grandis | 33/2 |
|  | 475 |  | $0.60 | Phragmipedium nitidissimum | 27/2 |
|  | 476 |  | $0.75 | Paphiopedilum boxalli v. atratum | 8/2 |
|  | 477 |  | $0.75 | Coelogyne sanderae | 56/2 |
|  | 478 |  | $0.80 | Dendrobium phalaenopsis | 42/2 |
|  | 479 |  | $0.85 | Paphiopedilum castleanum | 45/2 |
|  | 480 |  | $0.90 | Gastorchis tuberculosa | 4/2 |
|  | 481 |  | $0.90 | Laelia anceps v. schroderiana | 13/2 |
|  | 482 |  | $1.30 | Paphiopedilum laucheanum & eyermannianum | 38/2 |
|  | 483 |  | $1.60 | Odontoglossum crispum v. mundyanum | 5/2 |
|  | 484 |  | $2.00 | Odontoglossum wattianum | 9/2 |
|  | 485 |  | $2.00 | Odontoglossum naevium | 44/2 |
|  | 486 |  | $3.00 | Dendrobium venus & cassiope | 50/2 |
|  | 487 |  | $3.20 | Dendrobium melanodiscus | 12/2 |
|  | 488 |  | $3.20 | Paphiopedilum lathamianum v. inversum | 10/2 |
|  | 489 |  | $3.50 | Miltoniopsis vexillaria | 29/2 |
|  | 490 |  | $3.60 | Cattleya labiata v. lueddemanniana | 34/2 |
|  | 491 |  | $3.90 | Laelia praestans | 6/2 |
|  | 492 |  | $0.25 | Laeliocattleya elegans v. bleheimensis | 20/2 |
|  | 493 |  | $0.40 | Laelia albida | #414 {68/1} RP, with new value |
|  | 494 |  | $0.40 | Dendrobium phalaenopsis v. statterianum | 7/2 |
|  | 495 |  | $0.50 | Laelia anceps v. schroderiana | #481 {13/2} RP, with new value |
|  | 496 |  | $0.80 | Gastorchis humblotii | #395 {17/1} RP, with new value |
|  | 497 |  | $0.85 | Disa uniflora | 15/2 |
|  | 498 |  | $0.90 | Dendrobium formosum | 3/2 |
|  | 499 |  | $1.20 | Phaius cooksonii | 14/2 |
|  | 500 |  | $1.30 | Miltonia bleuana | 32/2 |
|  | 501 |  | $1.50 | Odontoglossum wilckeanum v. rothschildianum | 22/2 |
|  | 502 |  | $3.20 | Lycaste skinneri v. armeniaca | 18/2 |
|  | 503 |  | $3.30 | Cattleya mendelii v. measuresiana | 28/2 |
| 1986/08/21 | 504 | --- | $0.40 | Catasetum pileatum | Booklet/ #469 {90/1} RP, with new value |
|  | 504a | Bookle | $50.00 | Catasetum | Booklet/ #1/1 thru #45/1 {Numberial or Alphabetical} |
|  | 504b | Bookle | $30.00 | Cattleya | Booklet/ #46/1 thru #96/1 {Numberial or Alphabetical} |
|  | 505 | --- | $0.45 | Cattleya guttata v. leopoldii | Booklet/ #386 {77/1} RP, with new value |
|  | 506 | --- | $0.45 | Oncidium splendidum | Booklet/ #449 {78/1} RP, with new value |
|  | 507 | --- | $0.45 | Odontoglossum luteo-purpureum v. prionopetalum | Booklet/ #411 {84/1} RP, with new value |
|  | 508 | --- | $0.45 | Cattleya rochellensis | Booklet/ #468 {85/1} RP, with new value |
|  | 509 | --- | $0.50 | Dendrobium wardianum | Booklet/ #392 {9/1} RP, with new value |
|  | 510 | --- | $0.50 | Rhynchostylis gigantea | Booklet/ #391 {22/1} RP, with new value |
|  | 511 | --- | $0.50 | Chondrorhyncha aromatica | Booklet/ #384 {53/1} RP, with new value |
|  | 512 | --- | $0.50 | Odontoglossum blandum | Booklet/ #459 {24/1} RP, with new value |
|  | 513 | --- | $0.50 | Paphiopedilum tautzianum | Booklet/ #413 {65/1} RP, with new value |

OMAN 1971 Unlisted; MALAWI 333; GHANA 404; GERMANY BERLIN 9N434; SAINT LUCIA 241; FRENCH POLYNESIA C120; BRITISH VIRGIN ISLANDS 401; NORTH KOREA M460; RWANDS 1089; AJMAN M430A; KAMPUCHEA M775; BURUNDI C140; NIUATO 8537 & 8538; ROMANIA 3535g; GUADELOUPE B2a;  CHRISTMAS ISLANDS 77; SAINT VINCENT-GRENADINES 8515; and BELIZE M610.

| DATE ISSUE | SCOTT/ MICHEL | GIBBON NUMBER | FACE VALUE | SPECIES NAME | BRIEF DESCRIPTION |
|---|---|---|---|---|---|
| **GUYANA {Continued}** | | | | | |
| 1986/08/21 | 514 | --- | $0.55 | Cattleya mendelii v. Duke of Marlborough | Booklet/ #452 {15/1} RP, with new value |
| | 515 | --- | $0.55 | Cattleya trianae v. alba | Booklet/ #389 {81/1} RP, with new value |
| | 516 | --- | $0.55 | Odontoglossum humeanum | Booklet/ #465 {82/1} RP, with new value |
| | 517 | --- | $0.55 | Paphiopedilum lemoinierianum | Booklet/ #412 {89/1} RP, with new value |
| | 518 | --- | $0.60 | Cattleya dowiana v. aurea | Booklet/ #410 {5/1}  RP, with new value |
| | 519 | --- | $0.60 | Dendrobium leechanum | Booklet/ #464 {50/1} RP, with new value |
| | 520 | --- | $0.60 | Paphiopedilum selligerum v. majus | Booklet/ #388 {54/1} RP, with new value |
| | 521 | --- | $0.60 | Miltoniopsis roezlii | Booklet/ #426 {69/1} RP, with new value |
| | 522 | --- | $0.60 | Dimorphorchis lowii | Booklet/ #383 {71/1} RP, with new value |
| | 523 | --- | $0.60 | Odontoglossum hebraicum v. aspersum | Booklet/ #458 {79/1} RP, with new value |
| | 524 | --- | $0.60 | Phalaenopsis leuchorrhoda | Booklet/ #450 {87/1} RP, with new value |
| | 525 | --- | $0.60 | Odontoglossum constictum | Booklet/ #467 {94/1} RP, with new value |
| | 526 | --- | $0.65 | Epidendrum prismatocarpum | Booklet/ #451 {76/1} RP, with new value |
| | 527 | --- | $0.65 | Cattleya dowiana v. chrysotoxa | Booklet/ #466 {80/1} RP, with new value |
| | 528 | --- | $0.65 | Oncidium tigrinum | Booklet/ #415 {88/1} RP, with new value |
| | 529 | --- | $0.65 | Odontoglossum reichenheimii | Booklet/ #387 {96/1} RP, with new value |
| | 530 | --- | $0.75 | Odontoglossum grande | Booklet/ #460 {60/1} RP, with new value |
| | 531 | --- | $0.75 | Paphiopedilum argus | Booklet/ #463 {83/1} RP, with new value |
| | 532 | --- | $0.75 | Dendrobium brymerianum | Booklet/ #390 {92/1} RP, with new value |
| | 533 | --- | $0.75 | Cattleya labiata v. warneri | Booklet/ #407 {95/1} RP, with new value |
| | 534 | --- | $0.80 | Dendrobium superbiens | Booklet/ #462 {39/1} RP, with new value |
| | 535 | --- | $0.80 | Vanda hookeriana | Booklet/ #461 {74/1} RP, with new value |
| | 536 | --- | $0.80 | Cattleya eldorado v. crocata | Booklet/ #408 {93/1} RP, with new value |
| | 537 | --- | $1.00 | Coelogyne cristata v. maxima | Booklet/ #431 {6/1}  RP, with new value |
| | 538 | --- | $1.00 | Masdevallia caudata & v. xanthocorys | Booklet/ #433 {13/1} RP, with new value |
| | 539 | --- | $1.00 | Encyclia citrina | Booklet/ #434 {20/1} RP, with new value |
| | 540 | --- | $1.00 | Maxillaria sanderiana | Booklet/ #432 {25/1} RP, with new value |
| | 541 | --- | $1.00 | Laelia harpophylla | Booklet/ #447 {40/1} RP, with new value |
| | 542 | --- | $1.00 | Phalaenopsis stuartiana | Booklet/ #446 {42/1} RP, with new value |
| | 543 | --- | $1.00 | Cattleya trianae v. ernesti | Booklet/ #455 {43/1} RP, with new value |
| | 544 | --- | $1.00 | Odontoglossum crispum v. kinlesideanum | Booklet/ #445 {45/1} RP, with new value |
| 1986/10/06 | --- | 1847 | $6.50 | Odontoglossum triumphans | #546 {86/1} SC & OP "12th World Orchid Conference" |
| 1986/10/23 | 545 | | $0.35 | Paphiopedilum castleanum | #479 {45/2} RP, with new value |
| | 546 | | $0.40 | Odontoglossum triumphans | #385 {86/1} RP, with new value |
| | 547 | | $0.50 | Oncidium macranthum | #394 {64/1} RP, with new value |
| | 548 | | $0.50 | Odontoglossum harryanum | #393 {49/1} RP, with new value |
| | 549 | | $0.50 | Disa uniflora | #497 {15/2} RP, with new value |
| | 550 | | $0.50 | Aerangis articulata | #403 {55/1} RP, with new value |
| | 551 | | $0.85 | Cattleya intermedia v. punctatissima | #558 {24/2} RP, with new value |
| | 552 | | $0.85 | Lycaste skinneri v. armeniaca | #502 {18/2} RP, with new value |
| | 553 | | $0.90 | Paphiopedilum lathamianum v. inversum | #488 {10/2} RP, with new value |
| | 554 | | $0.90 | Phragmipedium nitidissimum | #475 {27/2} RP, with new value |
| | 555 | | $0.90 | Cattleya bowringiana | #557 {2/2}  RP, with new value |
| | 556 | | $1.80 | Odontoglossum ramosissimum | 41/2 |
| | 557 | | $2.00 | Cattleya bowringiana | 2/2 |
| | 558 | | $2.25 | Cattleya intermedia v. punctatissima | 24/2 |
| | 559 | | $2.30 | Laelia purpurata | 25/2 |
| | 560 | | $3.00 | Cattleya victoria-regina | 85/2 |
| | 561 | | $3.30 | Thunia brymeriana | 82/2 |
| | 562 | | $4.25 | Laelia autumnalis v. alba | 87/2 |
| | 563 | | $4.40 | Spathoglottis kimballiana | 88/2 |
| | 564 | | $5.90 | Cattleya mossiae v. reineckiana | 52/2 |
| | 565 | | $6.50 | Arachnis clarkei | 65/2 |
| 1986/10/30 | --- | 1864 | $3.20 | Odontoglossum blandum | #459 {24/1} SC & OP "Columbus 1492-1992" >Red and Black< |
| | --- | 1865 | $3.20 | Odontoglossum blandum | #459 {24/1} SC & OP "Columbus 1432-1992" >Red< |
| 1986/11/10 | --- | E1 | $12.00 | Paphiopedilum tautzianum | #1598 {65/1} SC & OP "EXPRESS and $12.00" >Red< |
| | --- | E2 | $15.00 | Odontoglossum triumphans | #385 {86/1} SC & OP "EXPRESS and $15.00" >ONTOGLOSSUM< |
| | --- | E2a | $15.00 | Odontoglossum triumphans | #385 {86/1} SC & OP "EXPRESS and $15.00" >ODontoglossum< |
| | --- | E4 | $25.00 | Chondrorhyncha aromatica | {53/1} unissued value [25c] SC & OP "$, + and EXPRESS" |
| 1986/11/26 | --- | 1897 | $0.30 | Sophronitis species | SS/ 12 stamps, 1 is #329d OP "1986" >Blue< |
| 1987/01/18 | --- | 1853 | $0.75 | Aerangis articulata | #409a {55/1} RP, with new value |
| 1987/01/19 | --- | 1930 | $2.25 | Chondrorhyncha aromatica | {53/1} unissued value [25c] SC & OP "2, GPOC and 1977-1987" |

| DATE ISSUE | SCOTT/ MICHEL | GIBBON NUMBER | FACE VALUE | SPECIES NAME | BRIEF DESCRIPTION |
|---|---|---|---|---|---|

## GUYANA {Continued}

| DATE ISSUE | SCOTT/ MICHEL | GIBBON NUMBER | FACE VALUE | SPECIES NAME | BRIEF DESCRIPTION |
|---|---|---|---|---|---|
| 1987/01/19 | --- | 1931 | $10.00 | Odontoglossum blandum | #459 {24/1} SC & OP "GPOC, $10 and 1977-1987" |
| 1987/02/09 | --- | 1932 | $2.00 | Catasetum pileatum | #504 {90/1} SC "two Fleur-de-lis and 200" >Red< |
|  | --- | 1933 | $2.00 | Laelia euspatha | #377 {8/1} SC "one large Fleur-de-lis and 200" |
|  | --- | 1934 | $2.00 | Phalaenopsis speciosa | #379 {51/1} SC "one large Fleur-de-lis and 200" |
| 1987/02/17 | --- | 2077 | $0.25 | Oncidium lanceanum | #548 SC & OP "P.O. Corp. 1977-1987 and 25c" |
|  | --- | 2078 | $0.60 | Oncidium lanceanum | #548 SC & OP "P.O. Corp. 1977-1987 and 60c" |
|  | --- | 2080 | $1.30 | Oncidium lanceanum | #548 SC & OP "P.O. Corp. 1977-1987 and 1.30" |
|  | Booklet B32 |  | $5.00 | Oncidium lanceanum | Booklet/ 4 panes, 1 is #2077/5 stamps |
|  | Booklet B33 |  | $20.00 | Oncidium & Zygopetalum | Booklet/ 4 panes of #2078/5, #2080/5 and #1930{53/1}/2 |
| 1987/03/01 | --- | 2084 | $1.30 | Paphiopedilum sanderianum | #427 {3/1} OP "1987" in schoolbook type |
|  | --- | 2085 | $1.30 | Coelogyne cristata v. maxima | #431 {6/1} OP "1987" in schoolbook type |
|  | --- | 2086 | $1.30 | Encyclia citrina | #434 {20/1} OP "1987" in schoolbook type |
|  | --- | 2087 | $1.30 | Chysis bractescens | #1536 {18/1} OP "1987" in schoolbook type |
|  | --- | 2088 | $1.30 | Odontoglossum crispum v. hrubyanum | #1537 {29/1} OP "1987" in schoolbook type |
|  | --- | 2089 | $1.30 | Oncidium concolor | #1538 {30/1} OP "1987" in schoolbook type |
|  | --- | 2090 | $1.30 | Zygopetalum intermedium | #435 {16/1} OP "1987" in schoolbook type |
|  | --- | 2091 | $1.30 | Cymbidium mastersii | #437 {66/1} OP "1987" in schoolbook type |
|  | --- | 2092 | $1.30 | Masdevallia caudata & v. xanthocorys | #1684 {13/1} OP "1987" in schoolbook type |
|  | --- | 2093 | $1.30 | Coelogyne cristata v. maxima | #431a {6/1} OP "1987" in schoolbook type |
|  | --- | 2094 | $1.30 | Encyclia citrina | #434a {20/1} OP "1987" in schoolbook type |
|  | --- | 2095 | $2.00 | Odontoglossum rossii | #453 {4/1} OP "1987" in schoolbook type |
|  | --- | 2096 | $2.00 | Angraecum sesquipedale | #454 {14/1} OP "1987" in schoolbook type |
|  | --- | 2097 | $2.00 | Oncidium jonesianum & v. phaeanthum | #456 {21/1} OP "1987" in schoolbook type |
|  | --- | 2098 | $2.00 | Odontoglossum luteo-purpureum | #457 {33/1} OP "1987" in schoolbook type |
|  | --- | 2099 | $2.00 | Cattleya trianae v. ernesti | #1658 {43/1} OP "1987" in schoolbook type |
|  | --- | 2100 | $2.00 | Odontoglossum hebraicum v. aspersum | #458 {79/1} OP "1987" in schoolbook type |
|  | --- | 2101 | $2.00 | Odontoglossum wattianum | #484 {9/2} OP "1987" in schoolbook type |
|  | --- | 2102 | $2.00 | Cattleya bowringiana | #557 {2/2} OP "1987" in schoolbook type |
|  | --- | 2103 | $2.50 | Vanda hookeriana | #461 {74/1} OP "1987" in schoolbook type |
|  | --- | 2104 | $2.60 | Dendrobium superbiens | #462 {39/1} OP "1987" in schoolbook type |
|  | --- | 2105a | $2.00 | Odontoglossum rossii | #1539a {4/1} OP "1987" in schoolbook type |
|  | --- | 2105b | $2.00 | Odontoglossum rossii | #1539b {4/1} OP "1987" in schoolbook type |
|  | --- | 2105c | $2.00 | Odontoglossum rossii | #1539c {4/1} OP "1987" in schoolbook type |
|  | --- | 2105d | $2.00 | Odontoglossum rossii | #1539d {4/1} OP "1987" in schoolbook type |
|  | --- | 2106a | $2.00 | Encyclia citrina | #1570a {20/1} OP "1987" in schoolbook type |
|  | --- | 2106b | $2.00 | Encyclia citrina | #1570b {20/1} OP "1987" in schoolbook type |
|  | --- | 2106c | $2.00 | Encyclia citrina | #1570c {20/1} OP "1987" in schoolbook type |
|  | --- | 2106d | $2.00 | Encyclia citrina | #1570d {20/1} OP "1987" in schoolbook type |
|  | --- | 2107 | $1.30 | Masdevallia caudata & v. xanthocorys | #433 {13/1} OP "1987" in schoolbook italic type |
|  | --- | 2108 | $1.30 | Maxillaria sanderiana | #432 {25/1} OP "1987" in schoolbook italic type |
|  | --- | 2109 | $1.30 | Cattleya ballantineana | #438 {91/1} OP "1987" in schoolbook italic type |
|  | --- | 2110 | $1.30 | Masdevallia caudata & v. xanthocorys | #433a {13/1} OP "1987" in schoolbook italic type |
|  | --- | 2111 | $1.30 | Maxillaria sanderiana | #432a {25/1} OP "1987" in schoolbook italic type |
| 1987/03/06 | --- | 1935 | $2.00 | Cattleya lawrenceana | #373 {12/1} SC & OP "TWO DOLLARS" |
|  | --- | 1936 | $2.00 | Paphiopedilum lo | #376 {23/1} SC & OP "TWO DOLLARS" |
| 1987/03/17 | --- | 1937 | $2.00 | Laelia albida | #493 {68/1} SC "two large/down Fleur-de-lis and 200" |
|  | --- | 1937a | $2.00 | Laelia albida | #493 {68/1} SC "two large/up Fleur-de-lis and 200" |
|  | --- | 1938 | $2.00 | Catasetum pileatum | #504 {90/1} SC "two large Fleur-de-lis and 200" >Black< |
|  | --- | 1939 | $2.00 | Dendrobium brymerianum | #390 {92/1} SC "two large Fleur-de-lis and 200" |
|  | --- | 1940 | $2.00 | Rhynchostylis gigantea | #510 {22/1} SC "two large Fleur-de-lis and 200" |
|  | --- | 1941 | $2.00 | Rhynchostylis gigantea | #391 {22/1} SC "two large Fleur-de-lis and 200" |
|  | --- | 1942 | $2.00 | Cattleya dowiana v. aurea | #518 {5/1} SC "two large Fleur-de-lis and 200" |
|  | --- | 1943 | $2.00 | Cattleya dowiana v. aurea | #410 {5/1} SC "two large Fleur-de-lis and 200" |
|  | --- | 1944 | $2.00 | Odontoglossum grande | #530 {60/1} SC "two large Fleur-de-lis and 200" |
|  | --- | 1945 | $2.00 | Dendrobium brymerianum | #532 {92/1} SC "two large Fleur-de-lis and 200" |
|  | --- | 1946 | $2.00 | Lycaste skinneri v. armeniaca | #552 {18/2} SC "two Fleur-de-lis and 200" |
|  | --- | 1947 | $2.00 | Catasetum pileatum | #469 {90/1} SC "two large Fleur-de-lis and 200" >Black< |
|  | --- | 1948 | $2.00 | Catasetum pileatum | #469a {90/1} SC "two Fleur-de-lis and 200" |
|  | --- | 1949 | $2.00 | Laeliocattleya elegans | #374 {52/1} SC "two Fleur-de-lis and 200" |
|  | --- | 1950 | $2.00 | Laelia euspatha | #377 {8/1} SC "two Fleur-de-lis and 200" |
|  | --- | 1951 | $2.00 | Cattleya warscewiczii | #375 {72/1} SC "two Fleur-de-lis and 200" |
|  | --- | 1952 | $2.00 | Dimorphorchis lowii | #383 {71/1} SC "two Fleur-de-lis and 200" |

## GUYANA {Continued}

| DATE ISSUE | SCOTT/ MICHEL | GIBBON NUMBER | FACE VALUE | SPECIES NAME | BRIEF DESCRIPTION |
|---|---|---|---|---|---|
| 1987/03/17 | --- | 1953 | $2.00 | Odontoglossum triumphans | #385 {86/1} SC "two Fleur-de-lis and 200" |
| | --- | 1954 | $2.00 | Chondrorhyncha aromatica | #384 {53/1} SC "two Fleur-de-lis and 200" |
| | --- | 1955 | $2.00 | Cattleya guttata v. leopoldii | #386 {77/1} SC "two Fleur-de-lis and 200" |
| | --- | 1956 | $2.00 | Odontoglossum triumphans | #546 {86/1} SC "two Fleur-de-lis and 200" |
| | --- | 1957 | $2.00 | Cattleya trianae v. alba | #389 {81/1} SC "two Fleur-de-lis and 200" |
| | --- | 1958 | $2.00 | Cattleya guttata v. leopoldii | #505 {77/1} SC "two Fleur-de-lis and 200" |
| | --- | 1959 | $2.00 | Oncidium splendidum | #506 {78/1} SC "two Fleur-de-lis and 200" |
| | --- | 1960 | $2.00 | Cattleya rochellensis | #508 {85/1} SC "two Fleur-de-lis and 200" |
| | --- | 1961 | $2.00 | Odontoglossum blandum | #512 {24/1} SC "two Fleur-de-lis and 200" |
| | --- | 1962 | $2.00 | Chondrorhyncha aromatica | #511 {53/1} SC "two Fleur-de-lis and 200" |
| | --- | 1963 | $2.00 | Paphiopedilum tautzianum | #513 {65/1} SC "two Fleur-de-lis and 200" |
| | --- | 1964 | $2.00 | Odontoglossum harryanum | #393 {49/1} SC "two Fleur-de-lis and 200" |
| | --- | 1965 | $2.00 | Gastorchis humblotii | #395 {17/1} SC "two Fleur-de-lis and 200" |
| | --- | 1966 | $2.00 | Odontoglossum harryanum | #393a {49/1} SC "two Fleur-de-lis and 200" |
| | --- | 1967 | $2.00 | Odontoglossum insleayi v. splendens | #396 {7/1} SC "two Fleur-de-lis and 200" |
| | --- | 1968 | $2.00 | Laelia autumnalis v. xanthotropis | #397 {10/1} SC "two Fleur-de-lis and 200" |
| | --- | 1969 | $2.00 | Masdevallia chimaera v. backhousiana | #400 {19/1} SC "two Fleur-de-lis and 200" |
| | --- | 1970 | $2.00 | Trichopilia suavis v. alba | #399 {31/1} SC "two Fleur-de-lis and 200" |
| | --- | 1971 | $2.00 | Sobralia xantholeuca | #401 {44/1} SC "two Fleur-de-lis and 200" |
| | --- | 1972 | $2.00 | Encyclia vitellina | #402 {47/1} SC "two Fleur-de-lis and 200" |
| | --- | 1973 | $2.00 | Vanda coerulea | #404 {57/1} SC "two Fleur-de-lis and 200" |
| | --- | 1974 | $2.00 | Oncidium lanceanum | #405 {73/1} SC "two Fleur-de-lis and 200" |
| | --- | 1975 | $2.00 | Cattleya labiata v. gaskelliana | #406 {75/1} SC "two Fleur-de-lis and 200" |
| | --- | 1976 | $2.00 | Dimorphorchis lowii | #522 {71/1} SC "two Fleur-de-lis and 200" |
| | --- | 1977 | $2.00 | Phalaenopsis leuchorrhoda | #524 {87/1} SC "two Fleur-de-lis and 200" |
| | --- | 1978 | $2.25 | Paphiopedilum lemoinierianum | #412 {89/1} SC "two Fleur-de-lis, 22 and large 5" |
| 1987/03/30 | --- | 1979 | $1.20 | Dendrobium wardianum | #509 {9/1} SC with script numbers |
| | --- | 1980 | $1.20 | Dendrobium wardianum | #392 {9/1} SC with script numbers |
| | --- | 1981 | $1.20 | Oncidium macranthum | #394 {64/1} SC with script numbers |
| | --- | 1982 | $1.20 | Oncidium macranthum | #394a {64/1} SC with script numbers |
| | --- | 1983 | $10.00 | Chondrorhyncha aromatica | {53/1} unissued value [25c] SC & OP "1987 and $10.00" |
| | --- | 1984 | $12.00 | Vanda hookeriana | #535 {74/1} SC & OP "1987 and $12.00" |
| | --- | 1985 | $15.00 | Dendrobium superbiens | #534 {39/1} SC & OP "1987 and $15.00" in script type |
| | --- | 1986 | $25.00 | Chondrorhyncha aromatica | {53/1} unissued value [25c] SC & OP "1987 and $" |
| 1987/04/12 | --- | 2138 | $6.50 | Dendrobium wardianum | #392 {9/1} SC & OP "12th World Orchid Conference Tokyo" |
| | --- | 2139 | $6.50 | Dendrobium wardianum | #392a {9/1} SC & OP "12th World Orchid Conference Tokyo" |
| 1987/04/24 | 583 | | $2.40 | Cattleya amethystoglossa | 47/2 |
| | 584 | | $2.60 | Cycnoches chlorochilon | 39/2 |
| | 585 | | $2.75 | Coelogyne pandurata | 58/2 |
| | 586 | | $3.90 | Odontoglossum leroyanum | 37/2 |
| | 587 | | $4.50 | Odontoglossum excellens | 19/2 |
| | 588 | | $4.60 | Oncidium loxense | 54/2 |
| | 589 | | $5.00 | Phragmipedium weidlichianum | 51/2 |
| | 590 | | $5.60 | Paphiopedilum Morganiae v. Burfordiense | 1/2 |
| | 591 | | $5.00 | Pescatoria klabochorum | 86/2 |
| | 592 | | $5.20 | Laeliocattleya Hon. Mrs. Astor | 89/2 |
| | 593 | | $20.00 | Miltonia spectabilis v. moreliana | 83/2 |
| | 594 | | $2.00 | Coelogyne swaniana | 92/2 |
| | 595 | | $2.00 | Cattleya arnoldiana | 48/2 |
| | 596 | | $2.00 | Paphiopedilum pollettianum & maynardii | 43/2 |
| | 597 | | $3.25 | Phalaenopsis sanderiana & intermedia v. portei | 68/2 |
| | 598 | | $4.00 | Europhia gigantea | 80/2 |
| | 599 | | $4.20 | Dendrobium gouldii | 95/2 |
| | 600 | | $4.80 | Paphiopedilum calypso | 77/2 |
| | 601 | | $5.75 | Oncidium superbiens | 60/2 |
| | 602 | | $6.00 | Encyclia atropurpureum v. randii | 94/2 |
| | 603 | | $25.00 | Cattleya rex | 72/2 |
| | 604 | | $2.55 | Dendrobium johnsoniae | 61/2 |
| | 605 | | $2.90 | Cymbidium lowianum | 53/2 |
| | 606 | | $3.75 | Vandopsis parishii v. mariottianum | 96/2 |
| | 607 | | $6.80 | Cattleya mendelii v. Quorndon House | 64/2 |
| | 608 | | $7.20 | Cattleya labiata | 49/2 |

## GUYANA {Continued}

| DATE ISSUE | SCOTT/ MICHEL | GIBBON NUMBER | FACE VALUE | SPECIES NAME | BRIEF DESCRIPTION |
|---|---|---|---|---|---|
| 1987/04/24 | 609 | | $7.50 | Huntleya meleagris | 66/2 |
| | 610 | | $8.00 | Miltoniopsis phalaenopsis | 79/2 #610a face value omitted |
| | 611 | | $8.50 | Masdevallia courtauldiana, geleniana, & measuresiana 76/2 #611a face value omitted | |
| 1987/06/01 | --- | 1191a | $2.25 | Cattleya labiata v. warneri | #407 {95/1} SC with large numbers |
| | --- | 1987 | $2.25 | Cattleya ballantineana | #471 {91/1} SC with large numbers |
| | --- | 1988 | $2.25 | Catasetum pileatum | #504 {90/1} SC with large numbers |
| | --- | 1989 | $2.25 | Rhynchostylis gigantea | #510 {22/1} SC with large numbers |
| | --- | 1989a | $2.25 | Dendrobium brymerianum | #390 {92/1} SC with large numbers |
| | --- | 1990 | $2.25 | Aerangis articulata | #403 {55/1} SC with large numbers |
| | --- | 1991 | $2.25 | Cattleya eldorado v. crocata | #408 {93/1} SC with large numbers |
| | --- | 1992 | $2.25 | Cattleya eldorado v. crocata | #536 {93/1} SC with large numbers |
| | --- | 1993 | $2.25 | Phalaenopsis stuartiana | #1657 {42/1} SC with large numbers |
| 1987/07/01 | --- | 1994 | $1.20 | Odontoglossum harryanum | #548 {49/1} SC and "Three bars" |
| | --- | 1995 | $1.20 | Oncidium macranthum | #547 {64/1} SC and "Three bars" |
| | --- | 1996 | $1.20 | Dendrobium wardianum | #509 {9/1} SC and "Three bars" |
| | --- | 1997 | $1.20 | Rhynchostylis gigantea | #510 {22/1} SC and "Three bars" |
| | --- | 1998 | $1.20 | Dendrobium formosum | #639 {3/2} SC and "Three bars" |
| | --- | 1999 | $1.20 | Laelia praestans | #640 {6/2} SC and "Three bars" |
| | --- | 2000 | $1.20 | Laeliocattleya elegans v. bleheimensis | #641 {20/2} SC and "Three bars" |
| | --- | 2001 | $1.20 | Miltonia bleuana | #642 {32/2} SC and "Three bars" |
| | --- | 2002 | $1.20 | Dendrobium wardianum | #392 {9/1} SC and "Three bars" |
| | --- | 2003 | $1.20 | Odontoglossum harryanum | #393 {49/1} SC and "Three bars" |
| | --- | 2004 | $1.20 | Oncidium macranthum | #394 {64/1} SC and "Three bars" |
| | --- | 2005 | $1.20 | Dendrobium wardianum | #392a {9/1} SC and "Three bars" |
| | --- | 2006 | $1.20 | Rhynchostylis gigantea | #391 {22/1} SC and "Three bars" |
| | --- | 2007 | $1.20 | Odontoglossum harryanum | #393a {49/1} SC and "Three bars" |
| | --- | 2008 | $1.20 | Oncidium macranthum | #394a {64/1} SC and "Three bars" |
| | --- | 2009 | $1.20 | Cattleya mendelii v. Duke of Marlborough | #514 {15/1} SC and "Three bars" |
| | --- | 2010 | $1.20 | Cattleya trianae v. alba | #515 {81/1} SC and "Three bars" |
| | --- | 2011 | $1.20 | Odontoglossum humeanum | #516 {82/1} SC and "Three bars" |
| | --- | 2012 | $1.20 | Paphiopedilum lemoinierianum | #517 {89/1} SC and "Three bars" |
| 1987/07/10 | --- | 2112 | $1.20 | Odontoglossum crispum | #420 {1/1} OP "1987" in block italic type |
| | --- | 2113 | $1.20 | Phalaenopsis amabilis | #419 {11/1} OP "1987" in block italic type |
| | --- | 2114 | $1.20 | Odontoglossum hallii v. xanthoglossum | #418 {28/1} OP "1987" in block italic type |
| | --- | 2115 | $1.20 | Odontoglossum hebraicum | #422 {37/1} OP "1987" in block italic type |
| | --- | 2116 | $1.20 | Cattleya trianae v. schroederiana | #421 {46/1} OP "1987" in block italic type |
| | --- | 2117 | $1.20 | Laelia anceps v. sanderiana | #424 {56/1} OP "1987" in block italic type |
| | --- | 2118 | $1.20 | Dendrobium nobile v. sanderiana | #425 {58/1} OP "1987" in block italic type |
| | --- | 2119 | $1.30 | Coelogyne cristata v. maxima | #431 {6/1} OP "1987" in block italic type |
| | --- | 2120 | $1.30 | Masdevallia caudata & v. xanthocorys | #433 {13/1} OP "1987" in block italic type |
| | --- | 2121 | $1.30 | Encyclia citrina | #434 {20/1} OP "1987" in block italic type |
| | --- | 2122 | $1.30 | Maxillaria sanderiana | #432 {25/1} OP "1987" in block italic type |
| | --- | 2123 | $1.50 | Laelia harpophylla | #447 {40/1} OP "1987" in block italic type >left< |
| | --- | 2124 | $1.50 | Odontoglossum crispum v. kinlesideanum | #445 {45/1} OP "1987" in block italic type >right< |
| | --- | 2125 | $1.50 | Phalaenopsis stuartiana | #1657 {42/1} OP "1987" in block italic type >left< |
| | --- | 2126 | $1.50 | Laelia harpophylla | #447a {40/1} OP "1987" in block italic type >right< |
| | --- | 2127 | $1.50 | Phalaenopsis stuartiana | #446 {42/1} OP "1987" in block italic type >right< |
| | --- | 2128 | $1.50 | Odontoglossum crispum v. kinlesideanum | #445a {45/1} OP "1987" in block italic type >left< |
| | --- | 2129 | $2.00 | Oncidium jonesianum & v. phaeanthum | #456 {21/1} OP "1987" in block italic type |
| | --- | 2130 | $2.00 | Cattleya trianae v. ernesti | #455 {43/1} OP "1987" in block italic type |
| | --- | 2131 | $2.00 | Cattleya trianae v. ernesti | #1658 {43/1} OP "1987" in block italic type |
| 1987/09/01 | --- | 2013 | $1.20 | Cattleya ballantineana | #471 {91/1} SC with condensed type |
| | --- | 2014 | $1.20 | Catasetum pileatum | #504 {90/1} SC with condensed type |
| | --- | 2015 | $1.20 | Odontoglossum harryanum | #548 {49/1} SC with condensed type |
| | --- | 2016 | $1.20 | Oncidium macranthum | #547 {64/1} SC with condensed type |
| | --- | 2017 | $1.20 | Dendrobium wardianum | #509 {9/1} SC with condensed type |
| | --- | 2018 | $1.20 | Rhynchostylis gigantea | #510 {22/1} SC with condensed type |
| | --- | 2019 | $1.20 | Odontoglossum blandum | #512 {24/1} SC with condensed type |
| | --- | 2020 | $1.20 | Chondrorhyncha aromatica | #511 {53/1} SC with condensed type |
| | --- | 2021 | $1.20 | Paphiopedilum tautzianum | #513 {65/1} SC with condensed type |
| | --- | 2022 | $1.20 | Dendrobium wardianum | #392a {9/1} SC with condensed type |
| | --- | 2023 | $1.20 | Rhynchostylis gigantea | #391 {22/1} SC with condensed type |

## GUYANA {Continued}

| DATE ISSUE | SCOTT/ MICHEL | GIBBON NUMBER | FACE VALUE | SPECIES NAME | BRIEF DESCRIPTION |
|---|---|---|---|---|---|
| 1987/09/01 | --- | 2024 | $1.20 | Odontoglossum harryanum | #393 {49/1} SC with condensed type |
| | --- | 2025 | $1.20 | Oncidium macranthum | #394 {64/1} SC with condensed type |
| | --- | 2026 | $1.20 | Cattleya percivaliana | #398 {2/1} SC with condensed type |
| | --- | 2027 | $1.20 | Laelia autumnalis v. xanthotropis | #397 {10/1} SC with condensed type |
| | --- | 2028 | $1.20 | Masdevallia chimaera v. backhousiana | #400 {19/1} SC with condensed type |
| | --- | 2029 | $1.20 | Trichopilia suavis v. alba | #399 {31/1} SC with condensed type |
| | --- | 2030 | $1.20 | Cattleya dowiana v. aurea | #518 {5/1} SC with condensed type |
| | --- | 2031 | $1.20 | Dendrobium leechanum | #519 {50/1} SC with condensed type |
| | --- | 2032 | $1.20 | Paphiopedilum selligerum v. majus | #520 {54/1} SC with condensed type |
| | --- | 2033 | $1.20 | Miltoniopsis roezlii | #521 {69/1} SC with condensed type |
| | --- | 2034 | $1.20 | Dimorphorchis lowii | #383 {71/1} SC with condensed type >facing out< |
| | --- | 2034a | $1.20 | Dimorphorchis lowii | #522 {71/1} SC with condensed type >facing in< |
| | --- | 2035 | $1.20 | Odontoglossum hebraicum v. aspersum | #523 {79/1} SC with condensed type |
| | --- | 2036 | $1.20 | Phalaenopsis leuchorrhoda | #524 {87/1} SC with condensed type >facing out< |
| | --- | 2036a | $1.20 | Phalaenopsis leuchorrhoda | #524 {87/1} SC with condensed type >facing in< |
| | --- | 2037 | $1.20 | Odontoglossum constictum | #525 {94/1} SC with condensed type |
| | --- | 2038 | $1.20 | Odontoglossum grande | #530 {60/1} SC with condensed type |
| | --- | 2039 | $1.20 | Paphiopedilum argus | #531 {83/1} SC with condensed type |
| | --- | 2040 | $1.20 | Dendrobium brymerianum | #532 {92/1} SC with condensed type |
| | --- | 2041 | $1.20 | Cattleya labiata v. warneri | #533 {95/1} SC with condensed type |
| | --- | 2042 | $2.00 | Cattleya guttata v. leopoldii | #505 {77/1} SC with condensed type |
| | --- | 2043 | $2.00 | Oncidium splendidum | #506 {78/1} SC with condensed type |
| | --- | 2044 | $2.00 | Odontoglossum luteo-purpureum v. prionopetalum | #507 {84/1} SC with condensed type |
| | --- | 2045 | $2.00 | Cattleya rochellensis | #508 {85/1} SC with condensed type |
| | --- | 2046 | $2.00 | Aerangis articulata | #550 {55/1} SC with condensed type |
| | --- | 2047 | $2.00 | Odontoglossum blandum | #512 {24/1} SC with condensed type |
| | --- | 2048 | $2.00 | Chondrorhyncha aromatica | #511 {53/1} SC with condensed type |
| | --- | 2049 | $2.00 | Paphiopedilum tautzianum | #513 {65/1} SC with condensed type |
| | --- | 2050 | $2.00 | Cattleya mendelii v. Duke of Marlborough | #514 {15/1} SC with condensed type |
| | --- | 2051 | $2.00 | Cattleya trianae v. alba | #515 {81/1} SC with condensed type |
| | --- | 2052 | $2.00 | Odontoglossum humeanum | #516 {82/1} SC with condensed type |
| | --- | 2053 | $2.00 | Paphiopedilum lemoinierianum | #517 {89/1} SC with condensed type |
| | --- | 2054 | $2.25 | Cattleya ballantineana | #471 {91/1} SC with condensed type |
| | --- | 2055 | $2.25 | Odontoglossum triumphans | #546 {86/1} SC with condensed type |
| | --- | 2055a | $2.25 | Odontoglossum triumphans | #546 {86/1} SC spelling error "Ontoglossum" |
| | --- | 2056 | $2.25 | Laelia albida | #493 {68/1} SC with condensed type |
| | --- | 2057 | $2.25 | Catasetum pileatum | #504 {90/1} SC with condensed type |
| | --- | 2058 | $2.25 | Epidendrum prismatocarpum | #526 {76/1} SC with condensed type |
| | --- | 2059 | $2.25 | Cattleya dowiana v. chrysotoxa | #527 {80/1} SC with condensed type |
| | --- | 2060 | $2.25 | Oncidium tigrinum | #528 {88/1} SC with condensed type |
| | --- | 2061 | $2.25 | Odontoglossum reichenheimii | #529 {96/1} SC with condensed type |
| | --- | 2062 | $6.00 | Gastorchis humblotii | #496 {17/1} SC with condensed type |
| | --- | 2063 | $6.00 | Dendrobium superbiens | #534 {39/1} SC with condensed type |
| | --- | 2064 | $6.00 | Vanda hookeriana | #535 {74/1} SC with condensed type |
| | --- | 2065 | $6.00 | Cattleya eldorado v. crocata | #536 {93/1} SC with condensed type |
| 1987/09/02 | E1 | | $15.00 | Paphinia rugosa & Promemae xanthina | 11/2 Express |
| | E2 | | $25.00 | Calanthe victor v. regina, bella & burfordiens | 63/2 Express |
| | E3 | | $45.00 | Odontoglossum chiriquense | 35/2 Express |
| 1987/10/05 | O 1 | | $2.25 | Masdevallia coccinea v. splendens | 26/2 Official |
| | O 2 | | $2.75 | Phaius amabilis & marthiae | 90/2 Official |
| | O 3 | | $3.20 | Cymbidium winnianum | 75/2 Official |
| | O 4 | | $3.30 | Paphiopedilum lawrenceanum v. hyeanum | 23/2 Official |
| | O 5 | | $6.00 | Angraecum humblotii | 70/2 Official |
| | O 6 | | $12.00 | Odontoglossum pescatorei | 71/2 Official |
| | O 7 | | $15.00 | Oncidium kramerianum | 84/2 Official |
| | O 8 | | $1.20 | Cattleya arnoldiana | #595 {48/2} RP, Official |
| | O 9 | | $1.30 | Coelogyne swaniana | #594 {92/2} RP, Official |
| | O10 | | $1.50 | Paphiopedilum pollettianum & maynardii | #596 {43/2} RP, Official |
| | O11 | | $2.00 | Dendrobium johnsoniae | #604 {61/2} RP, Official |
| | O12 | | $2.30 | Phalaenopsis sanderiana & intermedia v. portei | #597 {68/2} RP, Official |
| | O13 | | $3.50 | Dendrobium gouldii | #599 {95/2} RP, Official |
| | O14 | | $1.40 | Cattleya granulosa v. schofieldiana | 36/2 Official |

## GUYANA {Continued}

| DATE ISSUE | SCOTT/ MICHEL | GIBBON NUMBER | FACE VALUE | SPECIES NAME | BRIEF DESCRIPTION |
|---|---|---|---|---|---|
| 1987/10/05 | O15 | | $1.75 | Paphiopedilum hybridium v. youngianum | 31/2 Official |
| | O16 | | $2.50 | Schomburgkia sanderiana | 59/2 Official |
| | O17 | | $2.60 | Phaius tankervilleae v. assamica | 69/2 Official |
| 1987/10/09 | --- | 2219 | $6.00 | Cattleya lueddemanniana v. alba | #2220 {74/2} SC with condensed type |
| | --- | 2219a | $6.00 | Cattleya lueddemanniana v. alba | 74/2 )se-tenant( pairs #2219 and #2220 |
| | --- | 2220 | $9.00 | Cattleya lueddemanniana v. alba | 74/2 |
| | --- | 2221 | $2.25 | Paphiopedilum tautzianum | #1854 {65/1} SC with large numbers |
| | --- | 2221a | $2.25 | Paphiopedilum tautzianum | #1598 {65/1} SC with large numbers |
| | --- | 2222 | $9.50 | Cattleya lueddemanniana v. alba | #2220 {74/2} SC & OP "Cristovao Colombo 1492-1992" |
| | --- | 2222a | $9.50 | Cattleya lueddemanniana v. alba | 74/2 )se-tenant( pairs #2222 and #2223 |
| | --- | 2223 | $9.50 | Cattleya lueddemanniana v. alba | #2220 {74/2} SC & OP "Christophe Colombus 1492-1992" |
| 1987/11/01 | --- | 2233 | $1.30 | Masdevallia caudata & v. xanthocorys | #1684 {13/1} OP "1987" with script numbers |
| | --- | 2233a | $1.30 | Masdevallia caudata & v. xanthocorys | #1684 {13/1} OP "1987" in serif type |
| 1987/11/09 | --- | 2232a | $2.25 | Rhynchostylis gigantea | #1619a {22/1} SC with large numbers |
| | --- | 2232b | $2.25 | Rhynchostylis gigantea | #1619b {22/1} SC with large numbers |
| | --- | 2232c | $2.25 | Rhynchostylis gigantea | #1619c {22/1} SC with large numbers |
| | --- | 2232d | $2.25 | Rhynchostylis gigantea | #1619d {22/1} SC with large numbers |
| 1987/11/20 | --- | 2234a | $6.00 | Coelogyne cristata v. maxima | #1685a {6/1} SC with block numbers |
| | --- | 2234b | $6.00 | Coelogyne cristata v. maxima | #1685b {6/1} SC with block numbers |
| | --- | 2234c | $6.00 | Coelogyne cristata v. maxima | #1685c {6/1} SC with block numbers |
| | --- | 2234d | $6.00 | Coelogyne cristata v. maxima | #1685d {6/1} SC with block numbers |
| 1987/11/26 | --- | 2243 | $0.75 | Laelia gouldiana | #382 {59/1} SC & OP "AIR and 75" in script type |
| 1987/12/01 | --- | 2132 | $1.20 | Plectrelminthus caudatus | #423 {67/1} OP "1987" in schoolbook lite type |
| | --- | 2133 | $1.30 | Chysis bractescens | #1536 {18/1} OP "1987" in schoolbook lite type |
| | --- | 2134 | $1.30 | Odontoglossum crispum v. hrubyanum | #1537 {29/1} OP "1987" in schoolbook lite type |
| | --- | 2135 | $1.30 | Oncidium concolor | #1538 {30/1} OP "1987" in schoolbook lite type |
| | --- | 2136 | $1.30 | Cymbidium mastersii | #437 {66/1} OP "1987" in schoolbook lite type |
| | --- | 2137 | $1.50 | Odontoglossum edwardii | #448 {26/1} OP "1987" in schoolbook lite type |
| | --- | 2265 | $0.60 | Aerangis articulata | #403 {55/1} OP "AIR" in gothic demi type |
| | --- | E11 | $15.00 | Odontoglossum triumphans | #E2 {86/1} OP "1987" in schoolbook lite type |
| | Booklet B36 | | $15.00 | Angraecum | Booklet/ #403 {55/1} OP "AIR" 1 stamp & 3 panes )Magenta |
| | Booklet B37 | | $15.00 | Angraecum | Booklet/ #403 {55/1} OP "AIR" 1 stamp & 3 panes )Green |
| 1987/12/09 | --- | 2247 | $0.30 | Sophronitis species | SS/ 12 stamps, 1 is #329d OP "1987" )Black( |
| | --- | 2256 | $1.20 | Plectrelminthus caudatus | #423 {67/1} OP "Protect Our Heritage 1987" |
| | --- | 2257 | $1.30 | Cymbidium mastersii | #437 {66/1} OP "Protect Our Heritage 1987" |
| | --- | 2258 | $1.50 | Odontoglossum edwardii | #448 {26/1} OP "Protect Our Heritage 1987" |
| | --- | 2259 | $1.80 | Cattleya mendelii v. Duke of Marlborough | #452 {15/1} OP "Protect Our Heritage 1987" |
| | --- | 2260 | $3.20 | Odontoglossum humeanum | #465 {82/1} OP "Protect Our Heritage 1987" |
| | --- | 2264 | $6.50 | Odontoglossum triumphans | #1847 {86/1} OP "Protect Our Heritage 1987" |
| 1988/01/03 | 677 | --- | $1.20 | Odontoglossum cervantesii v. decorum | #612b {46/2} RP )could be either #612a, 612c or 612d( |
| 1988/02/23 | --- | 2273 | $1.20 | Oncidium lanceanum | #548 SC & OP "Republic Day 1988" |
| 1988/04/24 | 612a | | $3.20 | Cattleya hardyana | 55/2 |
| 1988/04/24 | 612b | | $3.30 | Odontoglossum cervantesii v. decorum | 46/2 |
| 1988/04/24 | 612c | | $3.50 | Aerides savageanum | 81/2 |
| 1988/04/24 | 612d | | $5.00 | Paphiopedilum leeanum v. giganteum | 57/2 |
| 1988/04/24 | 613a | | $3.20 | Odontoglossum cervantesii v. decorum | 46/2 |
| | 613b | | $3.30 | Cattleya hardyana | 55/2 |
| | 613c | | $3.50 | Paphiopedilum leeanum v. giganteum | 57/2 |
| | 613d | | $5.00 | Aerides savageanum | 81/2 |
| | 614a | | $3.20 | Aerides savageanum | 81/2 |
| | 614b | | $3.30 | Paphiopedilum leeanum v. giganteum | 57/2 |
| | 614c | | $3.50 | Cattleya hardyana | 55/2 |
| | 614d | | $5.00 | Odontoglossum cervantesii v. decorum | 46/2 |
| | 615a | | $3.20 | Paphiopedilum leeanum v. giganteum | 57/2 |
| | 615b | | $3.30 | Aerides savageanum | 81/2 |
| | 615c | | $3.50 | Odontoglossum cervantesii v. decorum | 46/2 |
| | 615d | | $5.00 | Cattleya hardyana | 55/2 |
| | 616 | | $3.20 | Phragmipedium grande | 16/2 |
| | 617 | | $3.50 | Cattleya lueddemanniana v. alba | #2220 {74/2} RP, with new value |
| | 618 | | $4.75 | Zygopetalum citrinum | 73/2 |
| | 619 | | $5.25 | Cattleya granulosa v. schofieldiana | #O14 {36/2} RP, with new value |
| | 620 | | $5.30 | Phaius tankervilleae v. assamica | #O17 {69/2} RP, with new value |

# GUYANA {Continued}

| DATE ISSUE | SCOTT/ MICHEL | GIBBON NUMBER | FACE VALUE | SPECIES NAME | BRIEF DESCRIPTION |
|---|---|---|---|---|---|
| 1988/04/24 | 621 | | $7.00 | Laeliocattleya behrensiana | 62/2 |
| | 622 | | $7.75 | Schomburgkia sanderiana | #016 {59/2} RP, with new value |
| | 623 | | $8.75 | Paphiopedilum hybridium v. youngianum | #015 {31/2} RP, with new value |
| | 624 | | $9.50 | Masdevallia chimaera v. mooreana | 78/2 |
| | 624A | | $10.00 | Cattleya O'Brieniana | 40/2 #624Aa face value omitted |
| | 624B | | $12.00 | Menadenium labiosum | 91/2 #624Ba face value omitted |
| | 624C | | $15.00 | Cattleya parthenia | 67/2 |
| | 631 | | $2.70 | Phaius amabilis & marthiae | #02 {90/2} RP, with new value |
| | 632 | | $3.60 | Oncidium kramerianum | #07 {84/2} RP, with new value |
| | 633 | | $5.50 | Angraecum humblotii | #05 {70/2} RP, with new value |
| | 634 | | $6.70 | Odontoglossum pescatorei | #06 {71/2} RP, with new value |
| 1988/05/17 | E4 | | $20.00 | Laeliocattleya phoebe | 93/2 Express |
| 1988/07/01 | --- | 2356 | $1.20 | Paphiopedilum rothschildianum | #378 {61/1} SC and 6 thin lines |
| | --- | 2357 | $1.20 | Dendrobium heterocarpum | #381 {63/1} SC and 6 thin lines |
| | --- | 2358 | $1.20 | Oncidium ampliatum v. majus | #380 {70/1} SC and 6 thin lines |
| | --- | 2359 | $1.20 | Laelia gouldiana | #382 {59/1} SC and 6 thin lines |
| | --- | 2359a | $1.20 | Laelia gouldiana | #382a {59/1} SC and 6 thin lines |
| | --- | 2360 | $1.20 | Dimorphorchis lowii | #383 {71/1} SC and 6 thin lines |
| | --- | 2361 | $1.20 | Chondrorhyncha aromatica | #384 {53/1} SC and 6 thin lines |
| | --- | 2362 | $1.20 | Odontoglossum triumphans | #385 {86/1} SC and 6 thin lines |
| | --- | 2363 | $1.20 | Rhynchostylis coelestis | #470 {30/2} SC and 6 thin lines |
| | --- | 2364 | $1.20 | Chondrorhyncha aromatica | #384a {53/1} SC and 6 thin lines |
| | --- | 2365 | $1.20 | Dendrobium phalaenopsis v. statterianum | #636 {7/2} SC and 6 thin lines |
| | --- | 2366 | $1.20 | Phaius cooksonii | #638 {14/2} SC and 6 thin lines )Lower( |
| | --- | 2367 | $1.20 | Phaius cooksonii | #638 {14/2} SC and 6 thin lines )Upper( |
| | --- | 2368 | $1.20 | Odontoglossum wilckeanum v. rothschildianum | #637 {22/2} SC and 6 thin lines |
| | --- | 2369 | $1.20 | Cattleya mendelii v. measuresiana | #635 {28/2} SC and 6 thin lines )Lower( |
| | --- | 2370 | $1.20 | Cattleya mendelii v. measuresiana | #635 {28/2} SC and 6 thin lines )Upper( |
| | --- | 2371 | $1.20 | Paphiopedilum castleanum | #545 {45/2} SC and 6 thin lines |
| | --- | 2372 | $1.20 | Cattleya guttata v. leopoldii | #386 {77/1} SC and 6 thin lines )Lower( |
| | --- | 2373 | $1.20 | Cattleya guttata v. leopoldii | #386 {77/1} SC and 6 thin lines )Upper( |
| | --- | 2374 | $1.20 | Odontoglossum reichenheimii | #387 {96/1} SC and 6 thin lines |
| | --- | 2375 | $1.20 | Cattleya ballantineana | #471 {91/1} SC and 6 thin lines )Lower( |
| | --- | 2376 | $1.20 | Cattleya ballantineana | #471 {91/1} SC and 6 thin lines )Upper( |
| | --- | 2377 | $1.20 | Odontoglossum triumphans | #546 {86/1} SC and 6 thin lines "Spelling Error" |
| | --- | 2378 | $1.20 | Laelia albida | #493 {68/1} SC and 6 thin lines )Upper( |
| | --- | 2379 | $1.20 | Laelia albida | #493 {68/1} SC and 6 thin lines )Lower( |
| | --- | 2380 | $1.20 | Catasetum pileatum | #504 {90/1} SC and 6 thin lines |
| | --- | 2381 | $1.20 | Paphiopedilum selligerum v. majus | #388 {54/1} SC and 6 thin lines |
| | --- | 2382 | $1.20 | Cattleya trianae v. alba | #389 {81/1} SC and 6 thin lines |
| | --- | 2383 | $1.20 | Odontoglossum coradinei | #472 {21/2} SC and 6 thin lines |
| | --- | 2384 | $1.20 | Dendrobium brymerianum | #390 {92/1} SC and 6 thin lines |
| | --- | 2385 | $1.20 | Laelia anceps v. schroderiana | #495 {13/2} SC and 6 thin lines |
| | --- | 2386 | $1.20 | Disa uniflora | #497 {15/2} SC and 6 thin lines |
| | --- | 2387 | $1.20 | Dendrobium wardianum | #509 {9/1} SC and 6 thin lines |
| | --- | 2388 | $1.20 | Rhynchostylis gigantea | #510 {22/1} SC and 6 thin lines |
| | --- | 2389 | $1.20 | Dendrobium formosum | #639 {3/2} SC and 6 thin lines |
| | --- | 2390 | $1.20 | Laelia praestans | #640 {6/2} SC and 6 thin lines |
| | --- | 2391 | $1.20 | Laeliocattleya elegans v. bleheimensis | #641 {20/2} SC and 6 thin lines |
| | --- | 2392 | $1.20 | Miltonia bleuana | #642 {32/2} SC and 6 thin lines |
| | --- | 2393 | $1.20 | Gastorchis humblotii | #395 {17/1} SC and 6 thin lines |
| | --- | 2394 | $1.20 | Cattleya percivaliana | #398 {2/1} SC and 6 thin lines |
| | --- | 2395 | $1.20 | Vanda coerulea | #404 {57/1} SC and 6 thin lines )Upper( |
| | --- | 2396 | $1.20 | Vanda coerulea | #404 {57/1} SC and 6 thin lines )Lower( |
| | --- | 2397 | $1.20 | Oncidium lanceanum | #405 {73/1} SC and 6 thin lines |
| | --- | 2398 | $1.20 | Cattleya labiata v. gaskelliana | #406 {75/1} SC and 6 thin lines )Right( |
| | --- | 2399 | $1.20 | Cattleya labiata v. gaskelliana | #406 {75/1} SC and 6 thin lines )Left( |
| | --- | 2400 | $1.20 | Cattleya labiata v. warneri | #407 {95/1} SC and 6 thin lines |
| | --- | 2401 | $1.20 | Cattleya eldorado v. crocata | #408 {93/1} SC and 6 thin lines |
| | --- | 2402 | $1.20 | Phragmipedium nitidissimum | #475 {27/2} SC and 6 thin lines |
| | --- | 2403 | $1.20 | Dendrobium leechanum | #519 {50/1} SC and 6 thin lines |
| | --- | 2404 | $1.20 | Paphiopedilum selligerum v. majus | #520 {54/1} SC and 6 thin lines |

## GUYANA {Continued}

| DATE ISSUE | SCOTT/ MICHEL | GIBBON NUMBER | FACE VALUE | SPECIES NAME | BRIEF DESCRIPTION |
|---|---|---|---|---|---|
| 1988/07/01 | --- | 2405 | $1.20 | Miltoniopsis roezlii | #521 {69/1} SC and 6 thin lines |
|  | --- | 2406 | $1.20 | Odontoglossum hebraicum v. aspersum | #523 {79/1} SC and 6 thin lines |
|  | --- | 2407 | $1.20 | Odontoglossum constictum | #525 {94/1} SC and 6 thin lines |
|  | --- | 2408 | $1.20 | Paphiopedilum boxalli v. atratum | #644 {8/2} SC and 6 thin lines |
|  | --- | 2409 | $1.20 | Odontoglossum wattianum | #646 {9/2} SC and 6 thin lines >Lower< |
|  | --- | 2410 | $1.20 | Odontoglossum wattianum | #646 {9/2} SC and 6 thin lines >Upper< |
|  | --- | 2411 | $1.20 | Dendrobium melanodiscus | #645 {12/2} SC and 6 thin lines >Upper< |
|  | --- | 2412 | $1.20 | Dendrobium melanodiscus | #645 {12/2} SC and 6 thin rules >Lower< |
|  | --- | 2413 | $1.20 | Cattleya schroederae v. alba | #643 {17/2} SC and 6 thin lines |
|  | --- | 2414 | $1.20 | Dendrobium superbiens | #534 {39/1} SC and 6 thin lines |
|  | --- | 2415 | $1.20 | Vanda hookeriana | #535 {74/1} SC and 6 thin lines |
|  | --- | 2416 | $1.20 | Cattleya eldorado v. crocata | #536 {93/1} SC and 6 thin lines |
|  | --- | 2417 | $1.20 | Paphiopedilum castleanum | #479 {45/2} SC and 6 thin lines |
|  | --- | 2418 | $1.20 | Cattleya intermedia v. punctatissima | #551 {24/2} SC and 6 thin lines |
|  | --- | 2419 | $1.20 | Disa uniflora | #497 {15/2} SC and 6 thin lines |
|  | --- | 2420 | $1.20 | Lycaste skinneri v. armeniaca | #552 {18/2} SC and 6 thin lines |
|  | --- | 2421 | $1.20 | Odontoglossum luteo-purpureum v. prionopetalum | #411 {84/1} SC and 6 thin lines |
|  | --- | 2422 | $1.20 | Paphiopedilum lemoinierianum | #412 {89/1} SC and 6 thin lines |
|  | --- | 2423 | $1.20 | Paphiopedilum lathamianum v. inversum | #553 {10/2} SC and 6 thin lines |
|  | --- | 2424 | $1.20 | Laelia anceps v. schroderiana | #481 {13/2} SC and 6 thin lines |
|  | --- | 2425 | $1.20 | Phragmipedium nitidissimum | #554 {27/2} SC and 6 thin lines |
|  | --- | 2426 | $1.20 | Cattleya bowringiana | #555 {2/2} SC and 6 thin lines |
|  | --- | 2427 | $2.00 | Dendrobium phalaenopsis | #478 {42/2} SC and 12 thin lines |
|  | --- | 2428 | $2.00 | Gastorchis tuberculosa | #480 {4/2} SC and 6 thin lines |
| 1988/07/09 | 703 |  | $1.30 | Zygopetalum citrinum | #618 {73/2} RP, "1985-1988" |
|  | 704 |  | $2.00 | Vandopsis parishii v. mariottianum | #606 {96/2} RP, "1985-1988" |
|  | 705 |  | $2.60 | Phragmipedium grande | #616 {16/2} RP, "1985-1988" |
|  | 706a |  | $1.20 | Aerides savageanum | #612c {81/2} RP, with new value |
|  | 706b |  | $1.20 | Paphiopedilum leeanum v. giganteum | #612d {57/2} RP, with new value |
|  | 706c |  | $1.20 | Cattleya hardyana | #612a {55/2} RP, with new value |
|  | 706d |  | $1.20 | Odontoglossum cervantesii v. decorum | #612b {46/2} RP, with new value |
|  | 707a |  | $1.50 | Paphiopedilum leeanum v. giganteum | #613c {57/2} RP, with new value |
|  | 707b |  | $1.50 | Aerides savageanum | #613d {81/2} RP, with new value |
|  | 707c |  | $1.50 | Odontoglossum cervantesii v. decorum | #613a {46/2} RP, with new value |
|  | 707d |  | $1.50 | Cattleya hardyana | #613b {55/2} RP, with new value |
|  | 708a |  | $2.25 | Odontoglossum cervantesii v. decorum | #614d {46/2} RP, with new value |
|  | 708b |  | $2.25 | Cattleya hardyana | #614c {55/2} RP, with new value |
|  | 708c |  | $2.25 | Paphiopedilum leeanum v. giganteum | #614b {57/2} RP, with new value |
|  | 708d |  | $2.25 | Aerides savageanum | #614a {81/2} RP, with new value |
|  | 709a |  | $3.05 | Cattleya hardyana | #615d {55/2} RP, with new value |
|  | 709b |  | $3.05 | Odontoglossum cervantesii v. decorum | #615c {46/2} RP, with new value |
|  | 709c |  | $3.05 | Aerides savageanum | #615b {81/2} RP, with new value |
|  | 709d |  | $3.05 | Paphiopedilum leeanum v. giganteum | #615a {57/2} RP, with new value |
| 1988/07/15 | --- | 2342 | $2.00 | Odontoglossum luteo-purpureum | #457 {33/1} OP "Conserve Water" in futura type |
|  | --- | 2343 | $2.00 | Odontoglossum hebraicum v. aspersum | #458 {79/1} OP "Conserve Water" in futura type |
|  | --- | 2344 | $2.25 | Odontoglossum blandum | #459 {24/1} OP "Conserve Water" in futura type |
|  | --- | 2345 | $3.50 | Odontoglossum constictum | #467 {94/1} OP "Conserve Water" in futura type |
| 1988/07/16 | --- | 2434 | $1.00 | Paphiopedilum tautzianum | #413 {65/1} OP "Conserve Our Resources" |
|  | --- | 2435 | $1.00 | Laelia albida | #414 {68/1} OP "Conserve Our Resources" |
|  | --- | 2436 | $1.00 | Oncidium tigrinum | #415 {88/1} OP "Conserve Our Resources" |
|  | --- | 2437 | $1.00 | Paphiopedilum tautzianum | #413a {65/1} OP "Conserve Our Resources" |
|  | --- | 2438 | $1.20 | Vanda teres | #416 {27/1} OP "Conserve Our Resources" |
|  | --- | 2439 | $1.20 | Laelia anceps v. percivaliana | #417 {36/1} OP "Conserve Our Resources" |
|  | --- | 2440 | $1.20 | Odontoglossum hebraicum | #422 {37/1} OP "Conserve Our Resources" |
|  | --- | 2441 | $1.20 | Laelia anceps v. sanderiana | #424 {56/1} OP "Conserve Our Resources" |
|  | --- | 2442 | $1.20 | Dendrobium nobile v. sanderiana | #425 {58/1} OP "Conserve Our Resources" |
|  | --- | 2443 | $1.20 | Plectrelminthus caudatus | #423 {67/1} OP "Conserve Our Resources" |
|  | --- | 2444 | $1.20 | Miltoniopsis roezlii | #426 {69/1} OP "Conserve Our Resources" |
|  | --- | 2445 | $1.30 | Paphiopedilum oenanthum v. superbum | #436 {38/1} OP "Conserve Our Resources" |
|  | --- | 2446 | $1.30 | Cymbidium mastersii | #437 {66/1} OP "Conserve Our Resources" |
|  | --- | 2447 | $1.30 | Cattleya ballantineana | #438 {91/1} OP "Conserve Our Resources" |
|  | --- | 2448 | $1.30 | Masdevallia caudata & v. xanthocorys | #433a {13/1} OP "Conserve Our Resources" & #2448a OP inverted |

<table>
<tr><td>DATE<br>ISSUE</td><td>SCOTT/<br>MICHEL</td><td>GIBBON<br>NUMBER</td><td>FACE<br>VALUE</td><td>SPECIES NAME</td><td>BRIEF DESCRIPTION</td></tr>
</table>

## GUYANA {Continued}

| DATE ISSUE | SCOTT/ MICHEL | GIBBON NUMBER | FACE VALUE | SPECIES NAME | BRIEF DESCRIPTION |
|---|---|---|---|---|---|
| 1988/07/16 | --- | 2449 | $1.30 | Encyclia citrina | #434a {20/1} OP "Conserve Our Resources" |
|  | --- | 2450 | $1.50 | Odontoglossum edwardii | #448 {26/1} OP "Conserve Our Resources" |
|  | --- | 2451 | $1.50 | Oncidium splendidum | #449 {78/1} OP "Conserve Our Resources" |
|  | --- | 2452 | $1.50 | Phalaenopsis leuchorrhoda | #450 {87/1} OP "Conserve Our Resources" |
|  | --- | 2453 | $1.50 | Epidendrum prismatocarpum | #451 {76/1} OP "Conserve Our Resources" |
|  | --- | 2454 | $2.50 | Vanda hookeriana | #461 {74/1} OP "Conserve Our Resources" |
| 1988/08/01 | --- | 2463 | $0.75 | Aerangis articulata | #409 {55/1} OP "AIR" in copperplate type |
|  | --- | 2464 | $0.75 | Cattleya dowiana v. aurea | #410 {5/1} OP "AIR" in copperplate type |
|  | --- | 2465 | $0.75 | Aerangis articulata | #409a {55/1} OP "AIR" in copperplate type |
|  | --- | 2466 | $0.75 | Paphiopedilum argus | #531 {83/1} OP "AIR" in copperplate type |
|  | --- | 2467 | $0.75 | Cattleya labiata v. warneri | #533 {95/1} OP "AIR" in copperplate type |
| 1988/08/03 | --- |  | $3.75 | Cattleya schroederae v. alba | #437 {17/2} SC & OP "Red Cross, 1948-1988 and Two bars" |
|  | --- |  | $4.24 | Cattleya schroederae v. alba | #437 {17/2} SC & OP "Red Cross, 1948-1988 and Two bars" |
| 1988/08/23 | --- |  | $1.30 | Odontoglossum coradinei | #472 {21/2} RP, with new value |
|  | --- |  | $1.40 | Rhynchostylis coelestis | #470 {30/2} RP, with new value |
|  | 635 | --- | $0.30 | Cattleya mendelii v. measuresiana | Booklet/ #503 {28/2} RP, with new value |
|  | 635a | Bookle | $70.00 | Paphiopedilum | Booklet/ #1/2 thru #48/2 {Numerical or Alphabetical} |
|  | 636 | --- | $0.30 | Dendrobium phalaenopsis v. statterianum | Booklet/ #494 {7/2} RP, with new value |
|  | 637 | --- | $0.30 | Odontoglossum wilckeanum v. rothschildianum | Booklet/ #501 {22/2} RP, with new value |
|  | 638 | --- | $0.30 | Phaius cooksonii | Booklet/ #499 {14/2} RP, with new value |
|  | 639 | --- | $0.50 | Dendrobium formosum | Booklet/ #498 {3/2} RP, with new value |
|  | 640 | --- | $0.50 | Laelia praestans | Booklet/ #491 {6/2} RP, with new value |
|  | 641 | --- | $0.50 | Laeliocattleya elegans v. bleheimensis | Booklet/ #492 {20/2} RP, with new value |
|  | 642 | --- | $0.50 | Miltonia bleuana | Booklet/ #500 {32/2} RP, with new value |
|  | 643 | --- | $0.70 | Cattleya schroederae v. alba | Booklet/ #473 {17/2} RP, with new value |
|  | 644 | --- | $0.70 | Paphiopedilum boxalli v. atratum | Booklet/ #476 {8/2} RP, with new value |
|  | 645 | --- | $0.70 | Dendrobium melanodiscus | Booklet/ #487 {12/2} RP, with new value |
|  | 646 | --- | $0.70 | Odontoglossum wattianum | Booklet/ #484 {9/2} RP, with new value |
|  | 647 | --- | $1.00 | Laelia grandis | Booklet/ #474 {33/2} RP, with new value |
|  | 648 |  | $1.00 | Odontoglossum naevium | Booklet/ #485 {44/2} RP, with new value |
|  | 649 |  | $1.30 | Dendrobium phalaenopsis | Booklet/ #478 {42/2} RP, with new value |
|  | 650 | --- | $1.30 | Miltoniopsis vexillaria | Booklet/ #489 {29/2} RP, with new value |
|  | 651 |  | $1.30 | Odontoglossum crispum v. mundyanum | Booklet/ #483 {5/2} RP, with new value |
|  | 652 | --- | $1.40 | Cattleya labiata v. lueddemanniana | Booklet/ #490 {34/2} RP, with new value |
|  | 653 | --- | $1.40 | Paphiopedilum laucheanum & eyermannianum | Booklet/ #482 {38/2} RP, with new value |
|  | 654 | --- | $1.40 | Laelia purpurata | Booklet/ #559 {25/2} RP, with new value |
|  | 655 | --- | $1.40 | Odontoglossum ramosissimum | Booklet/ #556 {41/2} RP, with new value |
|  | 656 |  | $1.40 | Gastorchis tuberculosa | Booklet/ #480 {4/2} RP, with new value |
|  | 657 | --- | $1.75 | Cattleya amethystoglossa | Booklet/ #583 {47/2} RP, with new value |
|  | 658 | --- | $1.75 | Cycnoches chlorochilon | Booklet/ #584 {39/2} RP, with new value |
|  | 659 | --- | $1.75 | Paphiopedilum Morganiae v. Burfordiense | Booklet/ #590 {1/2} RP, with new value |
|  | 660 | --- | $1.75 | Odontoglossum excellens | Booklet/ #587 {19/2} RP, with new value |
|  | 661 | --- | $1.75 | Odontoglossum leroyanum | Booklet/ #586 {37/2} RP, with new value |
|  | 662 |  | $2.00 | Paphiopedilum lawrenceanum v. hyeanum | Booklet/ #04 {23/2} RP, with new value |
|  | 663 |  | $2.00 | Masdevallia coccinea v. splendens | Booklet/ #01 {26/2} RP, with new value |
|  | 664 |  | $2.00 | Paphinia rugosa & Promemae xanthina | Booklet/ #E1 {11/2} RP, with new value |
|  | 665 | --- | $2.25 | Cattleya hardyana | Booklet/ #614c {55/2} RP >could be #614a, 614b or 614d< |
|  | 666 | --- | $2.50 | Cattleya O'Brieniana | Booklet/ #624A {40/2} RP, with new value |
|  | 667 |  | $3.80 | Odontoglossum chiriquense | Booklet/ #E3 {35/2} RP, with new value |
|  | 668 |  | $1.60 | Dendrobium venus & cassiope | #486 {50/2} RP, with new value |
|  | 669 |  | $1.75 | Phragmipedium weidlichianum | #589 {51/2} RP, with new value |
|  | 670 |  | $2.50 | Miltoniopsis phalaenopsis | #610 {79/2} RP, with new value |
|  | 671 |  | $2.80 | Laeliocattleya behrensiana | #621 {62/2} RP, with new value |
|  | 672 |  | $2.85 | Calanthe victor v. regina, bella & burfordiens | #E2 {63/2} RP, with new value |
|  | 673 |  | $2.00 | Cymbidium winnianum | #03 {75/2} RP, with new value |
|  | 674 |  | $2.00 | Laeliocattleya phoebe | #E4 {93/2} RP, with new value |
| 1988/09/01 | --- | 2429 | $1.20 | Cattleya warscewiczii | #375 {72/1} SC and dingbat >Black< |
| 1988/09/05 | --- | 2472 | $2.00 | Angraecum sesquipedale | #454 {14/1} OP "1928-1988 Cricket Jubilee" |
|  | --- | 2473 | $2.00 | Odontoglossum hebraicum v. aspersum | #458 {79/1} SC & OP "1928-1988 Cricket Jubilee" |
|  | --- | 2474 | $8.00 | Phalaenopsis leuchorrhoda | #450 {87/1} SC & OP "1928-1988 Cricket Jubilee" |
|  | --- | 2475 | $8.00 | Odontoglossum crispum v. mundyanum | #483 {5/2} SC & OP "1928-1988 Cricket Jubilee" |
|  | Booklet B34 |  | $20.00 | Phalaenopsis & Angraecum | Booklet/ 2 panes #2474/2 & #2472/2 "Cricket Diamond Jubilee" |

ALAND 44; UPPER VOLTA C276; WALLIS & FUTUNA ISLANDS 283; SABAH 17; GRENADA 666; LIECHTENSTEIN 467; NORFOLK ISLANDS 337;  SAINT PIERRE & MIQUELON 360; VANUATU 326; UNITED STATES 1975; SWITZERLAND B128; SOLOMON ISLANDS 600; GIBRALATAR 340; RUSSIA 1976 Postcard; CHILE 795a; PHILIPPINES 1188; NORTH VIETNAM M841; BELGIUM CONGO 268; KATANGA M28a; RUANDA-URUNDI 119; ROSS DEPENDENCY L19; and BARBUDA 8625.

## GUYANA {Continued}

| DATE ISSUE | SCOTT/ MICHEL | GIBBON NUMBER | FACE VALUE | SPECIES NAME | BRIEF DESCRIPTION |
|---|---|---|---|---|---|
| 1988/09/05 | Booklet B35 | | $20.00 | Phalaenopsis & Odontoglossum | Booklet/ 2 panes #2474/2 & #2473/2 "Cricket Diamond Jubilee" |
| 1988/09/16 | --- | 2476 | $1.20 | Cattleya trianae v. schroederiana | #421 {46/1} OP "Olympic Games 1988" |
| | --- | 2477 | $1.30 | Paphiopedilum laucheanum & eyermannianum | #482 {38/2} OP "Olympic Games 1988" |
| | --- | 2478 | $1.50 | Phalaenopsis leuchorrhoda | #450 {87/1} OP "Olympic Games 1988" |
| | --- | 2479 | $2.00 | Odontoglossum luteo-purpureum | #457 {33/1} OP "Olympic Games 1988" |
| | --- | 2480 | $3.00 | Paphiopedilum argus | #463 {83/1} OP "Olympic Games 1988" |
| | --- | 2481 | $3.00 | Cattleya labiata v. lueddemanniana | #490 {34/2} SC & OP "Olympic Games 1988" |
| | --- | 2482 | $3.20 | Paphiopedilum lathamianum v. inversum | #488 {10/2} OP "Olympic Games 1988" |
| | --- | 2483 | $3.30 | Thunia brymeriana | #561 {82/2} OP "Olympic Games 1988" |
| | --- | 2484 | $3.50 | Odontoglossum constictum | #467 {94/1} OP "Olympic Games 1988" |
| | --- | 2485 | $3.50 | Miltoniopsis vexillaria | #489 {29/2} OP "Olympic Games 1988" |
| 1988/10/01 | --- | 2430 | $2.40 | Rhynchostylis coelestis | {30/2} unissued value [140] SC in helvetica bold type |
| | --- | 2431 | $2.40 | Cattleya labiata v. lueddemanniana | #652 {34/2} SC in helvetica bold type |
| | --- | 2432 | $2.40 | Laelia autumnalis v. alba | #562 {87/2} SC in helvetica bold type |
| | --- | 2433 | $2.60 | Catasetum pileatum | #469 {90/1} SC in helvetica bold type |
| 1988/10/12 | --- | 2496 | $3.20 | Dendrobium leechanum | #464 {50/1} OP "V Centenary of Landing of Columbus" |
| | --- | 2497 | $15.00 | Cattleya rochellensis | #468 {85/1} SC & OP "V Centenary Landing of Columbus" |
| 1988/11/10 | --- | 2512 | $1.50 | Cattleya violacea | #440 {32/1} OP "Season's Greetings" in copperplate type |
| | --- | 2513 | $1.50 | Vanda sanderiana | #439 {62/1} OP "Season's Greetings" in copperplate type |
| | --- | 2514 | $2.25 | Odontoglossum grande | #460 {60/1} OP "Season's Greetings" in copperplate type |
| | --- | 2515 | $2.60 | Dendrobium superbiens | #462 {39/1} OP "Season's Greetings" in copperplate type |
| | --- | 2516 | $3.20 | Odontoglossum humeanum | #465 {82/1} OP "Season's Greetings" in copperplate type |
| | --- | 2517 | $3.30 | Cattleya dowiana v. chrysotoxa | #466 {80/1} OP "Season's Greetings" in copperplate type |
| | --- | 2518 | $3.60 | Cattleya rochellensis | #468 {85/1} OP "Season's Greetings" in copperplate type |
| | --- | 2519 | $1.20 | Coelogyne cristata v. maxima | #537 {6/1} SC & OP "Season's Greetings" dingbat >Blue< |
| | --- | 2520 | $1.20 | Masdevallia caudata & v. xanthocorys | #538 {13/1} SC & OP "Season's Greetings" dingbat >Blue< |
| | --- | 2521 | $1.20 | Encyclia citrina | #539 {20/1} SC & OP "Season's Greetings" dingbat >Blue< |
| | --- | 2522 | $1.20 | Maxillaria sanderiana | #540 {25/1} SC & OP "Season's Greetings" dingbat >Blue< |
| | --- | 2523 | $1.20 | Laelia harpophylla | #541 {40/1} SC & OP "Season's Greetings" dingbat >Blue< |
| | --- | 2524 | $1.20 | Phalaenopsis stuartiana | #542 {42/1} SC & OP "Season's Greetings" dingbat >Blue< |
| | --- | 2525 | $1.20 | Cattleya trianae v. ernesti | #543 {43/1} SC & OP "Season's Greetings" dingbat >Blue< |
| | --- | 2526 | $1.20 | Odontoglossum crispum v. kinlesideanum | #544 {45/1} SC & OP "Season's Greetings" dingbat >Blue< |
| | --- | 2527 | $2.25 | Odontoglossum blandum | #459 {24/1} OP "Season's Greetings 1988" |
| | --- | 2528 | $2.25 | Odontoglossum grande | #460 {60/1} OP "Season's Greetings 1988" |
| | --- | 2529 | $2.25 | Odontoglossum blandum | #459a {24/1} OP "Season's Greetings 1988" |
| | --- | 2530 | $2.25 | Paphiopedilum tautzianum | #2221 {65/1} OP "Season's Greetings 1988" |
| | --- | 2531a | $2.25 | Rhynchostylis gigantea | #2232a {22/1} OP "Season's Greetings 1988" |
| | --- | 2531b | $2.25 | Rhynchostylis gigantea | #2232b {22/1} OP "Season's Greetings 1988" |
| | --- | 2531c | $2.25 | Rhynchostylis gigantea | #2232c {22/1} OP "Season's Greetings 1988" |
| | --- | 2531d | $2.25 | Rhynchostylis gigantea | #2232d {22/1} OP "Season's Greetings 1988" |
| | --- | 2532 | $2.40 | Cattleya mendelii v. Duke of Marlborough | #452 {15/1} SC & OP "Season's Greetings" dingbat >Black< |
| 1989/01/03 | --- | | $5.50 | Paphiopedilum Morganiae v. Burfordiense | #590 {1/2} SC & OP "Saluting Winners Olympic Games 1988" |
| | --- | | $9.00 | Lycaste skinneri v. armeniaca | #502 {18/2} SC & OP "Saluting Winners Olympic Games 1988" |
| | --- | | $10.50 | Dendrobium leechanum | #464 {50/1} SC & OP "Saluting Winners Olympic Games 1988" |
| | 676 | --- | $1.00 | Coelogyne sanderae | Booklet/ #477 {56/2} RP, with new value |
| | 676a | Bookle | $137.75 | Cattleya | Booklet/ #49/2 thru #96/2 {Numerical or Alphabetical} |
| | 677 | --- | $1.20 | Aerides savageanum | Booklet/ #706a {81/2} RP >could be #706b, 706c or 706d< |
| | 678 | --- | $1.40 | Cattleya mossiae v. reineckiana | Booklet/ #564 {52/2} RP, with new value |
| | 679 | --- | $1.40 | Arachnis clarkei | Booklet/ #656 {65/2} RP, with new value |
| | 680 | --- | $1.75 | Coelogyne pandurata | Booklet/ #585 {58/2} RP, with new value |
| | 680a | --- | $1.75 | Oncidium loxense | Booklet/ #588 {54/2} RP, with new value |
| | 681 | --- | $2.00 | Cattleya labiata | Booklet/ #608 {49/2} RP, with new value |
| | 682 | --- | $2.00 | Cymbidium lowianum | Booklet/ #605 {53/2} RP, with new value |
| | 683 | --- | $2.00 | Oncidium superbiens | Booklet/ #601 {60/2} RP, with new value |
| | 684 | --- | $2.00 | Cattleya mendelii v. Quorndon House | Booklet/ #607 {64/2} RP, with new value |
| | 685 | --- | $2.25 | Odontoglossum cervantesii v. decorum | Booklet/ #708a {81/2} RP >could be #708b, 708c or 708d< |
| | 685a | --- | $2.00 | Cymbidium winnianum | Booklet/ #03 {75/2} RP, with new value |
| | 686 | --- | $2.50 | Masdevallia courtauldiana, geleniana, & measuresiana | Booklet/ #611 {76/2} RP, new value |
| | 687 | --- | $2.50 | Thunia brymeriana | Booklet/ #561 {82/2} RP, with new value |
| | 688 | --- | $2.50 | Cattleya victoria-regina | Booklet/ #560 {85/2} RP, with new value |
| | 689 | --- | $2.50 | Laelia autumnalis v. alba | Booklet/ #562 {87/2} RP, with new value |
| | 690 | --- | $2.50 | Spathoglottis kimballiana | Booklet/ #563 {88/2} RP, with new value |

<table>
<tr><td>DATE<br>ISSUE</td><td>SCOTT/<br>MICHEL</td><td>GIBBON<br>NUMBER</td><td>FACE<br>VALUE</td><td>SPECIES NAME</td><td>BRIEF DESCRIPTION</td></tr>
</table>

# GUYANA {Continued}

| DATE ISSUE | SCOTT/ MICHEL | GIBBON NUMBER | FACE VALUE | SPECIES NAME | BRIEF DESCRIPTION |
|---|---|---|---|---|---|
| 1989/01/03 | 691 | --- | $2.50 | Menadenium labiosum | Booklet/ #624B {91/2} RP, with new value |
| | 692 | --- | $2.80 | Huntleya meleagris | Booklet/ #609 {66/2} RP, with new value |
| | 693 | --- | $2.80 | Cattleya parthenia | Booklet/ #624C {67/2} RP, with new value |
| | 694 | --- | $2.80 | Masdevallia chimaera v. mooreana | Booklet/ #624 {78/2} RP, with new value |
| | 695 | --- | $3.00 | Cattleya rex | Booklet/ #603 {72/2} RP, with new value |
| | 696 | --- | $3.00 | Paphiopedilum calypso | Booklet/ #600 {77/2} RP, with new value |
| | 697 | --- | $3.00 | Europhia gigantea | Booklet/ #598 {80/2} RP, with new value |
| | 698 | --- | $3.00 | Encyclia atropurpureum v. randii | Booklet/ #602 {94/2} RP, with new value |
| | 699 | --- | $3.05 | Cattleya hardyana | Booklet/ #612a {55/2} RP >could be #612b, 612c or 612d< |
| | 700 | --- | $3.50 | Miltonia spectabilis v. moreliana | Booklet/ #593 {83/2} RP, with new value |
| | 701 | --- | $3.50 | Pescatoria klabochorum | Booklet/ #591 {86/2} RP, with new value |
| | 702 | --- | $3.50 | Laeliocattleya Hon. Mrs. Astor | Booklet/ #592 {89/2} RP, with new value |
| 1989/03/01 | --- | 2576 | $1.20 | Laelia purpurata | #654 {25/2} SC and dingbat >Red< |
| | --- | 2577 | $1.20 | Cattleya mossiae v. reineckiana | #687 {52/2} SC and dingbat >Red< |
| | --- | 2578 | $1.20 | Arachnis clarkei | #679 {65/2} SC and dingbat >Red< |
| | --- | 2579 | $1.20 | Oncidium loxense | #680a {54/2} SC and dingbat >Red< |
| | --- | 2580 | $1.20 | Paphiopedilum laucheanum & eyermannianum | #653 {38/2} SC and "Two bars" |
| | --- | 2581 | $1.20 | Odontoglossum ramosissimum | #655 {41/2} SC and "Two bars" |
| | --- | 2582 | $1.70 | Coelogyne pandurata | #680 {58/2} SC and "Two bars" |
| | --- | 2583 | $2.50 | Huntleya meleagris | #692 {66/2} SC and "Two bars" |
| | --- | 2584 | $2.50 | Cattleya parthenia | #693 {67/2} SC and "Two bars" |
| | --- | 2585 | $3.00 | Cymbidium lowianum | #605 {53/2} SC and "Two bars" |
| 1989/03/22 | --- | 2590a | $1.25 | Dendrobium melanodiscus | #487 {12/2} SC & OP "Easter" and 6 thin lines |
| | --- | 2590b | $2.50 | Dendrobium melanodiscus | #487 {12/2} SC & OP "Easter" and 6 thin lines |
| | --- | 2590c | $3.00 | Dendrobium melanodiscus | #487 {12/2} SC & OP "Easter" and 6 thin lines |
| | --- | 2590d | $3.50 | Dendrobium melanodiscus | #487 {12/2} SC & OP "Easter" and 6 thin lines |
| 1989/04/01 | --- | | $1.25 | Cattleya granulosa v. schofieldiana | #014 {36/2} SC & OP "Postage and Two bars" |
| | --- | | $1.25 | Coelogyne swaniana | #09 {92/2} SC & OP "Postage and Two bars" |
| | --- | | $1.50 | Paphiopedilum hybridium v. youngianum | #015 {31/2} SC & OP "Postage and Two bars" |
| | --- | | $1.50 | Paphiopedilum pollettianum & maynardii | #010 {43/2} OP "Postage" in copperplate type |
| | --- | | $2.50 | Masdevallia coccinea v. splendens | #01 {26/2} SC & OP "Postage and Two bars" >Bottom< |
| | --- | | $2.50 | Masdevallia coccinea v. splendens | #01 {26/2} SC & OP "Postage and Two bars" >Top< |
| | --- | | $2.50 | Phaius tankervilleae v. assamica | #017 {69/2} SC & OP "Postage and Two bars" >Center< |
| | --- | | $2.50 | Phaius tankervilleae v. assamica | #017 {69/2} SC & OP "Postage and Two bars" >Top< |
| | --- | | $2.50 | Phalaenopsis sanderiana & intermedia v. portei | #012 {68/2} SC & OP "Postage and Two bars" |
| | --- | | $2.50 | Schomburgkia sanderiana | #016 {59/2} OP "Postage" in copperplate type |
| | --- | | $3.00 | Phaius amabilis & marthiae | #02 {90/2} SC & OP "Postage and Two bars" |
| | --- | | $3.50 | Dendrobium gouldii | #013 {95/2} OP "Postage" >Left< in copperplate type |
| | --- | | $3.50 | Dendrobium gouldii | #013 {95/2} OP "Postage" >Right< in copperplate type |
| | --- | | $3.50 | Paphiopedilum lawrenceanum v. hyeanum | #04 {23/2} SC & OP "Postage and Two bars" |
| | --- | | $6.00 | Angraecum humblotii | #05 {70/2} OP "Postage" in copperplate type |
| | --- | | $12.00 | Odontoglossum pescatorei | #06 {71/2} OP "Postage" in copperplate type |
| | --- | | $15.00 | Oncidium kramerianum | #07 {84/2} OP "Postage" in copperplate type |
| 1989/04/03 | --- | | $2.50 | Coelogyne sanderae | #477 {56/2} SC & OP "All For Heath and Two bars" |
| | --- | | $2.50 | Coelogyne sanderae | #477 {56/2} SC & OP "Heath For All and Two bars" |
| | --- | | $6.75 | Cattleya labiata | #608 {49/2} SC & OP "All For Heath and Two bars" |
| | --- | | $6.75 | Cattleya labiata | #608 {49/2} SC & OP "Heath For All and Two bars" |
| 1989/04/11 | --- | | $2.50 | Laelia grandis | #474 {33/2} SC & OP "Boy Scouts 1909-1989 and Two bars" |
| | --- | | $2.50 | Laelia grandis | #474 {33/2} SC & OP "Girl Guides 1924-1989 and Two bars" |
| | --- | | $3.00 | Dendrobium venus & cassiope | #486 {50/2} OP "Boy Scouts 1909-1989" |
| | --- | | $3.00 | Dendrobium venus & cassiope | #486 {50/2} OP "Girl Guides 1924-1989" |
| 1989/05/02 | --- | | $3.00 | Coelogyne sanderae | #477 {56/2} SC & OP "I.L.O. 1919-1989 and Two bars" |
| | --- | | $6.40 | Cattleya labiata | #___ {49/2} SC "All For Health" |
| | --- | | $6.40 | Cattleya labiata | #___ {49/2} SC "Health for All" |
| 1989/05/11 | --- | | $2.50 | Laelia grandis | #647 {33/2} SC & OP "Boy Scouts 1909-1989" and 6 lines |
| | --- | | $2.50 | Laelia grandis | #647 {33/2} SC & OP "Girl Guides 1924-1989" and 6 lines |
| | --- | | $25.00 | Laeliocattleya behrensiana | #621 {62/2} SC & OP "Lady Baden Powell 1889-1989" |
| | --- | | $25.00 | Laeliocattleya behrensiana | #671 {62/2} SC & OP "Lady Baden Powell 1889-1989" |
| 1989/05/15 | --- | | $5.50 | Laelia praestans | #491 {6/2} SC & OP "Photography 1839-1989 and Two bars" |
| | --- | | $6.50 | Laelia praestans | #491 {6/2} SC & OP "Photography 1839-1989 and 6 thin lines" |
| | --- | | $6.50 | Laelia praestans | #491 {6/2} SC & OP "Photography 1839-1989 and Two bars" |
| 1989/06/26 | --- | | $1.25 | Odontoglossum naevium | #485 {44/2} SC & OP "Caricom Day and Two bars" |

## GUYANA {Continued}

| DATE ISSUE | SCOTT/ MICHEL | GIBBON NUMBER | FACE VALUE | SPECIES NAME | BRIEF DESCRIPTION |
|---|---|---|---|---|---|
| 1989/06/26 | --- | | $1.25 | Odontoglossum naevium | #485 {44/2} SC & OP "Caricom Day" and 6 thin lines |
| 1990/03/01 | --- | | 90+120 | Cattleya bowringiana | #555 and #2426 {2/2} se-tenant |
| | --- | | 85+120 | Cattleya intermedia v. punctatissima | #551 and #2418 {24/2} se-tenant |
| | --- | | 30+120 | Cattleya mendelii v. measuresiana | #635 and #2370 {28/2} se-tenant |
| | --- | | 70+120 | Cattleya schroederaem v. alba | #643 and #2413 {17/2} se-tenant |
| | --- | | 50+120 | Dendrobium formosum | #639 and #2389 {3/2} se-tenant |
| | --- | | 70+120 | Dendrobium melanodiscus | #645 and #2411 {12/2} se-tenant |
| | --- | | 30+120 | Dendrobium phalaenopsis v. statterianum | #636 and #2365 {7/2} se-tenant |
| | --- | | 50+120 | Disa uniflora | #497 and #2419 {15/2} se-tenant |
| | --- | | 50+120 | Laelia anceps v. schroderiana | #481 and #2424 {13/2} se-tenant |
| | --- | | 50+120 | Laelia praestans | #640 and #2390 {6/2} se-tenant |
| | --- | | 50+120 | Laeliocattleya elegans v. bleheimensis | #641 and #2391 {20/2} se-tenant |
| | --- | | 85+120 | Lycaste skinneri v. armeniaca | #552 and #2420 {18/2} se-tenant |
| | --- | | 50+120 | Miltonia bleuana | #642 and #2392 {32/2} se-tenant |
| | --- | | 45+120 | Odontoglossum coradinei | #472 and #2383 {21/2} se-tenant |
| | --- | | 70+120 | Odontoglossum wattianum | #646 and #2410 {9/2} se-tenant |
| | --- | | 30+120 | Odontoglossum wilckeanum v. rothschildianum | #637 and #2368 {22/2} se-tenant |
| | --- | | 70+120 | Paphiopedilum boxalli v. atratum | #644 and #2408 {8/2} se-tenant |
| | --- | | 35+120 | Paphiopedilum castleanum | #479 and #2417 {45/2} se-tenant |
| | --- | | 90+120 | Paphiopedilum lathamianum v. inversum | #553 and #2423 {10/2} se-tenant |
| | --- | | 30+120 | Phaius cooksonii | #638 and #2367 {14/2} se-tenant |
| | --- | | 60+120 | Phragmipedium nitidissimum | #554 and #2425 {27/2} se-tenant |
| | --- | | 30+120 | Rhynchostylis coelestis | #470 and #2363 {30/2} se-tenant |
| 1990/05/01 | --- | | $0.80 | Dendrobium wardianum | #392 {9/1} SC & OP "Rotary Dist 405 9th Conf 5/90 Georgetown" |
| | --- | | $0.80 | Odontoglossum harryanum | #393 {49/1} SC & OP "Rotary Dist 405 9th Conf 5/90 Georgetown" |
| | --- | | $0.80 | Oncidium macranthum | #394 {61/1} SC & OP "Rotary Dist 405 9th Conf 5/90 Georgetown" |
| | --- | | $6.40 | Coelogyne cristata v. maxima | #431 {6/1} SC & OP "Rotary Dist 405 9th Conf 5/90 Georgetown" |
| | --- | | $6.40 | Maxillaria sanderiana | #432 {25/1} SC & OP "Rotary Dist 405 9th Conf 5/90 Georgetown" |
| | --- | | $7.65 | Maxillaria sanderiana | #432 {25/1} SC & OP "Rotary Dist 405 9th Conf 5/90 Georgetown" |
| 1990/09/12 | | | $8.90 | Catasetum macrocarpum | Background of trogon birds |
| | | | $9.75 | Barkeria cyclotella | Background of trogon birds |
| | | | $11.40 | Maxillaria setigera | Background of aracari birds |
| | | | $12.65 | Catasetum macrocarpum | Background of train bearer birds |
| | | | $12.80 | Scutacaria hadwenii | Background of hermit birds |
| | | | $13.90 | Coelogyne | Background of hummingbirds |
| | | | $15.30 | Coryanthes | Background of hummingbirds |
| | | | $17.80 | Scuticaria hadwenii | Background of jacobin birds |
| | | | $19.20 | Lacaena | Background of topaz birds |
| | | | $22.95 | Rodriguezia | Background of coquette birds |
| | | | $26.70 | Paphinia cristata | Background of pied-tail birds |
| | | | $30.00 | Acacallis cyanea | Background of quetzal birds |
| | | | $50.00 | Laelia jongheana | Background of brilliant birds |
| | | | $100.00 | Lycaste skinneri v. alba | Background of hummingbirds |
| | | | $190.00 | Zygopetalum | Background of hummingbirds |
| | | | $225.00 | Peristeria | Background of hummingbirds |
| 1990/11/01 | | | $10.00 | Aspasia variegata | |
| | | | $10.00 | Brassia caudata | |
| | | | $10.00 | Brassoavola nodosa | |
| | | | $10.00 | Cattleya deckeri | |
| | | | $10.00 | Cattleya violacea | |
| | | | $10.00 | Caularthron bicornumtum | |
| | | | $10.00 | Cryptarrhena lunata | |
| | | | $10.00 | Cyropodium punctatum | |
| | | | $10.00 | Dichea muricata | |
| | | | $10.00 | Epidendrum rigidum | |
| | | | $10.00 | Galenandra devoniana | |
| | | | $10.00 | Octomeria erosilabia | |
| | | | $10.00 | Oncidium carthagenense | |
| | | | $10.00 | Pleurothallis diffusa | |
| | | | $10.00 | Spiranthes orchiodes | |
| | | | $10.00 | Stenia pallida | SS/ 16 stamps #___ thru #___ |
| | | | $190.00 | Ionopsis utricularioides | SS/ 1 stamp |

## GUYANA {Continued}

| DATE ISSUE | SCOTT/ MICHEL | GIBBON NUMBER | FACE VALUE | SPECIES NAME | BRIEF DESCRIPTION |
|---|---|---|---|---|---|
| 1991/01/01 | | | $7.65 | Vanilla indora | Sheetlet 10 stamps |
| | | | $8.90 | Epidendrum ibaguense | Sheetlet 10 stamps |
| | | | $12.80 | Maxillaria parkeri | Sheetlet 10 stamps |
| | | | $15.30 | Epidendrum nocturnum | Sheetlet 10 stamps |
| | | | $17.80 | Catasetum discolor | Sheetlet 10 stamps |
| | | | $20.00 | Scuticaria hadwenii | Sheetlet 10 stamps |
| | | | $25.00 | Epidendrum fragrans | Sheetlet 10 stamps |
| | | | $100.00 | Epistephium parviflorum | Sheetlet 10 stamps |

## HAITI

| DATE ISSUE | SCOTT/ MICHEL | FACE VALUE | SPECIES NAME | BRIEF DESCRIPTION |
|---|---|---|---|---|
| 1960/12/17 | C171 | $0.20 | Cattleya labiata | |
| | C175 | 1 gourde | Cattleya labiata | |
| | C176a | SS | Cattleya labiata | SS/ 3 stamps, 1 is #C175 |
| 1961/03/17 | CO4 | 1 gourde | Cattleya labiata | #C175 OP "Officiel" )Canceled only< |
| | CO5a | SS | Cattleya labiata | SS/ #C176a OP "Officiel" )Canceled only< |
| 1961/09/30 | CB32 | $0.25 | Cattleya labiata | #C171 OP "18e Conference Internationale di Scoutisme" |
| | CB32a | $0.25 | Cattleya labiata | Inverted OP |
| | CB33 | $0.25 | Cattleya labiata | #C175 OP "18e Conference Internationale di Scoutisme" |
| | CB34a | SS | Cattleya labiata | SS/ #C176a OP "18e Conference Internationale di Scoutisme" |
| 1970/04/03 | 636 | $0.10 | Laeliopsis dominguensis | |
| | 637 | $0.20 | Oncidium haitiense | |
| | 638 | $0.25 | Oncidium calochilum | |
| | C354 | $0.50 | Tetramicra elegans | |
| | C355 | 1.5 gour | Epidendrum truncatum | |
| | C356 | 2 gourde | Oncidium desertorum | |

## HONDURAS

| DATE ISSUE | SCOTT/ MICHEL | FACE VALUE | SPECIES NAME | BRIEF DESCRIPTION |
|---|---|---|---|---|
| 1943/09/14 | C136 | $0.21 | Cattleya gigas v. warscewiczii | |
| 1944/10/12 | C143 | $0.21 | Cattleya trianae | |
| 1972/05/19 | C510 | $0.09 | Brassavola digbyana | 150th Anniversary of Independence |
| | C511 | $0.10 | Brassavola digbyana | |
| | C519 | 2 lempir | Brassavola digbyana | |
| | C519a | SS | Brassavola digbyana | SS/ 3 stamps, #C510 thru #C512 |
| 1977/08/29 | C640 | 2 lempir | Brassavola digbyana | |

## HONG KONG

| DATE ISSUE | SCOTT/ MICHEL | FACE VALUE | SPECIES NAME | BRIEF DESCRIPTION |
|---|---|---|---|---|
| 1971/11/02 | 267 | $1.00 | Cymbidium | Stylized |
| 1977/10/12 | 342 | $0.20 | Spathoglottis pubescens | |
| | 343 | $1.30 | Paphiopedilum purpuratum | |
| | 344 | $2.00 | Habenaria susannae | |

## HUNGARY

| DATE ISSUE | SCOTT/ MICHEL | GIBBON NUMBER | FACE VALUE | SPECIES NAME | BRIEF DESCRIPTION |
|---|---|---|---|---|---|
| 1961/06/23 | 1393 | | 1.70 for | Ophrys holosericea | Sheetlet/ 4 stamps )SILVER< |
| 1961/08/19 | 1397 | | 1.70 for | Ophrys holosericea | Sheetlet/ 4 stamps )GOLD< |
| 1965/10/11 | 1707 | | 30 fille | Cattleya warscewiczii v. gigas | |
| | 1709 | | 70 fille | Paphiopedilum hybrid | |
| | 1711 | | 1 forint | Laeliocattleya elegans | |
| 1973/05/11 | 2222 | | 60 forin | Ophrys holosericea | #1397 RP, stamp on stamp |
| 1984/02/01 | Post | 1005/8 | 1 forint | Paphiopedilum hybrid | Postcard/ Picture side has orchid and stamp has letterbox |
| 1984/06/04 | 2851 | | 1 forint | Goodyera repens | Background of butterfly |
| | 2852 | | 1 forint | Ansellia gigantea | Background of butterfly |
| | 2854 | | 2 forint | Stanhopea | Background of butterfly |
| | 2855 | | 4 forint | Angraecum | Background of butterfly |
| 1985/02/01 | Post | 1005/8 | 2 forint | Paphiopedilum hybrid | Postcard/ Picture side has orchid and stamp has letterbox |
| 1986/04/17 | Post | --- | 2 forint | Cymbidium & Phalaenopsis | Postcard/ Stamp and cachet has orchids |
| 1987/02/01 | Post | 1005/8 | 2 forint | Paphiopedilum hybrid | Postcard/ Picture side has orchid and stamp has letterbox |
| 1987/10/29 | 3087 | | 2 forint | Cypripedium calceolus | |
| | 3088 | | 2 forint | Orchis purpurea | |
| | 3089 | | 4 forint | Himantoglossum hircinum | |
| | 3090 | | 4 forint | Ophrys scolopax v. cornuta | |
| | 3091 | | 5 forint | Cephalanthera rubra | |
| | 3092 | | 6 forint | Epipactis atrorubens | |

## HUNGARY {Continued}

| DATE ISSUE | SCOTT/ MICHEL | GIBBON NUMBER | FACE VALUE | SPECIES NAME | BRIEF DESCRIPTION |
|---|---|---|---|---|---|
| 1987/10/29 | 3093 | | 20 forin | Orchis italica & Dactylorhiza romana | SS/ 1 stamp |
| 1988/02/01 | Post | 1005/8 | 2 forint | Paphiopedilum hybrid | Postcard/ Picture side has orchid & stamp has pinetree branch |
| 1988/03/28 | Post | 20748/ | 2 forint | Cattleya | Postcard/ Picture side has two orchids on a blue egg |
| 1989/03/01 | Post | 19248/ | 3 forint | Cattleya Gyurics Eva | Postcard/ Picture side has single orchid |
| | Post | 20074/ | 3 forint | Laeliocattleya Katona Gyorgyi | Postcard/ Picture side has two orchids |
| 1989/11/01 | Post | 1173/8 | 2 forint | Cymbidium | Postcard/ Picture side has orchid and single candle |
| 1990 | Post | 1328/9 | 5 forint | Phalaenopsis | Postcard/ Candy stripped orchid, stamp has christmas scene |
| 1990 | Post | 1563/8 | 3 forint | Cymbidium | Postcard/ Three orchids, tall sprig, candle and pine greens |
| 1990 | Post | 4341 | 3 forint | Phalaenopsis | Postcard/ Candy stripped orchid on sea shell, stamp has map |
| 1990/03/01 | Post | 880120 | 3 forint | Cymbidium | Postcard/ Picture side has >Lime Green< orchid and two eggs |

## HUTT RIVER PROVINCE

| DATE ISSUE | SCOTT/ MICHEL | GIBBON NUMBER | FACE VALUE | SPECIES NAME | BRIEF DESCRIPTION |
|---|---|---|---|---|---|
| 1979/04/23 | NS | --- | $0.15 | Thelymitra villosa | |

## ICELAND

| DATE ISSUE | SCOTT/ MICHEL | GIBBON NUMBER | FACE VALUE | SPECIES NAME | BRIEF DESCRIPTION |
|---|---|---|---|---|---|
| 1968/01/17 | 394 | | 2.50 kro | Dactylorhiza maculata | |

## INDONESIA

| DATE ISSUE | SCOTT/ MICHEL | GIBBON NUMBER | FACE VALUE | SPECIES NAME | BRIEF DESCRIPTION |
|---|---|---|---|---|---|
| 1957/12/03 | B108 | | 75 sen | Dendrobium phalaenopsis v. amabilis | |
| 1959/06/01 | 475 | | 20 sen | Phalaenopsis | Lower left |
| 1962/12/20 | B146 | | 1 rupiah | Vanda tricolor | |
| | B147 | | 1.5 rupi | Phalaenopsis amabilis | |
| | B148 | | 3 rupiah | Dendrobium phalaenopsis | |
| | B149 | | 6 rupiah | Paphiopedilum praestans | |
| 1975/07/21 | 944 | | 40 rupia | Dendrobium Pakarena | |
| | 945 | | 70 rupia | Aeridachnis Bogor v. Apple Blossum Pink | |
| | 946 | | 85 rupia | Vanda genta v. Pride O'Lanka | |
| 1976/09/07 | 978 | | 25 rupia | Arachnis flos-aeris v. insignis | |
| | 979 | | 40 rupia | Vanda Putri-serang | |
| | 980 | | 100 rupi | Coelogyne pandurata | |
| | 978a | | 25 rupia | Arachnis flos-aeris v. insignis | SS/ 1 stamp |
| 1977/10/28 | 1010 | | 25 rupia | Taeniophyllum species | |
| | 1011 | | 40 rupia | Phalaenopsis violacea | |
| | 1012 | | 100 rupi | Dendrobium spectabile | |
| | 1012a | | 100 rupi | Dendrobium spectabile | SS/ 1 stamp, #1012 with color changed |
| 1977/12/10 | Formula SD36 | --- | | Dendrobium phalaenopsis | Aerogram/ Cachet has orchid |
| | Formula SD40 | --- | | Dendrobium phalaenopsis | Aerogram/ #SD36 RP, Also without black type and code numbers |
| 1978/12/22 | 1036 | | 40 rupia | Phalaenopsis Sri Rejeki | |
| | 1037 | | 75 rupia | Dendrobium macrophyllum | |
| | 1038 | | 100 rupi | Dendrobium macrophyllum | |
| | 1038a | | 100 rupi | Dendrobium macrophyllum | SS/ 1 stamp |
| 1979/03/22 | 1045 | | 60 rupia | Paphiopedilum lowii | |
| | 1046 | | 100 rupi | Vanda limbata | |
| | 1047 | | 125 rupi | Phalaenopsis gigantea | |
| | 1047a | | 125 rupi | Phalaenopsis gigantea | SS/ 1 stamp |
| 1979/05/24 | 1047b | | SS | Paphiopedilum | SS/ 2 stamps, #1045 and #1046 with new values |
| 1980/12/10 | 1107 | | 75 rupia | Dendrobium insigne | |
| | 1108 | | 100 rupi | Dendrobium discolor | |
| | 1109 | | 200 rupi | Dendrobium lasianthera | |
| | 1110 | | SS | Dendrobium | SS/ 2 stamps, #1108 and #1109 with new values |
| 1988/05/17 | 1348 | | 400 rupe | Dendrobium none | |
| | 1349 | | 500 rupe | Dendrobium abang | |

## IRAN

| DATE ISSUE | SCOTT/ MICHEL | GIBBON NUMBER | FACE VALUE | SPECIES NAME | BRIEF DESCRIPTION |
|---|---|---|---|---|---|
| 1989/03/11 | --- | 2515 | 10 rials | Cephalanthera kurdica | |
| | --- | 2516 | 10 rials | Dactylorhiza romana v. georgica | |
| | --- | 2517 | 10 rials | Comperia comperiana | |
| | --- | 2518 | 10 rials | Orchis mascula | |

## ISLE OF MAN

| DATE ISSUE | SCOTT/ MICHEL | GIBBON NUMBER | FACE VALUE | SPECIES NAME | BRIEF DESCRIPTION |
|---|---|---|---|---|---|
| 1986/04/10 | 306a | | 12 pence | Neotinea intacta | |

## ISRAEL

| DATE ISSUE | SCOTT/ MICHEL | GIBBON NUMBER | FACE VALUE | SPECIES NAME | BRIEF DESCRIPTION |
|---|---|---|---|---|---|
| 1970/05/06 | 414 | | 12 agora | Orchis laxiflora | Descriptive tab |

## IVORY COAST

| DATE ISSUE | SCOTT/ MICHEL | GIBBON NUMBER | FACE VALUE | SPECIES NAME | BRIEF DESCRIPTION |
|---|---|---|---|---|---|
| 1961/09/30 | 187 | | 25 franc | Polystachya cucullata | #187a Red omitted |
| 1977/12/15 | MC532 | 519 | 60 franc | Arachnis flos-aeris | |
| | MD532 | 520 | 65 franc | Renanthera storiei | |
| 1979/02/24 | 496 | | 60 franc | Vanda Josephine | |
| | 497 | | 65 franc | Renanthera storiei | |

## JAMAICA

| DATE ISSUE | SCOTT/ MICHEL | GIBBON NUMBER | FACE VALUE | SPECIES NAME | BRIEF DESCRIPTION |
|---|---|---|---|---|---|
| 1973/10/08 | 375 | | $0.05 | Broughtonia sanguinea | |
| | 376 | | $0.10 | Arpophyllum jamaicense | |
| | 377 | | $0.20 | Oncidium pulchellum | |
| | 378 | | $1.00 | Brassia maculata | |
| | 378a | | SS | Broughtonia | SS/ 4 stamps, #375 thru #378 |
| 1981/07/29 | 500 | | $0.20 | Vanda species | #500a Wmk and #500b >Perf 15x14<   Sheetlet/ 5 stamps, 1 label |
| | 502a | | $0.60 | Broughtonia sanguinea | Sheetlet/ Left border design |
| | Booklet B3 | | $6.25 | Vanda species | Booklet/ 1 pane of 4 stamps, 1 is #500 |
| 1984/10/22 | 594 | | $1.00 | Brassia | Background of snake |
| | 594a | | SS | Brassia | SS/ 4 stamps, 1 is #594 |
| 1988/12/15 | 709 | | $4.00 | Broughtonia sanguinea | |

## JAPAN

| DATE ISSUE | SCOTT/ MICHEL | GIBBON NUMBER | FACE VALUE | SPECIES NAME | BRIEF DESCRIPTION |
|---|---|---|---|---|---|
| 1935/04/02 | 218 | | 1.5 sen | Cymbidium goeringii | Sheetlet/ 20 stamps |
| | 220 | | 6 sen | Cymbidium goeringii | Sheetlet/ 20 stamps |
| 1942/09/15 | 346 | | 20 sen | Cymbidium ensifolium>C & goeringii>L | 10th Anniversary of Manchukuo Independence |
| 1950/06/15 | Post | HG94c | 2 yen | Cattleya & Dendrobium | Postcard/ Picture side has seven orchids |
| 1973/09/12 | Post | --- | 10 yen | Cymbidium goeringii | Postcard/ Stamp has two plants and single orchid |
| 1982/02/01 | Post | --- | 40 yen | Potinara Medea | Advertising Postcard/ Akatsuki Botanical Gardens, two orchids |
| 1982/08/02 | Post | --- | 40 yen | Odontoglossum | Advertising Postcard/ Silk Flowers for Fukui Corp. |
| 1982/12/01 | Post | --- | 40 yen | Orchis graminifolia | Advertising Postcard/ Tochigi Publishers, single orchid spray |
| 1984/06/15 | Post | --- | 40 yen | Habenaria radiata | Postcard/ Cachet has two plants and three orchids |
| 1985/09/02 | Post | --- | 40 yen | Dendrobium phalaenopsis | Advertising Postcard/ Lemon tea, with single orchid |
| 1987/03/19 | 1730 | | 60 yen | Calanthe izuinsularis | Sheetlet/ 20 stamps |
| | 1731 | | 60 yen | Neofinetia falcata | Sheetlet/ 20 stamps |
| | Post | --- | 40 yen | Calanthe discolor | Private Postcard/ Cachet has three orchid sprays |
| | Post | --- | 40 yen | Cymbidium goeringii | Private Postcard/ Cachet has single plant with two orchids |
| | Post | --- | 40 yen | Cypripedium japonicum | Private Postcard/ Cachet has single orchid |
| | Post | --- | 40 yen | Dendrobium moniliforme | Private Postcard/ Cachet has two orchid plants |
| | Post | --- | 40 yen | Orchis graminifolia | Private Postcard/ Cachet has three orchid sprays |
| 1988/02/01 | Post | --- | 40 yen | Dendrobium | Postcard/ Picture side has orchid sprays |
| 1988/10/01 | Post | --- | 40 yen | Dendrobium phalaenopsis | Advertising Postcard/ on Meito's Lemon Tea can, single spray |
| 1989/08/25 | 1840 | | 62 yen | Phalaenopsis aphrodite | Sheetlet/ 20 stamps |
| 1989/11/01 | Post | | 41 yen | Cymbidium goeringii | Advertising Posdtcard/ |
| 1990/11/20 | Booklet | | 740 yen | Cephalanthera | Booklet/ Cover design {Issued only at Chi Chibu Post Office} |
| 1991/03/01 | Booklet | | 740 yen | Cymbidium species | Booklet/ Cover design has five orchid flowers on a sprig |
| | Booklet | | 740 yen | Cymbidium species | Booklet/ Cover design has seven orchid flowers on a sprig |
| | Booklet | | 740 yen | Cymbidium species | Booklet/ Cover design has six orchids & two buds on a sprig |

## JERSEY

| DATE ISSUE | SCOTT/ MICHEL | GIBBON NUMBER | FACE VALUE | SPECIES NAME | BRIEF DESCRIPTION |
|---|---|---|---|---|---|
| 1972/01/18 | 63 | | 7.5 penc | Orchis laxiflora | |
| 1973/09/10 | Booklet B13 | | 30 pence | Orchis laxiflora | Booklet/ Cover design >Black< |
| 1984/11/15 | 346 | | 9 pence | Brassolaeliocattleya St. Helier | |
| | 347 | | 12 pence | Odontioda Mt. Bingham | |
| 1987/09/21 | Aero | | 26 pence | Lycaste Auburn Ditchling | Aerogram/ Cachet has five orchids |
| 1988/01/12 | 442 | | 11 pence | Cymbidium Pontac | |
| | 443 | | 15 pence | Odontioda Eric Young | |
| | 444 | | 29 pence | Lycaste Auburn Seaford & Ditchling | |
| | 445 | | 31 pence | Odontoglossum St. Brelade v. Montmillais | |
| | 446 | | 34 pence | Cymbidium Mavourneen v. Jester | |

<table>
<tr><td>DATE<br>ISSUE</td><td>SCOTT/<br>MICHEL</td><td>GIBBON<br>NUMBER</td><td>FACE<br>VALUE</td><td>SPECIES NAME</td><td>BRIEF DESCRIPTION</td></tr>
</table>

## JOHORE {Malaysia}

| | | | | |
|---|---|---|---|---|
| 1965/11/15 169 | | 1 sen | Vanda hookeriana | #169a Black omitted and #169b Wmk sideways |
| 170 | | 2 sen | Arundina graminifolia | |
| 171 | | 5 sen | Paphiopedilum niveum | #171a Yellow omitted |
| 172 | | 6 sen | Spathoglottis plicata | #172a Shifted perfs |
| 173 | | 10 sen | Arachnis flos-aeris | #173a Green omitted and #173b Wmk sideways |
| 174 | | 15 sen | Rhynchostylis retusa | #174a Green omitted |
| 175 | | 20 sen | Phalaenopsis violacea | #175a Magenta omitted |

## JUGOSLAVIA

| | | | |
|---|---|---|---|
| 1957/05/25 476 | 70 dinar | Orchis morio | |
| 1989/03/20 1956 | 3,000 di | Orchis simia | |

## KAMPUCHEA {Cambodia}

| | | | | |
|---|---|---|---|---|
| 1984/02/10 M554 | 510 | 80 sen | Dendrobium | Background of birds |
| 1986/06/19 M775 | 733 | 3 riels | Cypripedium macranthos | Background of butterfly |
| 1988/10/10 --- | 929 | 20 sen | Cattleya aclandiae | |
| --- | 930 | 50 sen | Odontoglossum Royal Sovereign | |
| --- | 931 | 80 sen | Cattleya labiata | |
| --- | 932 | 1 riel | Ophrys apifera | |
| --- | 933 | 1.50 rie | Laelia anceps | |
| --- | 934 | 2 riels | Laelia pumila | |
| --- | 935 | 3 riels | Stanhopea tigrina | |

## KATANGA

| | | | |
|---|---|---|---|
| 1960/09/22 M28 | $0.50 | Eurychone galeandrae | Belgian Congo #268 OP "Katanga" and #M28a OP Inverted |
| M32 | 2 francs | Ansellia gigantea | Belgian Congo #274 OP "Kananga" |

## KEDAH {Malaysia}

| | | | |
|---|---|---|---|
| 1965/11/15 106 | 1 sen | Vanda hookeriana | #106a Black omitted and #106b Wmk sideways |
| 107 | 2 sen | Arundina graminifolia | #107a Yellow omitted and #107b Green omitted |
| 108 | 5 sen | Paphiopedilum niveum | #108a Black omitted and #108b Red omitted |
| 109 | 6 sen | Spathoglottis plicata | |
| 110 | 10 sen | Arachnis flos-aeris | #110a Red omit #110b Green omit and #110c Wmk sideways |
| 111 | 15 sen | Rhynchostylis retusa | |
| 112 | 20 sen | Phalaenopsis violacea | #112a Purple omitted and #112b Yellow omitted |

## KELANTAN {Malaysia}

| | | | |
|---|---|---|---|
| 1965/11/15 91 | 1 sen | Vanda hookeriana | #91a Magenta omitted and #91b Wmk sideways |
| 92 | 2 sen | Arundina graminifolia | |
| 93 | 5 sen | Paphiopedilum niveum | |
| 94 | 6 sen | Spathoglottis plicata | |
| 95 | 10 sen | Arachnis flos-aeris | #95a Yellow omit #95b Red Brown omit #95c Wmk sideway |
| 96 | 15 sen | Rhynchostylis retusa | |
| 97 | 20 sen | Phalaenopsis violacea | #97a Magenta omitted and #97b Yellow omitted |

## LAOS

| | | | |
|---|---|---|---|
| 1971/07/07 216 | 30 kip | Dendrobium aggregatum | |
| 217 | 50 kip | Ascocentrum miniatum | |
| 218 | 70 kip | Trichoglottis fasciata | |
| C79 | 125 kip | Laeliocattleya hybrid | |
| 1972/05/05 230 | 40 kip | Rhynchostylis gigantea | |
| 231 | 60 kip | Paphiopedilum exul | |
| 232 | 80 kip | Cattleya labiata | |
| C89 | 150 kip | Vanda teres | |
| 1983/06/10 467 | 1 kip | Dendrobium draconis | |
| 468 | 2 kip | Aerides odoratum | |
| 469 | 3 kip | Dendrobium aggregatum | |
| 470 | 4 kip | Dendrobium secundum | |
| 471 | 5 kip | Dendrobium moschatum | |
| 472 | 6 kip | Dendrobium farmeri | |
| 1985/07/05 637 | $0.50 | Cattleya percivaliana | |
| 638 | 1 kip | Odontoglossum luteo-purpureum | |
| 639 | 2 kip | Cattleya lueddemanniana | |

## LAOS {Continued}

| DATE ISSUE | SCOTT/ MICHEL | GIBBON NUMBER | FACE VALUE | SPECIES NAME | BRIEF DESCRIPTION |
|---|---|---|---|---|---|
| 1985/07/05 | 640 | | 2 kip | Maxillaria sanderiana | |
| | 641 | | 3 kip | Miltoniopsis vexillaria | |
| | 642 | | 4 kip | Oncidium varicosum | |
| | 643 | | 8 kip | Cattleya dowiana v. aurea | |
| | 644 | | 10 kip | Catasetum fimbriatum | SS/ 1 stamp |
| 1987/10/08 | 796 | | 3 kip | Vanda teres | |
| | 796a | | 7 kip | Laeliocattleya species | |
| | 796b | | 10 kip | Paphiopedilum hybrid | |
| | 796c | | 39 kip | Sobralia species | |
| | 796d | | 44 kip | Paphiopedilum hybrid | |
| | 796e | | 47 kip | Paphiopedilum hybrid | |
| | 796f | | 50 kip | Cattleya trianae | |
| | 796g | | 95 kip | Vanda tricolor | SS/ 1 stamp |

## LESOTHO

| DATE ISSUE | SCOTT/ MICHEL | GIBBON NUMBER | FACE VALUE | SPECIES NAME | BRIEF DESCRIPTION |
|---|---|---|---|---|---|
| 1982/07/01 | 374 | | 75 lisen | Odontoglossum | Bridal Bouquet Di's {Birthday} |
| 1985/11/11 | 501 | | 1 maloti | Disa crassicornis | |
| 1990/02/26 | 773 | | 5 maloti | Ansellia gigantea | SS/ 1 stamp, background of butterfly |
| 1990/03/12 | 756 | | 12 sente | Satyrium princeps | |
| | 757 | | 16 sente | Huttronaea pulchra | |
| | 758 | | 55 sente | Herschelia graminifolia | |
| | 759 | | 1 maloti | Ansellia gigantea | |
| | 760 | | 1.55malo | Polystachya pubescens | |
| | 761 | | 2.40malo | Penthea filicornis | |
| | 762 | | 3 maloti | Disperis capensis | |
| | 763 | | 4 maloti | Disa uniflora | |
| | 764 | | 5 maloti | Stenoglottis longifolia | SS/ 1 stamp |

## LIBERIA

| DATE ISSUE | SCOTT/ MICHEL | GIBBON NUMBER | FACE VALUE | SPECIES NAME | BRIEF DESCRIPTION |
|---|---|---|---|---|---|
| 1955/09/28 | 352 | | $0.08 | Plectrelminthus caudatus | |

## LIECHTENSTEIN

| DATE ISSUE | SCOTT/ MICHEL | GIBBON NUMBER | FACE VALUE | SPECIES NAME | BRIEF DESCRIPTION |
|---|---|---|---|---|---|
| 1970/04/30 | 467 | | 30 rappe | Ophrys holosericea | Descriptive tabs |
| 1987/06/09 | Post | --- | 50 rappe | Dactylorhiza & Nigritella | Postcard/ Picture side has orchid sprays |

## LUXEMBOURG

| DATE ISSUE | SCOTT/ MICHEL | GIBBON NUMBER | FACE VALUE | SPECIES NAME | BRIEF DESCRIPTION |
|---|---|---|---|---|---|
| 1975/12/04 | B303 | | 1 franc | Ophrys insectifera | |
| | B304 | | 3 francs | Anacamptis pyramidalis | |
| | B305 | | 4 francs | Epipactis palustris | |
| | B307 | | 15 franc | Ophrys apifera | |
| 1976/12/06 | B310 | | 6 francs | Cephalanthera rubra | |
| | B311 | | 12 franc | Ophrys holosericea | |
| 1977/12/05 | B316 | | 12 franc | Ophrys sphegodes | |
| | B317 | | 20 franc | Dactylorhiza maculata | |

## MACAU

| DATE ISSUE | SCOTT/ MICHEL | GIBBON NUMBER | FACE VALUE | SPECIES NAME | BRIEF DESCRIPTION |
|---|---|---|---|---|---|
| 1953/09/22 | 375 | | 10 avos | Phaius tankervilleae | |

## MADAGASCAR

| DATE ISSUE | SCOTT/ MICHEL | GIBBON NUMBER | FACE VALUE | SPECIES NAME | BRIEF DESCRIPTION |
|---|---|---|---|---|---|
| 1957/03/12 | 299 | | 12 franc | Vanilla planifolia | |
| | 299a | --- | SS | Vanilla planifolia | SS/ 3 stamps, 1 is #299 |

## MADERIA {Portugal}

| DATE ISSUE | SCOTT/ MICHEL | GIBBON NUMBER | FACE VALUE | SPECIES NAME | BRIEF DESCRIPTION |
|---|---|---|---|---|---|
| 1980/09/17 | 70 | | 5 escudo | Cymbidium hybrid | |
| | 72 | | 8 escudo | Cymbidium hybrid | |
| 1981/10/06 | 77 | | 7 escudo | Dactylorchis foliosa | |
| | Booklet 80a | | $85.50 | Dactylorchis foliosa | Booklet/ 1 pane of 4 stamps, 1 is #77 |
| 1982/08/31 | 82 | | 9 escudo | Goodyera macrophylla | |
| | Booklet 85a | | $79.50 | Goodyera macrophylla | Booklet/ 1 pane of 4 stamps, 1 is #82 |

## MALACCA {Malaysia}

| DATE ISSUE | SCOTT/ MICHEL | GIBBON NUMBER | FACE VALUE | SPECIES NAME | BRIEF DESCRIPTION |
|---|---|---|---|---|---|
| 1965/11/15 | 67 | | 1 sen | Vanda hookeriana | #67a Wmk sideways |
| | 68 | | 2 sen | Arundina graminifolia | |

## MALACCA {Malaysia} {Continued}

| DATE ISSUE | SCOTT/ MICHEL | FACE VALUE | SPECIES NAME | BRIEF DESCRIPTION |
|---|---|---|---|---|
| 1965/11/15 | 69 | 5 sen | Paphiopedilum niveum | #69a Red omitted, #69b Yellow omitted and #69c Wmk sideways |
| | 70 | 6 sen | Spathoglottis plicata | |
| | 71 | 10 sen | Arachnis flos-aeris | #71a Wmk sideways |
| | 72 | 15 sen | Rhynchostylis retusa | |
| | 73 | 20 sen | Phalaenopsis violacea | |

## MALAGASY

| DATE ISSUE | SCOTT/ MICHEL | FACE VALUE | SPECIES NAME | BRIEF DESCRIPTION |
|---|---|---|---|---|
| 1963/10/04 | 344 | 8 francs | Gastorchis humblotii | |
| | 345 | 10 franc | Eulophiella roempleriana | |
| | 346 | 12 franc | Angraecum sesquipedale | |
| 1965/01/27 | 348 | 5 francs | Vanilla planifolia | Heraldic sign for state of Artalaha |
| 1973/08/06 | 495 | 10 franc | Paphiopedilum hybrid | |
| | 498 | 100 fran | Paphiopedilum hybrid | |
| 1981/03/23 | 612 | 5 francs | Angraecum sesquipedale | |
| | 613 | 80 franc | Angraecum ramosum | |
| | 614 | 170 fran | Angraecum leonis | |
| 1984/11/20 | 706 | 20 franc | Disa incarnata | |
| | 707 | 235 fran | Eulophiella roempleriana | |
| | 708 | 400 fran | Gastorchis tuberculosa | SS/ 1 stamp |
| | C180 | 50 franc | Eulophiella elizabethae | |
| | C181 | 50 franc | Grammangis ellisii | |
| | C182 | 50 franc | Grammangis spectabilis | |
| 1985/11/08 | 735 | 20 franc | Aeranthes grandiflorus | |
| | 736 | 45 franc | Angraecum magdalenae | |
| | 737 | 50 franc | Aerangis stylosa | |
| | 738 | 100 fran | Angraecum eburneum v. longicalcar | |
| | 739 | 100 fran | Angraecum sesquipedale | |
| | 740 | 400 fran | Angraecum eburneum v. superbum | SS/ 1 stamp |
| 1988/04/18 | 840a | 550 fran | Vanilla planifolia | SS/ 1 stamp, lower left |
| 1989/02/28 | 910 | 5 francs | Sobennikoffia robusta | |
| | 911 | 10 franc | Grammangis fallax | |
| | 912 | 80 franc | Cymbidiella humblotii | |
| | 913 | 80 franc | Angraecum sororium | |
| | 914 | 250 fran | Oeonia oncidiiflora | |
| | 915 | 1000 fra | Aerangis curnowiana | SS/ 1 stamp |

## MALAWI

| DATE ISSUE | SCOTT/ MICHEL | FACE VALUE | SPECIES NAME | BRIEF DESCRIPTION |
|---|---|---|---|---|
| 1969/07/09 | 114 | 4 pence | Holothrix longiflora | |
| | 115 | 9 pence | Disa ornithantha | |
| | 116 | 1/6 shil | Ansellia gigantea | |
| | 117 | 3 shilli | Disa hamatopetala | |
| | 117a | SS | Holothrix | SS/ 4 stamps, #114 thru #117 |
| 1975/06/06 | 255 | 3 tambal | Habenaria splendens | |
| | 256 | 10 tamba | Eulophia cucullata | |
| | 257 | 20 tamba | Disa welwitchii | |
| | 258 | 40 tamba | Angraecum conchiferum | |
| | 258a | SS | Habenaria | SS/ 4 stamps, #255 thru #258 |
| 1979/01/02 | 327 | 1 tambal | Vanilla polylepis | |
| 1979/01/02 | 328 | 2 tambal | Cirrhopetalum umbellatum | |
| | 329 | 5 tambal | Calanthe natalensis | |
| | 330 | 7 tambal | Ansellia gigantea | |
| | 331 | 8 tambal | Tridactyle bicaudata | |
| | 332 | 10 tamba | Acampe pachyglossa | |
| | 333 | 15 tamba | Eulophia quartiniana | |
| | 334 | 20 tamba | Cyrtorchis arcuata | |
| | 335 | 30 tamba | Eulophia tricristata | |
| | 336 | 50 tamba | Disa hamatopetala | |
| | 337 | 75 tamba | Cyrtorchis glandulosa | |
| | 338 | 1 kwacha | Aerangis kotschyana | |
| | 339 | 1.50 kwa | Polystachya dendrobiiflora | |
| | 340 | 2 kwacha | Disa ornithantha | |
| | 341 | 4 kwacha | Cyrtorchis praetermissa | |

LIBERIA 352; ALBANIA 2285; NORTH VIETNAM M861; CHAD 515b; MAURITIUS 639; MADERIA 77; BELGIUM B502; AUSTRALIA 998; COLOMBIA 582; CEYLON 342; REUNION 224; ARGENTINA 1348; SURINAME 665; TOGO 461; MACAU 375; CONGO 339; AZORES 327; CHINA 1092; DENMARK 561; GUINEA 937; NEW GUINEA B20; VENEZUELA C1049; SALVADOR 794; SOUTH MOLUCASS 1977 Unlisted; SINGAPORE 250; BOTSWANA 224; ard BRITISH HONDURAS 155.

## MALAWI {Continued}

| DATE ISSUE | SCOTT/ MICHEL | GIBBON NUMBER | FACE VALUE | SPECIES NAME | BRIEF DESCRIPTION |
|---|---|---|---|---|---|
| 1990/10/01 | 578 | | 15 tamba | Aerangis kotschyana | |
| | 579 | | 40 tamba | Angraecum eburneum | |
| | 580 | | 50 tamba | Aerangis luteo-alba v. rhodostica | |
| | 581 | | 2 kwacha | Cyrtorchis arcuata v. whytei | |
| | 581a | | SS | Cyrtorchis arcuata v. whytei | SS/ 4 stamps #578 thru #581 |

## MALAYSIA

| DATE ISSUE | SCOTT/ MICHEL | GIBBON NUMBER | FACE VALUE | SPECIES NAME | BRIEF DESCRIPTION |
|---|---|---|---|---|---|
| 1963/10/03 | 4 | | 6 sen | Vanda teres v. alba, Arandas & Arachnis | |
| | 5 | | 25 sen | Vanda teres v. alba, Arandas & Arachnis | |
| 1964/01/01 | Enve | E1 | 15 sen | Rhynchostylis retusa | Envelope/ Stamp has orchid |
| 1965/12/01 | Post | P1 | 10 sen | Arachnis flos-aeris | Postcard/ Small crest on left, stamp has orchids |
| | Post | P2 | 10 sen | Arachnis flos-aeris | Postcard/ Large crest on left, stamp has orchids |
| 1984/02/01 | 274 | | 80 sen | Arachnis species | |

## MALDIVES

| DATE ISSUE | SCOTT/ MICHEL | GIBBON NUMBER | FACE VALUE | SPECIES NAME | BRIEF DESCRIPTION |
|---|---|---|---|---|---|
| 1984/09/21 | 1062 | | 10 rupee | Dendrobium bigibbum | |
| | 1063 | | 15 rupee | Thelymitra aristata | SS/ 1 stamp |
| 1985/08/20 | 1096 | | 3 rupees | Dendrobium | Bouquet Queen Mother's {Birthday} |
| 1986/01/04 | 1095 | | 1 rupee | Dendrobium | Bouquet Queen Mother's {Birthday}  Sheetlet/ 5 stamps, 1 label |
| 1987/01/29 | 1238 | | 10 rupee | Spathoglottis plicata | |
| 1990/12/01 | 1446 | | 20 laari | Spathoglottis plicata | |

## MANAMA

| DATE ISSUE | SCOTT/ MICHEL | GIBBON NUMBER | FACE VALUE | SPECIES NAME | BRIEF DESCRIPTION |
|---|---|---|---|---|---|
| 1972 | M800 | --- | 5 dirham | Phalaenopsis | Bridal Bouquet JFKennedy {Wedding} |
| 1972 | NS | --- | 2 riyals | Angraecum | MS/ 1 stamp, selvage design |
| | NS | --- | 1 riyal | Odontoglossum | MS/ 1 stamp, selvage design |
| | NS | --- | 1.50 riy | Vanda | MS/ 1 stamp, selvage design |

## MANCHUKUO

| DATE ISSUE | SCOTT/ MICHEL | GIBBON NUMBER | FACE VALUE | SPECIES NAME | BRIEF DESCRIPTION |
|---|---|---|---|---|---|
| 1937/03/01 | 111 | | 3 fen | Cymbidium goeringii | Right side |
| 1937/09/16 | 116 | | 2 fen | Cymbidium goeringii | Top left |
| | 118 | | 10 fen | Cymbidium goeringii | Top left |
| 1937/12/01 | 122 | | 4 fen | Cymbidium goeringii | Top left |
| | 123 | | 8 fen | Cymbidium goeringii | Top left |
| | 124 | | 10 fen | Cymbidium goeringii | Top left |
| | 126 | | 20 fen | Cymbidium goeringii | Top left |
| 1942/09/15 | Post | HG49a | 3 fen | Cymbidium goeringii | Postcard/ Japanese Slogan "Name should be written carefully... |
| | Post | HG49b | 3 fen | Cymbidium goeringii | Postcard/ Chinese Slogan "Name should be written carefully..." |
| | Post | HG50a | 3 fen | Cymbidium goeringii | Postcard/ Japanese Slogan "Let's build the country up..." |
| | Post | HG50b | 3 fen | Cymbidium goeringii | Postcard/ Chinese Slogan "Let's build the country up..." |
| 1944/04/01 | Post | HG51 | 3 fen | Cymbidium goeringii | Postcard/ Single card with NO slogans, stamp has orchids |
| 1944/10/01 | Post | HG52 | 5 fen | Cymbidium goeringii | Postcard/ #51a SC {two different types of surcharge} >Magenta< |
| | Post | HG53 | 5 fen | Cymbidium goeringii | Postcard/ No slogans, stamp has orchids |
| | Post | HG54 | 3 fen | Cymbidium goeringii | Postcard/ Double reply and NO slogans, stamp has orchids |
| 1945/07/01 | Post | HG55 | 5 fen | Cymbidium goeringii | Postcard/ Has 4 blocks for address, making reuse impossible |

## MAUTITIUS

| DATE ISSUE | SCOTT/ MICHEL | GIBBON NUMBER | FACE VALUE | SPECIES NAME | BRIEF DESCRIPTION |
|---|---|---|---|---|---|
| 1982/07/01 | 550 | | 5 rupees | Odontoglossum | Bridal Bouqeut Di's {Birthday} |
| 1986/10/03 | 638 | | $0.25 | Cryptopus elatus | |
| | 639 | | 2 rupees | Jumellea recta | |
| | 640 | | 2.50 rup | Angraecum mauritianum | |
| | 641 | | 10 rupee | Bulbophyllum longifolium | |

## MEXICO

| DATE ISSUE | SCOTT/ MICHEL | GIBBON NUMBER | FACE VALUE | SPECIES NAME | BRIEF DESCRIPTION |
|---|---|---|---|---|---|
| 1980/03/08 | C633 | | 1.60 pes | Vanilla planifolia | |

## MONACO

| DATE ISSUE | SCOTT/ MICHEL | GIBBON NUMBER | FACE VALUE | SPECIES NAME | BRIEF DESCRIPTION |
|---|---|---|---|---|---|
| 1976/11/09 | 1047 | | $0.80 | Odontoglossum | |
| 1977/11/09 | 1085 | | 1 franc | Phalaenopsis | |
| 1979/11/12 | 1190 | | 1 franc | Phalaenopsis Princesse Grace | |
| 1984/11/08 | 1441 | | 3 francs | Vanda coerulea & Aerides crassifolium | |
| 1990/05/03 | 1706 | | 2 francs | Phalaenopsis Princesse Grace | |
| | 1707 | | 3 francs | Paphiopedilum Prince Rainier III | |
| | 1709 | | 4 francs | Cattleya Principessa Grace | |

## MONTSERRAT

| DATE ISSUE | SCOTT/ MICHEL | GIBBON NUMBER | FACE VALUE | SPECIES NAME | BRIEF DESCRIPTION |
|---|---|---|---|---|---|
| 1985/05/09 | 554 | | $0.90 | Oncidium urophyllum | |
| | 555 | | $1.15 | Epidendrum difforme | |
| | 556 | | $1.50 | Epidendrum ciliare | |
| | 557 | | $2.50 | Brassavola cucullata | |
| | 557a | | SS | Oncidium | SS/ 4 stamps, #554 thru #557 |
| 1987/11/13 | 658 | | $0.90 | Oncidium variegatum | |
| | 659 | | $1.15 | Vanilla planifolia | |
| | 660 | | $1.50 | Gongora quinquenervis | |
| | 661 | | $3.50 | Brassavola nodosa | |
| | 662 | | $5.00 | Oncidium lanceanum | SS/ 1 stamp |

## MOROCCO

| DATE ISSUE | SCOTT/ MICHEL | GIBBON NUMBER | FACE VALUE | SPECIES NAME | BRIEF DESCRIPTION |
|---|---|---|---|---|---|
| 1965/12/13 | 129 | | $0.25 | Ophrys speculum | Sheetlet/ 10 stamps, also descriptive tabs |
| | 130 | | $0.40 | Ophrys fusca | Sheetlet/ 10 stamps, also descriptive tabs |
| | 131 | | $0.60 | Ophrys tenthredinifera | Sheetlet/ 10 stamps, also descriptive tabs |

## MOZAMBIQUE

| DATE ISSUE | SCOTT/ MICHEL | GIBBON NUMBER | FACE VALUE | SPECIES NAME | BRIEF DESCRIPTION |
|---|---|---|---|---|---|
| 1978/05/16 | 594 | | 1.50 esc | Eulophia speciosa | |
| 1981/12/21 | 797 | | 7.5 meti | Ansellia gigantea | |

## NANUMAGE {Tuvalu}

| DATE ISSUE | SCOTT/ MICHEL | GIBBON NUMBER | FACE VALUE | SPECIES NAME | BRIEF DESCRIPTION |
|---|---|---|---|---|---|
| 1985/05/03 | 8512 | --- | $0.30 | Vanda coerulea | |
| | 8516 | --- | $0.50 | Thelymitra venosa | |

## NANUMEA {Tuvalu}

| DATE ISSUE | SCOTT/ MICHEL | GIBBON NUMBER | FACE VALUE | SPECIES NAME | BRIEF DESCRIPTION |
|---|---|---|---|---|---|
| 1987/11/20 | 8702 | --- | $0.60 | Cattleya | Bridal Bouaqet QE2 {40th Wedding Anniversary} |

## NEGRI SEMBILAN {Malaysia}

| DATE ISSUE | SCOTT/ MICHEL | GIBBON NUMBER | FACE VALUE | SPECIES NAME | BRIEF DESCRIPTION |
|---|---|---|---|---|---|
| 1965/11/15 | 76 | | 1 sen | Vanda hookeriana | #76a Wmk sideways |
| | 77 | | 2 sen | Arundina graminifolia | |
| | 78 | | 5 sen | Paphiopedilum niveum | #78a Yellow omitted |
| | 79 | | 6 sen | Spathoglottis plicata | |
| | 80 | | 10 sen | Arachnis flos-aeris | |
| | 81 | | 15 sen | Rhynchostylis retusa | |
| | 82 | | 20 sen | Phalaenopsis violacea | |

## NEVIS

| DATE ISSUE | SCOTT/ MICHEL | GIBBON NUMBER | FACE VALUE | SPECIES NAME | BRIEF DESCRIPTION |
|---|---|---|---|---|---|
| 1984/08/08 | 8441 | | $0.20 | Epidendrum ciliare | |
| 1985/04/02 | O8502 | | $0.20 | Epidendrum ciliare | #8441 OP "Officiel" |
| 1986/05/01 | 8441a | | $0.20 | Epidendrum ciliare | #8441 RP, with "1986" added in selvage |
| 1990/11/19 | 626 | | $0.10 | Cattleya deckeri | |
| | 627 | | $0.15 | Epidendrum ciliare | |
| | 628 | | $0.20 | Epidendrum fragrans | |
| | 629 | | $0.40 | Epidendrum ibaguense | |
| | 630 | | $0.60 | Epidendrum latifolium | |
| | 631 | | $1.20 | Maxillaria conferta | |
| | 632 | | $2.00 | Epidendrum strobiliferum | |
| | 633 | | $3.00 | Brassavola cucullata | |
| | 634 | | $5.00 | Rodriguezia lanceolata | SS/ 1 stamp |

## NEW CALEDONIA

| DATE ISSUE | SCOTT/ MICHEL | GIBBON NUMBER | FACE VALUE | SPECIES NAME | BRIEF DESCRIPTION |
|---|---|---|---|---|---|
| 1975/05/30 | 408 | | 8 francs | Calanthe triplicata | |
| | 409 | | 11 franc | Lyperanthus gigas | |
| | C125 | | 42 franc | Eriaxis rigida | |
| 1977/01/15 | C136 | | 11 franc | Vanda teres | Lower left |
| 1977/05/23 | 425 | | 22 franc | Phaius daenikeri | |
| | 426 | | 44 franc | Dendrobium finetianum | |
| 1983/02/02 | 482A | | 10 franc | Dendrobium oppositifolium | |
| | 482B | | 15 franc | Dendrobium muricatum v. munificum | |
| | 482C | | 29 franc | Dendrobium fractiflexum | |
| 1984/07/19 | 502 | | 16 franc | Diplocaulobium ou-hinnae | |
| | 503 | | 38 franc | Acianthus atepalus | |
| | 543 | | 44 franc | Coelogyne lycastoides | |
| | 544 | | 58 franc | Calanthe langei | |

## NEW GUINEA

| DATE ISSUE | SCOTT/ MICHEL | GIBBON NUMBER | FACE VALUE | SPECIES NAME | BRIEF DESCRIPTION |
|---|---|---|---|---|---|
| 1959/11/16 | B20 | | $0.10 | Dendrobium antennatum | |

## NEW HEBRIDES {British & French}

| DATE ISSUE | SCOTT/ MICHEL | GIBBON NUMBER | FACE VALUE | SPECIES NAME | BRIEF DESCRIPTION |
|---|---|---|---|---|---|
| 1973/02/26 | 171 | | $0.25 | Dendrobium teretifolium | #171a Wmk inverted {British} |
| | 172 | | $0.30 | Ephemerantha comata | British |
| | 173 | | $0.35 | Spathoglottis petri | #173a Wmk Inverted {British} |
| | 174 | | $0.65 | Dendrobium mohlianum | British |
| | 190 | | $0.25 | Dendrobium teretifolium | French |
| | 191 | | $0.30 | Ephemerantha comata | French |
| | 192 | | $0.35 | Spathoglottis petri | French |
| | 193 | | $0.65 | Dendrobium mohlianum | French |

## NEW ZEALAND

| DATE ISSUE | SCOTT/ MICHEL | GIBBON NUMBER | FACE VALUE | SPECIES NAME | BRIEF DESCRIPTION |
|---|---|---|---|---|---|
| 1980/02/07 | 705 | | $0.25 | Earina autumnalis & Thelymitra venosa | |
| 1988 | Enve | --- | Prepaid | Cymbidium pumilum | Envelope/ Stamp has orchid >Whangarei Orchid Society< |
| | Enve | --- | Prepaid | Pterostylis banksii | Envelope/ Stamp has orchid >Kaitaia Orchid Society< |
| | Formula | --- | --- | Brassocattleya Thalie | Advertising Aerogram/ World Orchid Conference |
| | Formula | --- | --- | Cymbidium Ormoulu | Advertising Aerogram/ World Orchid Conference |
| | Formula | --- | --- | Miltonia Melissa Baker | Advertising Aerogram/ World Orchid Conference |
| | Formula | --- | --- | Paphiopedilum hirsutissimum v. album | Advertising Aerogram/ World Orchid Conference |
| 1989 | Letter | --- | Prepaid | Peterostylis banksii | Lettercard/ Stamp has orchid >Canterbury Orchid Society< |
| 1990/04/18 | 986a | | $0.40 | Thelymitra pulchella | |
| | 986b | | $0.40 | Corybas macranthus | |
| | 986c | | $0.40 | Dendrobium cunninghamii | |
| | 986d | | $0.40 | Pterostylis banksii | |
| | 986e | | $0.80 | Aporostylis bifolia | SS/ 5 stamps #986a thru #986e |

## NICARAGUA

| DATE ISSUE | SCOTT/ MICHEL | GIBBON NUMBER | FACE VALUE | SPECIES NAME | BRIEF DESCRIPTION |
|---|---|---|---|---|---|
| 1962/03/30 | RA66 | | $0.05 | Hexisea bidentata | |
| | RA67 | | $0.05 | Schomburgkia tibicinis | |
| | RA68 | | $0.05 | Stanhopea ecornuta | |
| | RA69 | | $0.05 | Lycaste macrophylla | |
| | RA70 | | $0.05 | Maxillaria tenuifolia | |
| | RA71 | | $0.05 | Cattleya skinneri | |
| | RA72 | | $0.05 | Cycnoches egertonianum | |
| | RA73 | | $0.05 | Bletia roezlii | |
| | RA74 | | $0.05 | Sobralia pleiantha | |
| | RA75 | | $0.05 | Oncidium cebolleta & ascendens | |
| 1964 | 842 | | $0.05 | Bletia roezlii | #RA73 OP "Correos" >Red< and #842a OP Inverted |
| 1965 | NS | --- | $0.05 | Bletia roezlii | #RA73 OP "Pensiones de Retiro y Montepio G.N." |
| | NS | --- | $0.05 | Cattleya skinneri | #RA71 OP "Pensiones de Retiro y Montepio G.N." |
| | NS | --- | $0.05 | Cycnoches egertonianum | #RA72 OP "Pensiones de Retiro y Montepio G.N." |
| | NS | --- | $0.05 | Hexisea bidentata | #RA66 OP "Pensiones de Retiro y Montepio G.N." |
| | NS | --- | $0.05 | Lycaste macrophylla | #RA69 OP "Pensiones de Retiro y Montepio G.N." |
| | NS | --- | $0.05 | Maxillaria tenuifolia | #RA70 OP "Pensiones de Retiro y Montepio G.N." |
| | NS | --- | $0.05 | Oncidium cebolleta & ascendens | #RA75 OP "Pensiones de Retiro y Montepio G.N." |
| | NS | --- | $0.05 | Schomburgkia tibicinis | #RA67 OP "Pensiones de Retiro y Montepio G.N." |
| | NS | --- | $0.05 | Sobralia pleiantha | #RA74 OP "Pensiones de Retiro y Montepio G.N." |
| | NS | --- | $0.05 | Stanhopea ecornuta | #RA68 OP "Pensiones de Retiro y Montepio G.N." |
| 1965/12/03 | 843 | | $0.05 | Hexisea bidentata | #RA66 OP "Camporee Scout 1965" |
| | 844 | | $0.05 | Schomburgkia tibicinis | #RA67 OP "Camporee Scout 1965" |
| | 845 | | $0.05 | Stanhopea ecornuta | #RA68 OP "Camporee Scout 1965" |
| | 846 | | $0.05 | Lycaste macrophylla | #RA69 OP "Camporee Scout 1965" |
| | 847 | | $0.05 | Maxillaria tenuifolia | #RA70 OP "Camporee Scout 1965" |
| | 848 | | $0.05 | Cattleya skinneri | #RA71 OP "Camporee Scout 1965" |
| | 849 | | $0.05 | Cycnoches egertonianum | #RA72 OP "Camporee Scout 1965" |
| | 850 | | $0.05 | Bletia roezlii | #RA73 OP "Camporee Scout 1965" |
| | 851 | | $0.05 | Sobralia pleiantha | #RA74 OP "Camporee Scout 1965" |
| | 852 | | $0.05 | Oncidium cebolleta & ascendens | #RA75 OP "Camporee Scout 1965" |
| 1967/11/20 | C626 | | $0.40 | Lycaste skinneri v. alba | |
| | C630 | | $0.40 | Cattleya skinneri | 5 stamps and 5 strips, #C626 and #C630 |
| 1969/07/07 | 855 | | $0.05 | Hexisea bidentata | #RA66 OP "Correo" >Black< |
| | 856 | | $0.05 | Schomburgkia tibicinis | #RA67 OP "Correo" >Black< |

## NICARAGUA {Continued}

| DATE ISSUE | SCOTT/ MICHEL | GIBBON NUMBER | FACE VALUE | SPECIES NAME | BRIEF DESCRIPTION |
|---|---|---|---|---|---|
| 1969/07/07 | 857 | | $0.05 | Lycaste macrophylla | #RA69 OP "Correo" >Black< |
| | 858 | | $0.05 | Cattleya skinneri | #RA71 OP "Correo" >Black< |
| 1969/09/30 | 859 | | $0.05 | Hexisea bidentata | #RA66 OP "O.I.T. 1919-1969" |
| | 860 | | $0.05 | Schomburgkia tibicinis | #RA67 OP "O.I.T. 1919-1969" |
| | 861 | | $0.05 | Stanhopea ecornuta | #RA68 OP "O.I.T. 1919-1969" |
| | 862 | | $0.05 | Lycaste macrophylla | #RA69 OP "O.I.T. 1919-1969" |
| | 863 | | $0.05 | Maxillaria tenuifolia | #RA70 OP "O.I.T. 1919-1969" |
| | 864 | | $0.05 | Cattleya skinneri | #RA71 OP "O.I.T. 1919-1969" |
| | 865 | | $0.05 | Cycnoches egertonianum | #RA72 OP "O.I.T. 1919-1969" |
| | 866 | | $0.05 | Bletia roezlii | #RA73 OP "O.I.T. 1919-1969" |
| | 867 | | $0.05 | Sobralia pleiantha | #RA74 OP "O.I.T. 1919-1969" |
| | 868 | | $0.05 | Oncidium cebolleta & ascendens | #RA75 OP "O.I.T. 1919-1969" |
| 1972/07/29 | 901 | | $0.05 | Hexisea bidentata | #RA66 OP "Correo" >Blue< |
| | 902 | | $0.05 | Schomburgkia tibicinis | #RA67 OP "Correo" >Blue< |
| | 903 | | $0.05 | Stanhopea ecornuta | #RA68 OP "Correo" >Blue< |
| | 904 | | $0.05 | Lycaste macrophylla | #RA69 OP "Correo" >Blue< |
| | 905 | | $0.05 | Cattleya skinneri | #RA71 OP "Correo" >Blue< |
| | 906 | | $0.05 | Cycnoches egertonianum | #RA72 OP "Correo" >Blue< |
| | 907 | | $0.05 | Bletia roezlii | #RA73 OP "Correo" >Blue< |
| | 908 | | $0.05 | Sobralia pleiantha | #RA74 OP "Correo" >Blue< |
| 1972/11/13 | C805 | | $0.25 | Cattleya | Story on back, Nero Wolf detective |
| 1973/07/26 | C844a | | SS | Houlletia tagrina, Odontoglossum suberuciforme & Kegeliella atropilosa/ 3 labels | |
| 1979/04/06 | C964 | | $0.55 | Paphiopedilum species | |
| | C968 | | 4 cordob | Cattleya | |
| 1982/11/13 | 1194 | | 2 cordob | Encyclia alatum | |
| 1983/02/05 | 1210 | | 1 cordob | Brassavola nodosa | |
| | 1211 | | 1 cordob | Cattleya lueddemanniana | |
| | 1214 | | 1 cordob | Laelia species | |
| | 1219 | | 1 cordob | Sobralia macrantha | |
| 1984/12/01 | Post | --- | 1 cordob | Sobralia macrantha | Postcard/ Christmas "Feliz ano Nuevo" Stamp has orchid |
| 1985/05/20 | M2590 | 2677 | 4 cordob | Vanilla planifolia | SS/ 6 stamps, 1 is #2677 |
| 1986/03/16 | M2651 | 2743 | 5 cordob | Brassavola nodosa | |
| | M2656 | 2752 | 5 cordob | Sobralia macrantha | |
| | M2662 | 2749 | 5 cordob | Cattleya lueddemanniana | |
| | M2667 | 2741 | 5 cordob | Laelia species | |
| 1987/03/25 | M2742 | 2834 | 10 cordo | Brassavola nodosa | |
| | M2746 | 2843 | 10 cordo | Sobralia macrantha | |
| | M2752 | 2840 | 10 cordo | Cattleya lueddemanniana | |
| | M2757 | 2832 | 10 cordo | Laelia species | |

## NIUE

| DATE ISSUE | SCOTT/ MICHEL | GIBBON NUMBER | FACE VALUE | SPECIES NAME | BRIEF DESCRIPTION |
|---|---|---|---|---|---|
| 1969/11/27 | 131 | | $0.30 | Vanda Miss Joaquim | |
| 1981/04/02 | 305 | | $0.02 | Phalaenopsis species | |
| | 306 | | $0.02 | Phalaenopsis species | Like values se-tenant |
| 1981/12/09 | 329 | | $1.00 | Phalaenopsis | Border design >GOLD< |
| | 330 | | $2.00 | Phalaenopsis | Also border design >GOLD< |
| | 331 | | $3.00 | Cattleya hybrid | Also Phalaenopsis, border design >GOLD< |
| 1982/01/15 | 332 | | $4.00 | Phalaenopsis | Border design >GOLD< |
| | 333 | | $6.00 | Phalaenopsis | Border design >GOLD< |
| 1982/03/12 | 334 | | $10.00 | Phalaenopsis | Border design >GOLD< |
| 1983/11/30 | 413E | | $3.70 | Cattleya hybrid | #331 Surcharged |
| 1984/02/20 | 417 | | $0.12 | Phalaenopsis species | |
| 1984/05/10 | 428 | | $2.30 | Dendrobium phalaenopsis | |
| | 429 | | $3.90 | Cattleya hybrid | |
| 1985/07/01 | O1 | | $0.12 | Phalaenopsis species | #417 OP "O.H.M.S." >Blue< |
| | O12 | | $2.30 | Dendrobium phalaenopsis | #428 OP "O.H.M.S." >Blue< |
| | O13 | | $3.90 | Cattleya hybrid | #429 OP "O.H.M.S." >Blue< |
| | O14 | | $4.00 | Phalaenopsis | #332 OP "O.H.M.S." >GOLD< |
| 1987/05/29 | O16 | | $6.00 | Phalaenopsis | #333 OP "O.H.M.S." >GOLD< |
| | O19 | | $10.00 | Phalaenopsis | #334 OP "O.H.M.S." >GOLD< |
| 1990/12/05 | 594 | | $10.00 | Phalaenopsis | #334 OP "Birdpex 90" >SILVER< |

## NIUTAO {Tuvalu}

| DATE ISSUE | SCOTT/ MICHEL | GIBBON NUMBER | FACE VALUE | SPECIES NAME | BRIEF DESCRIPTION |
|---|---|---|---|---|---|
| 1985/09/04 | 8537 | --- | $0.15 | Cymbidium | Queen Mothers Birthday/ Left |
| | 8538 | --- | $0.15 | Cymbidium | Queen Mothers Birthday/ Right |
| | 8539 | --- | $0.35 | Cymbidium | Queen Mothers Birthday/ Left |
| | 8540 | --- | $0.35 | Cymbidium | Queen Mothers Birthday/ Right |
| | 8541 | --- | $0.70 | Cymbidium | Queen Mothers Birthday/ Left |
| | 8542 | --- | $0.70 | Cymbidium | Queen Mothers Birthday/ Right |
| | 8543 | --- | $0.95 | Cymbidium | Queen Mothers Birthday/ Left |
| | 8544 | --- | $0.95 | Cymbidium | Queen Mothers Birthday/ Right |
| | 8544A | --- | $1.05 | Cymbidium | SS/ 2 stamps, Queen Mothers Birthday |
| 1986/01/10 | 8545 | --- | $1.50 | Cymbidium | SS/ 2 stamps, Queen Mothers Birthday |
| | 8546 | --- | $4.00 | Cymbidium | SS/ 2 stamps, Queen Mothers Birthday |

## NORFOLK ISLANDS

| DATE ISSUE | SCOTT/ MICHEL | GIBBON NUMBER | FACE VALUE | SPECIES NAME | BRIEF DESCRIPTION |
|---|---|---|---|---|---|
| 1984/01/10 | 325 | | $0.03 | Phreatia crassiuscula | |
| 1984/03/27 | 337 | | $3.00 | Oberonia titania | |

## NORTH BORENO

| DATE ISSUE | SCOTT/ MICHEL | GIBBON NUMBER | FACE VALUE | SPECIES NAME | BRIEF DESCRIPTION |
|---|---|---|---|---|---|
| 1961/02/01 | 286 | | $0.20 | Phalaenopsis amabilis | #286a Wmk block |

## NORTH KOREA

| DATE ISSUE | SCOTT/ MICHEL | GIBBON NUMBER | FACE VALUE | SPECIES NAME | BRIEF DESCRIPTION |
|---|---|---|---|---|---|
| 1963/03/21 | M460 | N453 | 40 chon | Cypripedium macranthum | |
| 1981/07/01 | M2175 | N2122 | 30 chon | Odontoglossum | SS/ 4 stamps, 1 has Bridal Bouquet Di's {Wedding} |
| | M2176 | N2123 | 70 chon | Odontoglossum | SS/ 4 stamps, 1 has Bridal Bouquet Di's {Wedding} |
| | NS | --- | 30 chon | Odontoglossum | SS/ 4 stamps, 1 has #M2175 OP "21st Birthday" |
| | NS | --- | 70 chon | Odontoglossum | SS/ 4 stamps, 1 has #M2176 OP "21st Birthday" |
| 1982/09/21 | --- | N2229 | 80 chon | Odontoglossum | SS/ 1 stamp, Bridal Bouquet Di's {1st Wedding Anniversary} |
| 1982/10/01 | MB131 | --- | 80 chon | Odontoglossum | SS/ >3D< Bridal Bouquet Di's {Wedding} Prince William's Birth |
| 1984/01/01 | M2442 | N2374 | 10 chon | Dendrobium phalaenopsis | Sheetlet/ 8 stamps |
| 1984/08/20 | M2481 | N2414 | 10 chon | Cattleya loddigesii | |
| | M2483 | N2415 | 20 chon | Thunia bracteata | |
| | M2484 | N2416 | 30 chon | Phalaenopsis amabilis | |
| | M2485 | N2417 | 80 chon | Dendrobium phalaenopsis | SS/ 1 stamp |
| 1984/12/30 | MB194 | | 10 chon | Dendrobium phalaenopsis & Cymbidium | SS/ ?? stamps, Bouquet in selvage |
| | MB195 | | 10 chon | Dendrobium phalaenopsis & Cymbidium | SS/ 3 stamps, Bouquet in selvage |
| | MB196 | | 10 chon | Dendrobium phalaenopsis & Cymbidium | SS/ 4 stamps, Bouquet in selvage |
| 1986/10/05 | --- | | 50 chon | Dendrobium phalaenopsis | Stamp on stamp, Flowers on sides >SILVER< |
| 1989/09/21 | --- | | 5 won | Dendrobium phalaenopsis | |

## NORTH VIET NAM

| DATE ISSUE | SCOTT/ MICHEL | GIBBON NUMBER | FACE VALUE | SPECIES NAME | BRIEF DESCRIPTION |
|---|---|---|---|---|---|
| 1966/01/10 | M425 | N422 | 12 xu | Dendrobium moschatum | |
| | M426 | N423 | 12 xu | Vanda teres | |
| | M427 | N424 | 12 xu | Dendrobium crystallinum | |
| | M428 | N425 | 12 xu | Dendrobium nobile | |
| | M429 | N426 | 20 xu | Vandopsis gigantea | |
| | M430 | N427 | 30 xu | Dendrobium patellaris | |
| 1976/01/25 | M841 | N848 | 6 xu | Dendrobium primulinum v. album | Blue |
| | M842 | N849 | 12 xu | Dendrobium primulinum v. album | Carmine |
| 1976/06/24 | M857 | N865 | 12 xu | Dendrobium devonianum | |
| | M858 | N864 | 12 xu | Habenaria rhodocheila | |
| | M859 | N866 | 20 xu | Dendrobium tortile | |
| | M860 | N867 | 30 xu | Doritis pulcherrima | |
| | M861 | N868 | 40 xu | Dendrobium farmeri | |
| | M862 | N869 | 50 xu | Dendrobium aggregatum | |
| | M863 | N870 | 60 xu | Eria pannea | |
| | M864 | N871 | 1 dong | Paphiopedilum concolor | |

## NORWAY

| DATE ISSUE | SCOTT/ MICHEL | GIBBON NUMBER | FACE VALUE | SPECIES NAME | BRIEF DESCRIPTION |
|---|---|---|---|---|---|
| 1990/02/23 | 970 | | 3.2 kron | Dactylorhiza fuchsii | |
| | 971 | | 3.2 kron | Epipactis atrorubens | |
| | Booklet 971a | | 32 krone | Epipactis | Booklet/ 1 pane of 10 se-tenant stamps #970 and #971 |

## OCCUSSI-AMBENO {Portugal Timor}

| DATE ISSUE | SCOTT/ MICHEL | GIBBON NUMBER | FACE VALUE | SPECIES NAME | BRIEF DESCRIPTION |
|---|---|---|---|---|---|
| 1978 | NS | --- | $2.00 | Cypripedium | SS/ 1 stamp, stylized background |

| DATE ISSUE | SCOTT/ MICHEL | GIBBON NUMBER | FACE VALUE | SPECIES NAME | BRIEF DESCRIPTION |
|---|---|---|---|---|---|

## OMAN STATE

| DATE ISSUE | SCOTT/ MICHEL | GIBBON NUMBER | FACE VALUE | SPECIES NAME | BRIEF DESCRIPTION |
|---|---|---|---|---|---|
| 1971/04/25 | NS | --- | 6 bugsha | Cypripedium calceolus | |
| 1973/08/30 | NS | --- | 10 baiza | Dendrobium | Background of birds |
| 1973/12/15 | --- | 358 | 1 baiza | Neottia nidus-avis | |
| | --- | 359 | 2 baiza | Spiranthes species | |
| | --- | 360 | 5 baiza | Epipactis helleborine | |
| | --- | 361 | 12 baiza | Gymnadenia conopsea | |
| | --- | 362 | 15 baiza | Liparis loeselii | |
| | --- | 363 | 20 baiza | Coeloglossum viride | |
| | --- | 364 | 25 baiza | Epipactis palustris | |
| | --- | 365 | 1 riyal | Listera ovata | |
| | --- | 366 | 2 riyal | Gymnadenia conopsea | SS/ 1 stamp |

## PAHANG {Malaysia}

| DATE ISSUE | SCOTT/ MICHEL | GIBBON NUMBER | FACE VALUE | SPECIES NAME | BRIEF DESCRIPTION |
|---|---|---|---|---|---|
| 1965/11/15 | 83 | | 1 sen | Vanda hookeriana | #83a Grey omitted and #83b Wmk sideways |
| | 84 | | 2 sen | Arundina graminifolia | |
| | 85 | | 5 sen | Paphiopedilum niveum | #85a Red omitted |
| | 86 | | 6 sen | Spathoglottis plicata | |
| | 87 | | 10 sen | Arachnis flos-aeris | #87a Red omitted and #87b Wmk sideways |
| | 88 | | 15 sen | Rhynchostylis retusa | |
| | 89 | | 20 sen | Phalaenopsis violacea | |

## PALAU

| DATE ISSUE | SCOTT/ MICHEL | GIBBON NUMBER | FACE VALUE | SPECIES NAME | BRIEF DESCRIPTION |
|---|---|---|---|---|---|
| 1987/03/12 | 145 | | $5.00 | Dendrobium palawense | |
| 1988/03/17 | 145A | | $10.00 | Dendrobium palawnese | Part of design |
| 1990/03/01 | 237 | | $0.45 | Corymborchis veratrifolia | |
| | 238 | | $0.45 | Malaxis setipes | |
| | 239 | | $0.45 | Dipodium freycinetanum | |
| | 240 | | $0.45 | Bulbophyllum micronesiacum | |
| | 241 | | $0.45 | Vanda teres v. hookeriana | |
| | 241a | | SS | Corymborchis | Sheetlet/ 3 strips of #237 thru #241 |

## PANAMA

| DATE ISSUE | SCOTT/ MICHEL | GIBBON NUMBER | FACE VALUE | SPECIES NAME | BRIEF DESCRIPTION |
|---|---|---|---|---|---|
| 1953/11/02 | C143 | | $0.25 | Peristeria elata | |
| 1960/02/06 | C227 | | $0.25 | Peristeria elata | #C143 OP "Naciones unicias eno Mundial Refugiados" |
| 1966/03/16 | C354 | | $0.30 | Sobralia panamensis | |
| | C354a | | SS | Sobralia panamensis | SS/ 2 stamps, 1 is #C354 |
| | C357 | | $0.40 | Peristeria elata | |
| | C357a | | SS | Peristeria elata | SS/ 2 stamps, 1 is #C357 |
| 1969/07/20 | MB70 | | $0.50 | Laeliocattleya Principe Negro | SS/ 1 stamp, Background >Pink< |
| | MB71 | | $0.50 | Laeliocattleya Principe Negro | SS/ 1 stamp, Background >Blue< |
| 1970/01/06 | 523 | | $0.13 | Peristeria elata | |

## PAPUA

| DATE ISSUE | SCOTT/ MICHEL | GIBBON NUMBER | FACE VALUE | SPECIES NAME | BRIEF DESCRIPTION |
|---|---|---|---|---|---|
| 1969/08/27 | 287 | | $0.05 | Dendrobium ostrinoglossum | |
| | 288 | | $0.10 | Dendrobium lawesii | |
| | 289 | | $0.20 | Dendrobium pseudofrigidum | |
| | 290 | | $0.30 | Dendrobium conanthum | |
| 1970/05/13 | 302 | | $0.10 | Dendrobium musiciforum | |
| | 303 | | $0.15 | Dendrobium | Tree limb |
| 1970/08/19 | 314 | | $0.20 | Phalaenopsis sanderiana | |
| 1974/11/20 | 402 | | $0.07 | Dendrobium bracteosum | |
| | 403 | | $0.10 | Dendrobium anosmum | |
| | 404 | | $0.20 | Dendrobium smillieae | |
| | 405 | | $0.30 | Dendrobium insigne | |
| 1986/08/04 | 651 | | 15 toea | Dendrobium vexillarius | |
| | 652 | | 35 toea | Dendrobium lineale | |
| | 653 | | 45 toea | Dendrobium johnsoniae | |
| | 654 | | 70 toea | Dendrobium cuthbertsonii | |

## PARAGUAY

| DATE ISSUE | SCOTT/ MICHEL | GIBBON NUMBER | FACE VALUE | SPECIES NAME | BRIEF DESCRIPTION |
|---|---|---|---|---|---|
| 1963/08/21 | MB45 | --- | 66 guara | Cattleya warscewiczii | SS/ 1 stamp |
| 1965/01/15 | MB65 | --- | 36 guara | Cattleya warscewiczii | SS/ 1 stamp >Lime Green< selvage design |
| | MB66 | --- | 36 guara | Cattleya warscewiczii | SS/ 1 stamp >Bright Orange< selvage design |

## PARAGUAY {Continued}

| DATE ISSUE | SCOTT/ MICHEL | GIBBON NUMBER | FACE VALUE | SPECIES NAME | BRIEF DESCRIPTION |
|---|---|---|---|---|---|
| 1965/07/28 | 699 | | $0.20 | Sobralia macrantha | Purple |
| | 700 | | $0.30 | Sobralia macrantha | Blue |
| | 701 | | $0.90 | Sobralia macrantha | Bright magenta |
| | 702 | | 1.50 gua | Sobralia macrantha | Green |
| | 703 | | 4.50 gua | Sobralia macrantha | Orange |
| 1973/12/31 | M2531 | --- | $0.75 | Cattleya | Descriptive tab |
| 1981/04/13 | M3375 | --- | 50 guara | Cattleya | International Year Children |
| | MB3373 | --- | 10 guara | Cattleya | SS/ 8 stamps, 2 labels with Orchid lower left selvage |
| 1981/12/04 | M3455 | --- | 25 guara | Miltonia | Stylized |
| | M3459 | --- | 3 guaran | Odontoglossum | Bridal Bouquet Di's {Wedding} |
| | M3462 | --- | 5 guaran | Odontoglossum | Bridal Bouquet Di's {Wedding} |
| | MB3461 | --- | 5 guaran | Odontoglossum | Sheetlet label/ 8 stamps, Bridal Bouquet Di's {Wedding} |
| | MB3466 | --- | 25 guara | Odontoglossum | SS/ 1 stamp, Bridal Bouquet Di's {Wedding} |
| 1983/11/24 | M3692 | --- | 25 guara | Miltonia hybrid | |

## PENANG {Malaysia}

| DATE ISSUE | SCOTT/ MICHEL | GIBBON NUMBER | FACE VALUE | SPECIES NAME | BRIEF DESCRIPTION |
|---|---|---|---|---|---|
| 1965/11/15 | 67 | | 1 sen | Vanda hookeriana | #67a Wmk sideways |
| | 68 | | 2 sen | Arundina graminifolia | |
| | 69 | | 5 sen | Paphiopedilum niveum | #69a Blue & yellow omit #69b Yellow omit #69c Magenta omit |
| | 70 | | 6 sen | Spathoglottis plicata | #70a Yellow omitted |
| | 71 | | 10 sen | Arachnis flos-aeris | #71a Green omitted and #71b Wmk sideways |
| | 72 | | 15 sen | Rhynchostylis retusa | #72a Green omitted |
| | 73 | | 20 sen | Phalaenopsis violacea | #73a Magenta omitted and #73b Yellow omitted |

## PENRHYN

| DATE ISSUE | SCOTT/ MICHEL | GIBBON NUMBER | FACE VALUE | SPECIES NAME | BRIEF DESCRIPTION |
|---|---|---|---|---|---|
| 1983/04/05 | 216 | | $0.48 | Vanda teres | |
| | 218 | | $2.00 | Vanda teres | SS/ 1 stamp |
| 1983/07/08 | 220 | | $0.48 | Vanda teres | #216 OP "XV World Jamboree Canada 1983" |
| | 222 | | $2.00 | Vanda teres | SS/ #218 OP "XV World Jamboree Canada 1983" |
| 1986/07/23 | 343 | | $2.50 | Vanda teres | Sheetlet >Top< Label/ 4 stamps, 2 labels |
| | 344 | | $3.50 | Vanda teres | Sheetlet >Top< Label/ 4 stamps, 2 labels |

## PERAK {Malaysia}

| DATE ISSUE | SCOTT/ MICHEL | GIBBON NUMBER | FACE VALUE | SPECIES NAME | BRIEF DESCRIPTION |
|---|---|---|---|---|---|
| 1965/11/15 | 139 | | 1 sen | Vanda hookeriana | #139a Wmk sideways |
| | 140 | | 2 sen | Arundina graminifolia | #140a Olive omitted |
| | 141 | | 5 sen | Paphiopedilum niveum | #141a Yellow omitted |
| | 142 | | 6 sen | Spathoglottis plicata | |
| | 143 | | 10 sen | Arachnis flos-aeris | #143a Magenta omitted and #143b Wmk sideways |
| | 144 | | 15 sen | Rhynchostylis retusa | #144a Lilac rose omitted and #144b Black omitted |
| | 145 | | 20 sen | Phalaenopsis violacea | #145a Magenta omitted |

## PERLIS {Malaysia}

| DATE ISSUE | SCOTT/ MICHEL | GIBBON NUMBER | FACE VALUE | SPECIES NAME | BRIEF DESCRIPTION |
|---|---|---|---|---|---|
| 1965/11/15 | 40 | | 1 sen | Vanda hookeriana | |
| | 41 | | 2 sen | Arundina graminifolia | |
| | 42 | | 5 sen | Paphiopedilum niveum | |
| | 43 | | 6 sen | Spathoglottis plicata | |
| | 44 | | 10 sen | Arachnis flos-aeris | #44a Black omitted |
| | 45 | | 15 sen | Rhynchostylis retusa | |
| | 46 | | 20 sen | Phalaenopsis violacea | |

## PERU

| DATE ISSUE | SCOTT/ MICHEL | GIBBON NUMBER | FACE VALUE | SPECIES NAME | BRIEF DESCRIPTION |
|---|---|---|---|---|---|
| 1971/09/27 | 553 | | 1.50 sol | Gongora portentosa | |
| | 554 | | 2 sol | Odontoglossum cristatum | |
| | 555 | | 2.50 sol | Mormolyca peruviana | |
| | 556 | | 3 sol | Trichocentrum pulchrum | |
| | 557 | | 3.50 sol | Oncidium sanderae | |
| 1972/12/29 | 603 | | 3.50 sol | Bletia catenulata | |
| 1973/09/27 | C377 | | 1.50 sol | Lycaste reichenbachii | |
| | C378 | | 2.50 sol | Masdevallia amabilis | |
| | C379 | | 3 sol | Sigmatostalix peruviana | |
| | C380 | | 3.50 sol | Porroglossum peruvianum | |
| | C381 | | 8 sol | Oncidium incurvum | |

| DATE ISSUE | SCOTT/ MICHEL | GIBBON NUMBER | FACE VALUE | SPECIES NAME | BRIEF DESCRIPTION |
|---|---|---|---|---|---|

# PHILIPPINES

| DATE ISSUE | SCOTT/ MICHEL | FACE VALUE | SPECIES NAME | BRIEF DESCRIPTION |
|---|---|---|---|---|
| 1932/05/03 | 360 | $0.32 | Vanda | Basket on left side |
| 1932/09/27 | C35 | $0.32 | Vanda | #360 OP "Round the World Flight vonGronau 1932" |
| 1935/05/26 | C51 | $0.32 | Vanda | #360 OP "Airmail" inside plane shape |
| 1952/08/19 | B6 | $0.05 | Cattleya | Corsage >Blue< |
|  | B7 | $0.06 | Cattleya | Corsage >Red< |
| 1962/03/09 | 850 | $0.05 | Vanda sanderiana |  |
|  | 851 | $0.06 | Phalaenopsis aphrodite |  |
|  | 852 | $0.10 | Dendrobium sanderae |  |
|  | 853 | $0.20 | Dendrobium anosmum |  |
|  | 853a | Block | Dendrobium | Block/ Se-tenant #850 thru #853, and #853b block imperf |
| 1962/12/23 | 872 | $0.05 | Cattleya | #B6 Surcharged |
| 1965/07/04 | 931 | $0.02 | Vanda sanderiana |  |
|  | 932 | $0.06 | Vanda sanderiana |  |
|  | 933 | $0.10 | Vanda sanderiana |  |
| 1973/04/23 | 1188 | $0.05 | Vanda sanderiana | #932 Surcharged |
| 1986/08/28 | 1808 | $0.60 | Vanda sanderiana |  |
|  | 1809 | 1.20 pes | Epigeneinum lyonii |  |
|  | 1810 | 2.40 pes | Paphiopedilum philippinense |  |
|  | 1811 | 3 pesos | Amesiella philippinensis |  |
| 1988/08/01 | 1941 | 1.90 pes | Paphiopedilum philippinense | #1810 Surcharged |
| 1990/06/30 | 2036 | 1 peso | Vanda sanderiana |  |

# POLAND

| DATE ISSUE | SCOTT/ MICHEL | FACE VALUE | SPECIES NAME | BRIEF DESCRIPTION |
|---|---|---|---|---|
| 1957/08/12 | 785 | 60 grosz | Cypripedium calceolus |  |
| 1962/08/08 | 1067 | 60 grosz | Platanthera bifolia |  |
| 1965/09/06 | 1346 | 20 grosz | Odontoglossum grande | #1346a value omitted, Sheetlet/ 8 stamps |
|  | 1347 | 30 grosz | Paphiopedilum hybrid | Sheetlet/ 8 stamps |
|  | 1348 | 40 grosz | Lycaste skinneri | Sheetlet/ 8 stamps |
|  | 1349 | 50 grosz | Cattleya warscewiczii v. gigas | Sheetlet/ 8 stamps |
|  | 1350 | 60 grosz | Vanda sanderiana | Sheetlet/ 8 stamps |
|  | 1351 | 1.35 zlo | Paphiopedilum hybrid | Sheetlet/ 8 stamps |
|  | 1352 | 4 zloty | Sobralia macrophylla | Sheetlet/ 8 stamps |
|  | 1353 | 5.60 zlo | Disa uniflora | Sheetlet/ 8 stamps |
|  | 1354 | 6.50 zlo | Cattleya labiata | Sheetlet/ 8 stamps |
| 1968/05/15 | 1581 | 60 grosz | Odontonia hybrid |  |
| 1973/08/30 | 1988 | 90 grosz | Dactylorhiza maculata | Lower left in field |

# REUNION

| DATE ISSUE | SCOTT/ MICHEL | FACE VALUE | SPECIES NAME | BRIEF DESCRIPTION |
|---|---|---|---|---|
| 1907 | J06 | $0.05 | Vanilla planifolia | Stylized >Carmine on yellow< |
|  | J07 | $0.10 | Vanilla planifolia | Stylized >Blue on blue< |
|  | J08 | $0.15 | Vanilla planifolia | Stylized >Bluish< |
|  | J09 | $0.20 | Vanilla planifolia | Stylized >Carmine< |
|  | J10 | $0.30 | Vanilla planifolia | Stylized >Green on greenish< |
|  | J11 | $0.50 | Vanilla planifolia | Stylized >Red on green< |
|  | J12 | $0.60 | Vanilla planifolia | Stylized >Carmine on blue< |
|  | J13 | 1 franc | Vanilla planifolia | Stylized >Violet< |
| 1927 | J14 | 2 francs | Vanilla planifolia | #J13 RP, >Red orange< surcharged |
|  | J15 | 3 francs | Vanilla planifolia | #J13 RP, >Red brown< surcharged |
| 1933/09/11 | J16 | $0.05 | Vanilla planifolia | Stylized >Deep violet< |
|  | J17 | $0.10 | Vanilla planifolia | Stylized >Dark green< |
|  | J18 | $0.15 | Vanilla planifolia | Stylized >Orange brown< |
|  | J19 | $0.20 | Vanilla planifolia | Stylized >Light red< |
|  | J20 | $0.30 | Vanilla planifolia | Stylized >Olive brown< |
|  | J21 | $0.50 | Vanilla planifolia | Stylized >Ultramarine< |
|  | J22 | $0.60 | Vanilla planifolia | Stylized >Black brown< |
|  | J23 | 1 franc | Vanilla planifolia | Stylized >Light violet< |
|  | J24 | 2 francs | Vanilla planifolia | Stylized >Deep blue< |
|  | J25 | 3 francs | Vanilla planifolia | Stylized >Carmine< |
| 1943/12/01 | 224 | $0.05 | Vanilla planifolia | Dull brown |
|  | 225 | $0.10 | Vanilla planifolia | Dark blue |
|  | 226 | $0.25 | Vanilla planifolia | Emerald |
|  | 227 | $0.30 | Vanilla planifolia | Deep orange |

PARAGUAY 703; POLAND 1354; ANGUILLA 404; JUGOSLAVIA 1956; SOUTH KOREA 1152; NANUMEA 8702; VENDA M47; SOUTH AFRICA 556; CANADA BK77; MADAGASCAR 299a; UMM AL QIWAIN 1973 Unlisted; ISRAEL 414; SWAZILAND 405; NIUE 413E; GREAT BRITIAN FB29; PERU 556; and TUVALU 455.

## REUNION {Continued}

| DATE ISSUE | SCOTT/ MICHEL | FACE VALUE | SPECIES NAME | BRIEF DESCRIPTION |
|---|---|---|---|---|
| 1943/12/01 | 228 | $0.40 | Vanilla planifolia | Dark slate green |
| | 229 | $0.80 | Vanilla planifolia | Rose brown |
| | 230 | 1 franc | Vanilla planifolia | Red brown |
| | 231 | 1.50 fra | Vanilla planifolia | Crimson |
| | 232 | 2 francs | Vanilla planifolia | Black |
| | 233 | 2.50 fra | Vanilla planifolia | Ultramarine and #233a background color omitted |
| | 234 | 4 francs | Vanilla planifolia | Dark violet |
| | 235 | 5 francs | Vanilla planifolia | Bistre |
| | 236 | 10 franc | Vanilla planifolia | Dark brown |
| | 237 | 20 franc | Vanilla planifolia | Dark green |
| 1945 | 240 | $0.50 | Vanilla planifolia | #224 Surcharged |
| | 241 | $0.60 | Vanilla planifolia | #224 Surcharged |
| | 242 | $0.70 | Vanilla planifolia | #224 Surcharged |
| | 243 | 1.20 fra | Vanilla planifolia | #224 Surcharged |
| | 244 | 2.40 fra | Vanilla planifolia | #226 Surcharged |
| | 245 | 3 francs | Vanilla planifolia | #226 Surcharged |
| | 246 | 4.50 fra | Vanilla planifolia | #226 Surcharged |
| | 247 | 15 franc | Vanilla planifolia | #233 Surcharged |

## RHODESIA

| DATE ISSUE | SCOTT/ MICHEL | FACE VALUE | SPECIES NAME | BRIEF DESCRIPTION |
|---|---|---|---|---|
| 1966/01/17 | 214 | 9 pence | Ansellia africana | Southern Rhodesia #101 OP "Independence Nov. 11, 1965" |
| | 214a | 9 pence | Ansellia africana | Double OP and #214b OP inverted |
| 1966/02/09 | 231 | 1/6 shil | Ansellia africana | Southern Rhodesia #101 RP, with new value and name change |
| 1968/03/11 | 247 | 1/6+15c | Ansellia africana | #231 RP, for currency change |

## ROMANIA

| DATE ISSUE | SCOTT/ MICHEL | FACE VALUE | SPECIES NAME | BRIEF DESCRIPTION |
|---|---|---|---|---|
| 1965/10/25 | 1780 | 10 bani | Stanhopea tigrina | |
| | 1781 | 20 bani | Paphiopedilum insigne | |
| 1968 | Enve | 55 bani | Cattleya | Envelope/ #68 Cachet with orchid plants in pots |
| 1969 | Post | 40 bani | Cattleya | Postcard/ #75 Gradina Botantical Gardens |
| 1971/06/19 | 2250 | 35 bani | Cypripedium macranthum | |
| 1972/06/05 | 2334 | 60 bani | Nigritella rubra v. miniata | |
| | 2336 | 2.90 lei | Cypripedium calceolus | |
| 1987/10/16 | 3465 | 1 leu | Cypripedium calceolus | SS/ 12 stamps, 1 is #3465i/5141a |
| 1988/10/24 | 3535 | SS | Oncidium | SS/ 12 stamps #3535a thru #35351 |
| | 3535a | 1 leu | Oncidium lanceanum | |
| | 3535b | 1 leu | Cattleya trianae | |
| | 3535c | 1 leu | Sophronitis cernua | |
| | 3535d | 1 leu | Bulbophyllum lobbii | |
| | 3535e | 1 leu | Lycaste cruenta | |
| | 3535f | 1 leu | Mormolyca ringens | |
| | 3535g | 1 leu | Phragmipedium schlimii | |
| | 3535h | 1 leu | Angraecum sesquipedale | |
| | 3535i | 1 leu | Laelia cripsa | |
| | 3535j | 1 leu | Encyclia atropurpurea | |
| | 3535k | 1 leu | Dendrobium nobile | |
| | 35351 | 1 leu | Oncidium splendidum | |
| | 3536 | SS | Brassavola | SS/ 12 stamps #3536a thru #35361 |
| | 3536a | 1 leu | Brassavola perrinii | |
| | 3536b | 1 leu | Paphiopedilum Maudiae | |
| | 3536c | 1 leu | Sophronitis coccinea | |
| | 3536d | 1 leu | Vandopsis lissochiloides | |
| | 3536e | 1 leu | Phalaenopsis lueddemmanniana | |
| | 3536f | 1 leu | Chysis bractescens | |
| | 3536g | 1 leu | Cochleanthes discolor | |
| | 3536h | 1 leu | Phalaenopsis amabilis | |
| | 3536i | 1 leu | Pleione pricei | |
| | 3536j | 1 leu | Sobralia macrantha | |
| | 3536k | 1 leu | Aspasia lunata | |
| | 35361 | 1 leu | Encyclia citrina | |

## ROSS DEPENDENCIES

| DATE ISSUE | SCOTT/ MICHEL | FACE VALUE | SPECIES NAME | BRIEF DESCRIPTION |
|---|---|---|---|---|
| 1982/01/20 | L19 | $0.40 | Vanda | Antarctic station's name |

# RUANDA-URUNDI

| DATE ISSUE | SCOTT/ MICHEL | GIBBON NUMBER | FACE VALUE | SPECIES NAME | BRIEF DESCRIPTION |
|---|---|---|---|---|---|
| 1953/03/01 | 119 | | $0.50 | Eurychone galeandrae | |
| | 125 | | 2 francs | Ansellia gigantea | |

# RUSSIA

| DATE ISSUE | SCOTT/ MICHEL | GIBBON NUMBER | FACE VALUE | SPECIES NAME | BRIEF DESCRIPTION |
|---|---|---|---|---|---|
| 1965/01/28 | Post | --- | 3 kupeck | Cattleya | Postcard/ Picture side has three orchids |
| 1967/03/29 | Aero | --- | 6 kupeck | Cattleya labiata | Aerogram/ Cachet has two orchids |
| 1969/03/11 | Enve | --- | 4 kupeck | Cattleya intermedia | Envelope/ Cachet has single orchid |
| 1969/05/15 | 3598 | | 10 kupec | Laeliocattleya hybrid | |
| 1969/06/11 | Enve | --- | 4 kupeck | Platanthera species | Envelope/ Cachet has two sprays of orchids |
| 1969/07/01 | Post | --- | 3 kupeck | Ephemerantha comata | Postcard/ Picture side has orchid |
| 1971/02/23 | Aero | --- | 6 kupeck | Phalaenopsis schilleriana | Aerogram/ Cachet has three orchids |
| 1971/03/22 | Aero | --- | 6 kupeck | Cattleya labiata | Aerogram/ Cachet has two orchids |
| 1971/03/29 | Enve | --- | 4 kupeck | Vanda pumila | Envelope/ Cachet has single orchid |
| 1971/12/15 | 3924 | | 1 kupeck | Vanda coerulea | |
| 1971/12/20 | Post | --- | 3 kupeck | Cattleya | Postcard/ Picture side has two orchids |
| 1971/12/30 | 3929 | | 10 kupec | Vanda coerulea | SS/ 4 stamps, 1 is #3929c |
| 1972/01/18 | Enve | --- | 4 kupeck | Vanda coerulea | Envelope/ Cachet has three orchids |
| 1973/06/07 | Enve | --- | 4 kupeck | Oncidium cebolleta | Envelope/ Cachet has four orchids |
| | Enve | --- | 4 kupeck | Vanda coerulea | Envelope/ Cachet has four orchids |
| 1973/07/02 | Enve | --- | 4 kupeck | Epidendrum radicans | Envelope/ Cachet has three orchids |
| 1973/07/12 | Enve | --- | 4 kupeck | Encyclia atropurpurea | Envelope/ Cachet has three orchids |
| 1973/09/05 | 4115 | | 4 kupeck | Dactylorhiza maculata | |
| 1973/09/05 | Aero | --- | 6 kupeck | Sophronitis coccinea | Aerogram/ Cachet has two orchids |
| 1974/05/13 | Enve | --- | 4 kupeck | Dendrobium falconeri | Envelope/ Cachet has single orchid |
| 1974/06/27 | Enve | --- | 4 kupeck | Cattleya mossiae | Envelope/ Cachet has single orchid |
| 1974/09/03 | Enve | --- | 4 kupeck | Odontoglossum grande | Envelope/ Cachet has two orchids |
| 1974/09/17 | Enve | --- | 10 kupec | Hexisea bilamellata | Envelope/ Cachet has one and a half orchids |
| 1975/01/01 | Post | --- | 3 kupeck | Cattleya | Postcard/ Picture side has two orchids framed-stylized design |
| 1975/07/09 | Post | --- | 3 kupeck | Cattleya mossiae | Postcard/ Picture side has three orchids |
| 1976/10/22 | Aero | --- | 6 kupeck | Cattleya | Aerogram/ Cachet has three orchids |
| 1976/11/30 | Post | --- | 3 kupeck | Cymbidium species | Postcard/ Picture side has three orchids |
| 1976/12/22 | Post | --- | 3 kupeck | Paphiopedilum species | Postcard/ Picture side has single orchid |
| 1977/12/06 | Enve | --- | 4 kupeck | Cattleya labiata | Envelope/ Cachet has single orchid |
| 1977/12/09 | Enve | --- | 4 kupeck | Calanthe vestita | Envelope/ Cachet has three orchids |
| 1979/03/11 | Enve | --- | 4 kupeck | Cattleya mossiae | Envelope/ Cachet has two and a half orchids |
| | Post | --- | 3 kupeck | Cattleya | Postcard/ Wedding invitation has two orchids |
| 1979/05/14 | Enve | --- | 4 kupeck | Vanilla barbella | Envelope/ Cachet has orchid |
| 1979/05/14 | Post | --- | 3 kupeck | Cymbidium species | Postcard/ Picture side has two orchids |
| 1981/04/27 | Enve | --- | 4 kupeck | Odontoglossum rossii | Envelope/ Cachet has single orchid |
| 1981/07/13 | Enve | --- | 4 kupeck | Cattleya mossiae | Envelope/ Cachet has single orchid |
| 1984/03/02 | Post | --- | 4 kupeck | Cattleya | Postcard/ Bowl of three orchids, with >Grey< background |
| 1986/03/13 | Enve | --- | 5 kupeck | Cattleya | Envelope/ With folded card inside, two Cattleyas on cover |
| 1988/06/09 | Enve | 890 | 5 kupeck | Dendrobium | Envelope/ Cachet has three orchids |
| 1988/08/12 | Enve | 89071 | 5 kupeck | Laelia purpurata | Envelope/ Cachet has three orchids |
| | Enve | 89072 | 5 kupeck | Odontoglossum grande | Envelope/ Cachet has two orchids |
| | Enve | 89073 | 5 kupeck | Chysis bractescens | Envelope/ Cachet has multiple orchid sprays |

# RWANDA

| DATE ISSUE | SCOTT/ MICHEL | GIBBON NUMBER | FACE VALUE | SPECIES NAME | BRIEF DESCRIPTION |
|---|---|---|---|---|---|
| 1966/03/14 | 156 | | 3 francs | Habenaria praestans | |
| 1968/09/09 | 256 | | $0.20 | Diaphananthe fragrantissima | |
| 1970/12/21 | 381 | | $0.20 | Brassocattleya Olympia v. alba | |
| | 382 | | $0.30 | Laeliocattleya callistoglossa | |
| | 383 | | $0.50 | Chondrorhyncha chestertoni | |
| | 384 | | 1 franc | Paphiopedilum hybrid | |
| | 385 | | 2 francs | Cymbidium hybrid | |
| | 386 | | 6 francs | Cattleya labiata | |
| | 387 | | 30 franc | Dendrobium nobile | |
| | 388 | | 60 franc | Laelia gouldiana | |
| 1975/10/25 | 692 | | 100 fran | Polystachya kermesiana | |
| 1976/11/22 | 779 | | $0.20 | Eulophia cucullata | |
| | 780 | | $0.30 | Eulophia streptopetala | |
| | 781 | | $0.50 | Disa stairsii | |

<table>
<tr><td>DATE<br>ISSUE</td><td>SCOTT/<br>MICHEL</td><td>GIBBON<br>NUMBER</td><td>FACE<br>VALUE</td><td>SPECIES NAME</td><td>BRIEF DESCRIPTION</td></tr>
</table>

## RWANDA {Continued}

| DATE ISSUE | SCOTT/MICHEL | GIBBON NUMBER | FACE VALUE | SPECIES NAME | BRIEF DESCRIPTION |
|---|---|---|---|---|---|
| 1976/11/22 | 782 | | 1 franc | Aerangis kotschyana | |
| | 783 | | 10 franc | Eulophia abyssinica | |
| | 784 | | 12 franc | Bonatea steudneri | |
| | 785 | | 26 franc | Ansellia gigantea | |
| | 786 | | 50 franc | Eulophia angolensis | |
| 1977/05/02 | 808 | | 100 fran | Polystachya kermesiana | #692 OP "Conference Mondiale de d'eau" |
| 1981/04/06 | 1010 | | $0.30 | Cyrtorchis praetermissa | |
| | 1012 | | 4 francs | Cynorkis kassnerana | |
| 1982/06/14 | 1089 | | 70 franc | Disa erubescens | |

## SABAH {Malaysia}

| DATE ISSUE | SCOTT/MICHEL | GIBBON NUMBER | FACE VALUE | SPECIES NAME | BRIEF DESCRIPTION |
|---|---|---|---|---|---|
| 1964/07/01 | 7 | | $0.20 | Phalaenopsis amabilis | North Boreno #286 OP "Sabah" |
| 1965/11/15 | 17 | | 1 sen | Vanda hookeriana | |
| | 18 | | 2 sen | Arundina graminifolia | #18a Olive omitted |
| | 19 | | 5 sen | Paphiopedilum niveum | |
| | 20 | | 6 sen | Spathoglottis plicata | |
| | 21 | | 10 sen | Arachnis flos-aeris | #21a Wmk sideways |
| | 22 | | 15 sen | Rhynchostylis retusa | |
| | 23 | | 20 sen | Phalaenopsis violacea | |

## SAINT HELENA

| DATE ISSUE | SCOTT/MICHEL | GIBBON NUMBER | FACE VALUE | SPECIES NAME | BRIEF DESCRIPTION |
|---|---|---|---|---|---|
| 1982/07/01 | 374 | | 29 pence | Odontoglossum | Bridal Bouquet Di's {Birthday} and #374a >Perf 13.5x14< |

## SAINT KILDA

| DATE ISSUE | SCOTT/MICHEL | GIBBON NUMBER | FACE VALUE | SPECIES NAME | BRIEF DESCRIPTION |
|---|---|---|---|---|---|
| 1969 | NS | --- | 2/6 shil | Dactylorhiza maculata | |
| 1970/09/01 | NS | --- | 2/6 shil | Dactylorhiza maculata | OP "European Conservation" |

## SAINT KITTS {St. Christopher, St. Kitts & Nevis}

| DATE ISSUE | SCOTT/MICHEL | GIBBON NUMBER | FACE VALUE | SPECIES NAME | BRIEF DESCRIPTION |
|---|---|---|---|---|---|
| 1971/03/01 | 241 | | $0.50 | Epidendrum ciliare | |
| 1980/02/04 | 395 | | $1.50 | Epidendrum difforme | |

## SAINT LUCIA

| DATE ISSUE | SCOTT/MICHEL | GIBBON NUMBER | FACE VALUE | SPECIES NAME | BRIEF DESCRIPTION |
|---|---|---|---|---|---|
| 1969/01/10 | 241 | | $0.10 | Chloraea species | |
| | 243 | | $0.25 | Chloraea species | |
| 1982/09/01 | 593 | | $4.00 | Odontoglossum | Bridal Bouquet Di's {Birthday} |
| 1986/06/14 | 826 | | $0.10 | Dendrobium | Bouquet QE2 {60th Birthday} |
| | 827 | | $0.45 | Dendrobium | Bouquet QE2 {60th Birthday} |
| | 828 | | $0.50 | Dendrobium | Bouquet QE2 {60th Birthday} |
| | 831 | | $5.00 | Dendrobium | Bouquet QE2 {60th Birthday} |
| | 833 | | $7.00 | Dendrobium | SS/ 1 stamp, Bouquet QE2 {60th Birthday} |

## SAINT PIERRE & MIQUELON

| DATE ISSUE | SCOTT/MICHEL | GIBBON NUMBER | FACE VALUE | SPECIES NAME | BRIEF DESCRIPTION |
|---|---|---|---|---|---|
| 1962/04/24 | 360 | | 25 franc | Cypripedium acaule | |
| | 361 | | 50 franc | Calopogon pulchellus | |

## SAINT THOMAS & PRINCE

| DATE ISSUE | SCOTT/MICHEL | GIBBON NUMBER | FACE VALUE | SPECIES NAME | BRIEF DESCRIPTION |
|---|---|---|---|---|---|
| 1982/07/31 | 8211 | --- | 75 dobra | Brassavola nodosa & Ansellia gigantea | Sheetlet labels >A and B< / 7 stamps |
| | 8212a | --- | 10 dobra | Brassavola nodosa & Ansellia gigantea | SS/ 1 stamp, 2 labels >A and B< |
| | 8212b | --- | 10 dobra | Brassavola nodosa & Ansellia gigantea | SS/ 2 stamps, 1 label >A< |
| | 8212c | --- | 10 dobra | Ansellia gigantea | SS/ 2 stamps, 1 label >B< |
| 1985 | MB1 | --- | 50 dobra | Brassavola nodosa & Ansellia gigantea | Sheetlet/ #8211 Surcharged |
| | MB2 | --- | 8 dobra | Brassavola nodosa & Ansellia gigantea | SS/ #8212a Surcharged |
| | MB3 | --- | 8 dobra | Brassavola nodosa & Ansellia gigantea | SS/ #8212b Surcharged |
| | MB4 | --- | 8 dobra | Ansellia gigantea | SS/ #8212c Surcharged |
| 1987/10/30 | 8715 | | SS | Oncidium nubigenum | SS/ 16 stamps, 1 is #8715f |
| 1989/10/15 | | | 20 dobra | Cattleya | Background of bird |
| | | | 20 dobra | Cattleya granulosa | |
| | | | 20 dobra | Dendrobium phalaenopsis | |
| | | | 50 dobra | Maxillaria eburnea & Diothonea imbricata | SS/ 1 stamp |
| 1989/12/20 | | | 100 dobr | Vanda tricolor | SS/ 1 stamp, Background of butterflies |

## SAINT VINCENT

| DATE ISSUE | SCOTT/MICHEL | GIBBON NUMBER | FACE VALUE | SPECIES NAME | BRIEF DESCRIPTION |
|---|---|---|---|---|---|
| 1977/02/07 | 483 | | 1/2 cent | Cattleya | Sheetlet label/ Bridal Bouquet QE2 {Silver Jubilee} |
| | 488 | | $0.10 | Cattleya | Sheetlet label/ Bridal Bouquet QE2 {Silver Jubilee} |

## SAINT VINCENT {Continued}

| DATE ISSUE | SCOTT/ MICHEL | FACE VALUE | SPECIES NAME | BRIEF DESCRIPTION |
|---|---|---|---|---|
| 1977/02/07 | 489 | $0.25 | Cattleya | Sheetlet label/ Bridal Bouquet QE2 {Silver Jubilee} |
| | 494 | $2.00 | Cattleya | Sheetlet label/ Bridal Bouquet QE2 {Silver Jubilee} |
| 1985/01/31 | 803 | $0.35 | Epidendrum ciliare | |
| | 804 | $0.45 | Ionopsis utricularioides | |
| | 805 | $1.00 | Epidendrum secundum | |
| | 806 | $3.00 | Oncidium altissimum | |
| 1990/11/01 | 1362 | $0.10 | Dendrophylax funalis & Dimerandra emarginata | |
| | 1363 | $0.15 | Epidendrum elongatum | Sheetlet/ 10 stamps |
| | 1364 | $0.45 | Comparettia falcata | Sheetlet/ 10 stamps |
| | 1365 | $0.60 | Brassia maculata v. guttata | |
| | 1366 | $1.00 | Encyclia cochleata & cordigera | |
| | 1367 | $2.00 | Cyrtopodium punctatum | Sheetlet/ 10 stamps |
| | 1368 | $4.00 | Cattleya labiata | Sheetlet/ 10 stamps |
| | 1369 | $5.00 | Bletia purpurea | |
| | 1370 | $6.00 | Ionopsis utricularioides | SS/ 1 stamp |
| | 1371 | $6.00 | Vanilla planifolia v. Jackson | SS/ 1 stamp |

## SAINT VINCENT-GRENADINES

| DATE ISSUE | SCOTT/ MICHEL | FACE VALUE | SPECIES NAME | BRIEF DESCRIPTION |
|---|---|---|---|---|
| 1985/03/13 | 8519 | $0.05 | Cypripedium calceolus | |
| | 8524 | $0.60 | Laelia anceps | |
| 1989/10/16 | 8939 | $0.05 | Doritis pulcherrima | Background of butterfly |
| 1990/11/23 | 9031 | $0.05 | Paphiopedilum Slipper | Sheetlet/ 10 stamps |
| | 9032 | $0.25 | Dendrobium phalaenopsis & Cymbidium hybrid | Sheetlet/ 10 stamps |
| | 9033 | $0.30 | Miltonia Candida | Sheetlet/ 10 stamps |
| | 9034 | $0.50 | Epidendrum ibaquense & Cymbidium Elliot Rogers v. Red Beauty | Sheetlet/ 10 stamps |
| | 9035 | $1.00 | Rossioglossum grande | Sheetlet/ 10 stamps |
| | 9036 | $2.00 | Phalaenopsis Elisa v. Chang Lou & Masdevallia coccinea | Sheetlet/ 10 stamps |
| | 9037 | $4.00 | Cypripedium acaule & calceolus | Sheetlet/ 10 stamps |
| | 9038 | $5.00 | Orchis spectabilis | Sheetlet/ 10 stamps |
| | 9039 | $6.00 | Dendrobium anosmum | SS/ 1 stamp |
| | 9040 | $6.00 | Epidendrum ibaquensis & Phalaenopsis hybrid | SS/ 1 stamp |

## SALVADOR

| DATE ISSUE | SCOTT/ MICHEL | FACE VALUE | SPECIES NAME | BRIEF DESCRIPTION |
|---|---|---|---|---|
| 1969/06/13 | 794 | $0.50 | Lycaste skinneri | Background of butterfly |
| 1976/02/19 | C374 | $0.25 | Caularthron bilamellatum | |
| | C375 | $0.25 | Oncidium oliganthum | |
| | C376 | $0.25 | Epidendrum ibaquense | |
| | C377 | $0.25 | Encyclia vitellina | |
| | C378 | $0.25 | Cyrtopodium punctatum | |
| | C379 | $0.25 | Pleurothallis schiedei | |
| | C380 | $0.25 | Lycaste cruenta | |
| | C381 | $0.25 | Spiranthes speciosa | |
| 1987/06/08 | 1131 | $0.20 | Maxillaria tenuifolia | Like values are se-tenant |
| | 1132 | $0.20 | Ponthieva maculata | |
| | 1133 | $0.25 | Meiracyllium trinasutum | |
| | 1134 | $0.25 | Encyclia vagans | |
| | 1135 | $0.70 | Encyclia cochleata | |
| | 1136 | $0.70 | Maxillaria atrata | |
| | 1137 | 1.50 col | Sobralia xantholeuca | |
| | 1138 | 1.50 col | Encyclia microcharis | |

## SAMOA {Western}

| DATE ISSUE | SCOTT/ MICHEL | FACE VALUE | SPECIES NAME | BRIEF DESCRIPTION |
|---|---|---|---|---|
| 1971/08/09 | 344 | 5 sene | Vanda | Lei |
| 1977/10/11 | 465 | 50 sene | Cattleya | Bed for Christ child |
| | 465a | SS | Cattleya | SS/ 4 stamps, 1 is #465 |
| 1985/01/23 | 637 | 48 sene | Dendrobium biflorum | |
| | 638 | 56 sene | Dendrobium vaupelianum | |
| | 639 | 67 sene | Glomera montana | |
| | 640 | 1 tala | Spathoglottis plicata | |
| 1989/01/31 | 751 | 15 sene | Phaius flavus | |
| | 752 | 45 sene | Calanthe triplicata | |
| | 753 | 60 sene | Luisia teretifolia | |
| | 754 | 3 tala | Dendrobium mohlianum | |

<table>
<tr><td>DATE<br>ISSUE</td><td>SCOTT/<br>MICHEL</td><td>GIBBON<br>NUMBER</td><td>FACE<br>VALUE</td><td>SPECIES NAME</td><td>BRIEF DESCRIPTION</td></tr>
</table>

## SAN MARINO

| DATE ISSUE | SCOTT/MICHEL | GIBBON NUMBER | FACE VALUE | SPECIES NAME | BRIEF DESCRIPTION |
|---|---|---|---|---|---|
| 1957/08/31 | 397 | | 4 lire | Cattleya trianae v. alba | |
| 1990/10/31 | 1219 | | 1000 lir | Ophrys bertolonii | Background of lizard |

## SARAWAK

| DATE ISSUE | SCOTT/MICHEL | GIBBON NUMBER | FACE VALUE | SPECIES NAME | BRIEF DESCRIPTION |
|---|---|---|---|---|---|
| 1932/01/01 | 094 | | $0.01 | Arachnis species | Indigo |
| | 095 | | $0.02 | Arachnis species | Green |
| | 096 | | $0.03 | Arachnis species | Violet |
| | 097 | | $0.04 | Arachnis species | Red-orange |
| | 098 | | $0.05 | Arachnis species | Deep Lake |
| | 099 | | $0.06 | Arachnis species | Scarlet |
| | 100 | | $0.08 | Arachnis species | Orange-yellow |
| | 101 | | $0.10 | Arachnis species | Black |
| | 102 | | $0.12 | Arachnis species | Deep ultramarine |
| | 103 | | $0.15 | Arachnis species | Chestnut |
| | 104 | | $0.20 | Arachnis species | Red-orange and Violet |
| | 105 | | $0.25 | Arachnis species | Orange-yellow and Chestnut |
| | 106 | | $0.30 | Arachnis species | Sepia and Vermilion |
| | 107 | | $0.50 | Arachnis species | Carmine-red and Olive-green |
| | 108 | | $1.00 | Arachnis species | Green and Carmine |

## SARAWAK {Malaysia}

| DATE ISSUE | SCOTT/MICHEL | GIBBON NUMBER | FACE VALUE | SPECIES NAME | BRIEF DESCRIPTION |
|---|---|---|---|---|---|
| 1965/11/15 | 228 | | 1 sen | Vanda hookeriana | #228a Grey omitted |
| | 229 | | 2 sen | Arundina graminifolia | #229a Olive omitted and #229b Black omitted |
| | 230 | | 5 sen | Paphiopedilum niveum | #230a Yellow omitted and #230b Black omitted |
| | 231 | | 6 sen | Spathoglottis plicata | #231a Black omitted |
| | 232 | | 10 sen | Arachnis flos-aeris | #232a Red brown omitted and #232b Magenta omitted |
| | 233 | | 15 sen | Rhynchostylis retusa | |
| | 234 | | 20 sen | Phalaenopsis violacea | |

## EYNHALLOW {Scotland}

| DATE ISSUE | SCOTT/MICHEL | GIBBON NUMBER | FACE VALUE | SPECIES NAME | BRIEF DESCRIPTION |
|---|---|---|---|---|---|
| 1982 | NS | --- | 2 pounds | Dendrobium | MS/ 1 stamp, Background of birds |
| | NS | --- | 2 pounds | Sobralia | SS/ 1 stamp |

## GRUNAY {Scotland}

| DATE ISSUE | SCOTT/MICHEL | GIBBON NUMBER | FACE VALUE | SPECIES NAME | BRIEF DESCRIPTION |
|---|---|---|---|---|---|
| 1982 | NS | --- | 1 pound | Calopogon | MS/ 1 stamp |
| | NS | --- | 10 pence | Orchis laxiflora | SS/ 4 stamps, 1 is an Orchid |

## STAFFA {Scotland}

| DATE ISSUE | SCOTT/MICHEL | GIBBON NUMBER | FACE VALUE | SPECIES NAME | BRIEF DESCRIPTION |
|---|---|---|---|---|---|
| 1982 | NS | --- | 40 pence | Cattleya aclandie | SS/ 4 stamps, 1 is an Orchid |
| | NS | --- | 40 pence | Cattleya superba | SS/ 4 stamps, 1 is an Orchid |
| | NS | --- | 25 pence | Encyclia cochleata | SS/ 4 stamps, 1 is an Orchid |
| | NS | --- | 75 pence | Orchis spectabilis | SS/ 6 stamps, 1 is an Orchid |
| | NS | --- | 2 pounds | Sophronitis grandiflora | SS/ 1 stamp |

## SELANGOR {Malaysia}

| DATE ISSUE | SCOTT/MICHEL | GIBBON NUMBER | FACE VALUE | SPECIES NAME | BRIEF DESCRIPTION |
|---|---|---|---|---|---|
| 1965/11/15 | 121 | | 1 sen | Vanda hookeriana | #121a Magenta omitted and #121b Wmk sideways |
| | 122 | | 2 sen | Arundina graminifolia | #122a Rose carmine omitted and #122b Yellow omitted |
| | 123 | | 5 sen | Paphiopedilum niveum | #123a Magenta omitted and #123b Yellow omitted |
| | 124 | | 6 sen | Spathoglottis plicata | #124a Red omitted and #124b Wmk sideways |
| | 125 | | 10 sen | Arachnis flos-aeris | #125a Red omitted and #125b Wmk sideways |
| | 126 | | 15 sen | Rhynchostylis retusa | #126a Green omitted |
| | 127 | | 20 sen | Phalaenopsis violacea | #127a Magenta omit #127b Green omit & #127c Yellow omit |
| | 127d | | 20 sen | Phalaenopsis violacea | Wmk Sideways |

## SEYCHELLES

| DATE ISSUE | SCOTT/MICHEL | GIBBON NUMBER | FACE VALUE | SPECIES NAME | BRIEF DESCRIPTION |
|---|---|---|---|---|---|
| 1962/02/21 | 199 | | $0.10 | Vanilla planifolia | #199a Wmk sideways |
| 1970/12/29 | 281 | | $0.50 | Vaniiia phaiaenopsis | |
| | 282 | | $0.85 | Angraecum brongniartianum | |
| | 283a | | SS | Vanilla | SS/ 4 stamps, 2 are #281 and #283 |
| 1978/02/06 | 391 | | $0.20 | Vanilla humblotii | |
| 1979/04/25 | Booklet 391A | | 5 rupees | Vanilla humblotii | Booklet/ 3 panes, 1 is #391/4 stamps |
| 1982 | 391a | | $0.20 | Vanilla humblotii | #391 RP, with "1982" added in selvage |
| 1983/11/17 | 527a | | SS | Phragmipedium | SS/ Stylized lower left selvage |
| 1986/04/21 | 592 | | $0.50 | Cattleya | Bridal Bouquet QE2 {60th Birthday} |

## SEYCHELLES {Continued}

| DATE ISSUE | SCOTT/ MICHEL | GIBBON NUMBER | FACE VALUE | SPECIES NAME | BRIEF DESCRIPTION |
|---|---|---|---|---|---|
| 1987/12/09 | 625 | | $0.50 | Cattleya | #592 OP "40th Wedding Anniversary" and #625a OP Inverted |
| 1988/12/21 | 661 | | 1 rupee | Dendrobium species | |
| | 662 | | 2 rupees | Arachnis hybrid | |
| | 663 | | 3 rupees | Vanda coerulea | |
| | 664 | | 10 rupee | Dendrobium phalaenopsis | |
| 1990/01/26 | 696 | | 1 rupree | Disperis tripetaloides | |
| | 697 | | 2 rupree | Vanilla phalaenopsis | |
| | 698 | | 3 rupree | Angraecum eburneum v. superbum | |
| | 699 | | 10 rupre | Polystachya concreta | |
| 1991/02/01 | 719 | | 1 rupee | Bulbophyllum intertextum | |
| | 720 | | 2 rupees | Agrostophyllum occidentale | |
| | 721 | | 3 rupees | Vanilla planifolia | |
| | 722 | | 10 rupee | Malaxis seychellarum | |

## SHARJAH

| DATE ISSUE | SCOTT/ MICHEL | GIBBON NUMBER | FACE VALUE | SPECIES NAME | BRIEF DESCRIPTION |
|---|---|---|---|---|---|
| 1972/12/28 | NS | --- | 1 riyal | Laelia | SS/ 12 stamps and labels, 1 is Laelia |
| | NS | --- | 1 riyal | Paphiopedilum | SS/ 12 stamps and labels, 1 is Paphiopedilum |

## SIERRA LEONE

| DATE ISSUE | SCOTT/ MICHEL | GIBBON NUMBER | FACE VALUE | SPECIES NAME | BRIEF DESCRIPTION |
|---|---|---|---|---|---|
| 1985/06/07 | 690 | | 1 leone | Eulophia cucullata | Bottom of frame |
| | 691 | | 1.70 leo | Eulophia cucullata | Bottom of frame |
| | 692 | | 10 leone | Eulophia cucullata | Bottom of frame |
| | 693 | | 12 leone | Eulophia cucullata | SS/ 1 stamp, Bottom of frame |
| 1987/11/15 | 919 | | 45 leone | Angraecum sesquipedale | |
| 1988/02/15 | 953 | | 65 leone | Cattleya | SS/ 1 stamp Bridal Bouquet QE2 {40th Wedding Anniversary} |
| 1989/09/08 | 1078 | | 3 leones | Bulbophyllum barbigerum | |
| | 1079 | | 6 leones | Bulbophyllum falcatum | |
| | 1080 | | 12 leone | Habenaria macrandra | |
| | 1081 | | 20 leone | Eurychone rothchildiana | |
| | 1082 | | 50 leone | Calyptrochilum christyanum | |
| | 1083 | | 60 leone | Bulbophyllum distans | |
| | 1084 | | 70 leone | Eulophia guineensis | |
| | 1085 | | 80 leone | Diaphananthe pellucida | |
| | 1086 | | 100 leon | Cyrtorchis arcuata | SS/ 1 stamp |
| | 1087 | | 100 leon | Eulophia cucullata | SS/ 1 stamp |
| 1990/08/20 | 1256 | | 250 leon | Odontoglossum | SS/ 1 stamp, Prince Charles & Diana's wedding background |

## SINGAPORE

| DATE ISSUE | SCOTT/ MICHEL | GIBBON NUMBER | FACE VALUE | SPECIES NAME | BRIEF DESCRIPTION |
|---|---|---|---|---|---|
| 1963/03/10 | 62 | | $0.01 | Arachnis Maggie Oei | #62a Wmk sideways |
| | 63 | | $0.08 | Vanda Tan Chay Yan | |
| | 64 | | $0.12 | Grammatophyllum speciosum | |
| | 65 | | $0.30 | Vanda Miss Joaquim | #65a Tan omitted |
| | Aero | A13 | $0.30 | Vanda Miss Joaquim | Aerogram/ Dotted line points to "R" of first fold |
| 1968/03/01 | Aero | A14 | $0.30 | Vanda Miss Joaquim | Aerogram/ #A13 RP, Dotted line points between "OL" of fold |
| 1969/03/01 | Aero | A15 | $0.30 | Vanda Miss Joaquim | Aerogram/ Stamp has two orchids >Green and Red much darker< |
| 1970/03/15 | 115 | | $1.00 | Odontoglossum rossii | |
| | 115a | | SS | Odontoglossum rossii | SS/ 4 stamps, 1 is #115 |
| 1976/06/20 | 247 | | $0.10 | Aranda Christine | |
| | 248 | | $0.35 | Aranda Majula | |
| | 249 | | $0.50 | Aranda Elizabeth Douglas-Home | |
| | 250 | | $0.75 | Aranda Noorah Alsagoff | |
| 1979/04/14 | 319 | | $0.10 | Rhyncovanda hybrid | |
| | 320 | | $0.35 | Vanda hybrid | |
| | 321 | | $0.50 | Vanda hybrid | |
| | 322 | | $0.75 | Vanda hybrid | |
| 1979/12/15 | 335 | | $1.00 | Vanda | Greenhouse |
| 1985/02/15 | Aero | A36 | $0.35 | Vanda Miss Joaquim | Aerogram/ Stamp has two orchids |
| 1986/05/02 | 486b | | $0.75 | Aranda | Garlands |
| 1987/08/08 | Aero | A37 | $0.35 | Vanda Miss Joaquim | Aerogram/ Chinese Wayang Dance Illustration/ Stamp has orchid |
| | Aero | A38 | $0.35 | Vanda Miss Joaquim | Aerogram/ Indian Classic Dance illustration/ Stamp has orchid |
| | Aero | A39 | $0.35 | Vanda Miss Joaquim | Aerogram/ Malay Candle Dance Illustration/ Stamp has orchid |
| 1990/02/17 | Aero | A45 | $0.34 | Oncidium & Vanda | Aerogram/ Design "Orchid Motif" back panel design |
| | Post | --- | $0.30 | Ascocenda Laikeun | Postcard/ Stamp and picture side has multiple orchids |

## SINGAPORE {Continued}

| DATE ISSUE | SCOTT/MICHEL | GIBBON NUMBER | FACE VALUE | SPECIES NAME | BRIEF DESCRIPTION |
|---|---|---|---|---|---|
| 1991/04/24 | | | $2.00 | Dendrobium anocha | Se-tenant with label |
| | | | $2.00 | Vanda Miss Joaquim | Se-tenant with label |

## SOLOMON ISLANDS

| DATE ISSUE | SCOTT/MICHEL | GIBBON NUMBER | FACE VALUE | SPECIES NAME | BRIEF DESCRIPTION |
|---|---|---|---|---|---|
| 1975/11/12 | 305 | | $0.20 | Spathoglottis plicata | Br.Solomon #241 OP with solid bar over "British" |
| | 306 | | $0.25 | Ephemerantha comata | Br.Solomon #242 OP with solid bar over "British" |
| | 307 | | $0.35 | Dendrobium cuthbertsonii | Br.Solomon #243 OP with solid bar over "British" |
| 1981/07/22 | 450 | | $0.08 | Ephemerantha comata, Spathoglottis plicata & Dendrobium cuthbertsonii/ Charles Wedding Wreath | |
| 1982/10/11 | 478 | | $0.12 | Phalaenopsis | Bouquet QE2 {Royal Visit} and #478a Pair |
| | 480a | | SS | Phalaenopsis | SS/ 3 stamps, 1 is #478 |
| | Booklet B5 | | $2.96 | Phalaenopsis | Booklet/ 2 panes of #480/8 stamps |
| 1987/09/23 | 598 | | $0.18 | Dendrobium conanthum | |
| | 599 | | $0.30 | Spathoglottis plicata | |
| | 600 | | $0.55 | Dendrobium gouldii | |
| | 601 | | $1.50 | Dendrobium goldfinchii | |
| 1989/01/20 | 631 | | $0.22 | Bulbophyllum dennisii | |
| | 632 | | $0.35 | Calanthe langei | |
| | 633 | | $0.55 | Bulbophyllum blumei | |
| | 634 | | $2.00 | Grammatophyllum speciosum | |

## SOUTH AFRICA

| DATE ISSUE | SCOTT/MICHEL | GIBBON NUMBER | FACE VALUE | SPECIES NAME | BRIEF DESCRIPTION |
|---|---|---|---|---|---|
| 1958/12/10 | Aero | K25 | 6 pence | Disa uniflora | Aerogram/ Design inside with single orchid |
| 1961/02/14 | Aero | K33 | $0.05 | Disa uniflora | #K25 Surcharged and #K33a SC shifted |
| 1961/05/31 | Aero | K36a | $0.05 | Disa uniflora | #K33 OP {22mm} 5c half way between bottom EP >Black< |
| | Aero | K36b | $0.05 | Disa uniflora | #K33 OP {22mm} 5c half way between bottom REP >Black< |
| | Aero | K36c | $0.05 | Disa uniflora | #K33 OP {21mm} 5c centered over bottom REP >Black< |
| | Aero | K36d | $0.05 | Disa uniflora | #K33 OP {21mm} 5c moved up between REP >Black< |
| | Aero | K36e | $0.05 | Disa uniflora | #K25 SC & OP {20mm} 5c down into REP >Black< |
| | Aero | K36f | $0.05 | Disa uniflora | #K25 SC & OP {20mm} 5c flushed left with REP >Black< |
| 1961/06/01 | Aero | K37 | $0.05 | Disa uniflora | #K25 SC & OP "Republic of South Africa" >Dark Purple< |
| 1962/02/01 | Aero | K43 | $0.05 | Disa uniflora | Aerogram/ Design inside and No descriptions >Baobab Tree Stamp |
| 1963/03/11 | Aero | K46 | $0.05 | Disa uniflora | Aerogram/ Design inside and Descriptive type lite >Jet Plane< |
| 1963/03/14 | 284 | | 2.5 cent | Disa uniflora | |
| 1966/05/14 | Aero | K47 | $0.05 | Disa uniflora | #K46 RP, Paper Pale Blue with Descriptive type lite >Jet Plane |
| 1967/05/14 | Aero | K48 | $0.05 | Disa uniflora | #K46 RP, Descriptive type heavier >Jet Plane< |
| 1979/03/30 | 516 | | $0.15 | Disa uniflora | Stylized on the salvage |
| | NS | --- | EXHIBIT | Disa uniflora | Exhibition sheet/ Stylized on top |
| 1981/09/11 | 553 | | $0.05 | Calanthe natalensis | |
| | 554 | | $0.15 | Eulophia speciosa | |
| | 555 | | $0.20 | Disperis fanniniae | |
| | 556 | | $0.25 | Disa uniflora | |
| | 556a | | SS | Calanthe | SS/ 4 stamps, #553 thru #556 |
| 1987/04/01 | Aero | --- | $0.16 | Disa uniflora | Aerogram/ Stamp WITHOUT frame and six address lines |
| | Aero | --- | $0.25 | Disa uniflora | Aerogram/ Stamp WITHOUT frame and six address lines |
| 1987/07/13 | Aero | --- | $0.30 | Disa uniflora | Aerogram/ Stamp with frame and six address lines |
| 1987/09/08 | Aero | --- | $0.16 | Disa uniflora | Aerogram/ Stamp with frame and six address lines |
| | Aero | --- | $0.25 | Disa uniflora | Aerogram/ Stamp with frame and six address lines |
| 1988/01/18 | Aero | --- | $0.16 | Disa uniflora | Aerogram/ #__RP, Stamp with frame and seven address lines |
| 1988/05/18 | Aero | --- | $0.30 | Disa uniflora | Aerogram/ #__RP, Stamp with frame and seven address lines |
| 1989/04/14 | Aero | --- | $0.18 | Disa uniflora | Aerogram/ Stamp with frame and seven address lines |
| 1989/08/21 | Aero | --- | $0.35 | Disa uniflora | Aerogram/ Stamp with frame and seven address lines |
| 1990/08/01 | Aero | --- | $0.40 | Disa uniflora | Aerogram/ Stamp with frame and seven address lines |
| 1990/10/01 | Aero | --- | $0.21 | Disa uniflora | Aerogram/ |
| 1990/12/09 | | | SS | Disa uniflora | SS/ 5 stamps, selvage design of flowers {Military Metals} |

## SOUTH KASAI

| DATE ISSUE | SCOTT/MICHEL | GIBBON NUMBER | FACE VALUE | SPECIES NAME | BRIEF DESCRIPTION |
|---|---|---|---|---|---|
| 1961 | K13 | --- | 10 franc | Ansellia gigantea | Belgian Congo #274 SC & OP "10fr Etat Autonome de Sud-Kasai" |

## SOUTH KOREA

| DATE ISSUE | SCOTT/MICHEL | GIBBON NUMBER | FACE VALUE | SPECIES NAME | BRIEF DESCRIPTION |
|---|---|---|---|---|---|
| 1979/05/02 | 1152 | | 20 won | Neofinetia falcata | |

## SOUTH MOLUCCAS

| DATE ISSUE | SCOTT/MICHEL | GIBBON NUMBER | FACE VALUE | SPECIES NAME | BRIEF DESCRIPTION |
|---|---|---|---|---|---|
| 1954 | NS | --- | 4 k | Arundina speciosa | |
| | NS | --- | 10 k | Phaius tankervilleae | |

## SOUTH MOLUCCAS {Continued}

| DATE ISSUE | SCOTT/ MICHEL | GIBBON NUMBER | FACE VALUE | SPECIES NAME | BRIEF DESCRIPTION |
|---|---|---|---|---|---|
| 1954 | NS | --- | 7.5 k | Spathoglottis plicata | |
| 1979/03/01 | NS | --- | 5 k | Arundina speciosa | #__ {4k}  SC & OP "IYC" and symbol of child |
| | NS | --- | 10 k | Phaius tankervilleae | #__ {10k} OP "IYC" and symbol of child |

## SOUTH VIET NAM

| DATE ISSUE | SCOTT/ MICHEL | FACE VALUE | SPECIES NAME |
|---|---|---|---|
| 1965/09/10 | 262 | $0.80 | Dendrobium nobile |
| 1974/08/18 | 490 | 10 dong | Rhynchostylis gigantea |
| | 491 | 20 dong | Paphiopedilum appletonianum |
| | 492 | 200 dong | Dendrobium nobile |

## SOUTHERN RHODESIA

| DATE ISSUE | SCOTT/ MICHEL | FACE VALUE | SPECIES NAME |
|---|---|---|---|
| 1964/02/19 | 101 | 9 pence | Anseliia gigantea |

## SRI LANKA

| DATE ISSUE | SCOTT/ MICHEL | GIBBON NUMBER | FACE VALUE | SPECIES NAME | BRIEF DESCRIPTION |
|---|---|---|---|---|---|
| 1976/12/12 | 497 | | $0.75 | Ipsea speciosa | |
| | 498a | | SS | Ipsea speciosa | SS/ 4 stamps, 1 is #497 |
| 1979/08/01 | Aero | --- | 1.75 rup | Cattleya | Aerogram/ Cachet has single orchid |
| 1981/04/01 | 631 | | 20 rupee | Phaius tankervilleae | |
| | 631a | | SS | Phaius tankervilleae | SS/ 4 stamps, 1 is #631 |
| 1981/07/07 | Aero | --- | 3.50 rup | Cattleya | Aerogram/ #__ SC & OP "Golden Jubilee of Universal Francise" |
| 1981/08/22 | Aero | --- | 3.50 rup | Cattleya | Aerogram/ #__ SC and "NO" overprint, Cachet has single orchid |
| 1983/06/23 | Post | --- | $0.35 | Dendrobium | Postcard/ Picture side has two orchid garlands |
| 1984/08/22 | 722 | | $0.60 | Vanda memorian v. Soysa Ernest | |
| | 723 | | 4.60 rup | Acanthephippium bicolor | |
| | 724 | | 5 rupees | Vanda tessellata v. rufescens | #724a/862B >Perf 13.5x13< |
| | 725 | | 10 rupee | Anoectochilus setaceus | |
| | 725a | | SS | Vanda | SS/ 4 stamps, #722 thru #725 |
| 1989/08/31 | 923 | | 5 rupees | Vanda Bank of Ceylon | |

## SUMMER ISLES

| DATE ISSUE | SCOTT/ MICHEL | GIBBON NUMBER | FACE VALUE | SPECIES NAME |
|---|---|---|---|---|
| 1979/03/21 | NS | --- | 25 pence | Dactylorhiza maculata |

## SURINAME

| DATE ISSUE | SCOTT/ MICHEL | FACE VALUE | SPECIES NAME | BRIEF DESCRIPTION |
|---|---|---|---|---|
| 1976/02/19 | 427 | $0.01 | Oncidium lanceanum | |
| | 428 | $0.02 | Epidendrum stenopetalum | |
| | 429 | $0.03 | Brassia lanceana | |
| | 430 | $0.04 | Epidendrum ibaguense | |
| | 431 | $0.05 | Encyclia fragrans | |
| 1977/01/19 | 460 | $0.20 | Ionopsis utricularioides | |
| | 461 | $0.30 | Rodriguezia secunda | |
| | 462 | $0.35 | Oncidium pusillum | |
| | 463 | $0.55 | Sobralia sessilis | |
| | 464 | $0.60 | Octomeria surinamensis | |
| 1979/02/07 | 520 | $0.10 | Rodriguezia candida | |
| | 521 | $0.20 | Stanhopea grandiflora | |
| | 522 | $0.35 | Scuticaria steelii | |
| | 523 | $0.60 | Bollea violacea | |
| 1980/11/19 | 562 | SS | Ionopsis | SS/ #460, #461, #462 and #464 lower left selvage |
| 1984/01/11 | 663 | $0.05 | Catasetum discolor | |
| | 664 | $0.10 | Menadenium labiosum | |
| | 665 | $0.40 | Comparettia falcata | |
| | 666 | $0.50 | Rodriguezia decorata | |
| | 667 | $0.70 | Oncidium papilio | |
| | 668 | $0.75 | Epidendrum porpax | |
| 1986/02/19 | 743 | $0.05 | Epidendrum ciliare | |
| | 744 | $0.15 | Cycnoches chlorochilon | |
| | 745 | $0.30 | Epidendrum anceps | |
| | 746 | $0.50 | Epidendrum vespa | |

## SWAZILAND

| DATE ISSUE | SCOTT/ MICHEL | FACE VALUE | SPECIES NAME | BRIEF DESCRIPTION |
|---|---|---|---|---|
| 1982/07/01 | 408 | $0.50 | Odontoglossum | Bridal Bouquet Di's {Birthday} |

## SWEDEN

| DATE ISSUE | SCOTT/ MICHEL | FACE VALUE | SPECIES NAME | BRIEF DESCRIPTION |
|---|---|---|---|---|
| 1955/07/21 | 484 | 20 ore | Cypripedium calceolus & Calypso bulbosa | Coil |

## SWEDEN {Continued}

| DATE ISSUE | SCOTT/ MICHEL | GIBBON NUMBER | FACE VALUE | SPECIES NAME | BRIEF DESCRIPTION |
| --- | --- | --- | --- | --- | --- |
| 1955/07/21 | 485 | | 1.40 kro | Cypripedium calceolus & Calypso bulbosa | |
| | 486 | | 20 ore | Cypripedium calceolus & Calypso bulbosa | >Perf 12.5< on three sides |
| | Booklet 486a | | 4 krona | Cypripedium calceolus & Calypso bulbosa | Booklets/ 2 different cover color types >Violet or Grey< |
| 1968/06/04 | 782 | | 45 ore | Platanthera bifolia | |
| | Booklet 786a | | 4.50 kro | Platanthera bifolia | Booklet/ 1 pane of 10 stamps, 2 are #782 >63 x 85mm< |
| | Booklet 786b | | 4.50 kro | Platanthera bifolia | Booklet/ 1 pane of 10 stamps, 2 are #782 >63 x 80mm< |
| 1982/10/09 | 1419a | | 1.65 kro | Orchis mascula | |
| | 1419b | | 1.65 kro | Cypripedium calceolus | |
| | 1419c | | 2.40 kro | Epipactis palustris | |
| | 1419d | | 2.70 kro | Dactylorhiza sambucina | SS/ 4 stamps, #1419a thru #1419d |
| 1985/03/14 | 1528 | | 2.20 kro | Nigritella nigra | |
| 1989/09/12 | 1763 | | 2.40 kor | Calypso bulbosa | |
| | Booklet 1763a | | 24 korna | Calypso bulbosa | Booklet/ 1 pane of 10 stamps, 5 are #1763 |

## SWITZERLAND

| DATE ISSUE | SCOTT/ MICHEL | GIBBON NUMBER | FACE VALUE | SPECIES NAME | BRIEF DESCRIPTION |
| --- | --- | --- | --- | --- | --- |
| 1880/11/17 | Post | HG12 | 5 pfenni | Vanilla | Advertising Postcard/ Word "Vanille" >Suchard Creme Glacee< |
| 1881/09/29 | Post | HG12 | 5 pfenni | Vanilla | Advertising Postcard/ Word "Vanille" >Suchard Creme auChocolat |
| 1929 | Post | HG161a | $0.10 | Words | Scenic Postcard/ Town name of Reichenbach {Botanist} |
| 1932 | Post | H&G | $0.25 | Words | Scenic Postcard/ Mountain name of Reichenbach {Botanist] >Red< |
| 1943/12/01 | B128 | | $0.20 | Cypripedium calceolus | Descriptive tabs/ 4 Different |

## SYRIA

| DATE ISSUE | SCOTT/ MICHEL | GIBBON NUMBER | FACE VALUE | SPECIES NAME | BRIEF DESCRIPTION |
| --- | --- | --- | --- | --- | --- |
| 1981/09/02 | 948 | | 100 pias | Dendrobium phalaenopsis | |

## TANZANIA

| DATE ISSUE | SCOTT/ MICHEL | GIBBON NUMBER | FACE VALUE | SPECIES NAME | BRIEF DESCRIPTION |
| --- | --- | --- | --- | --- | --- |
| 1989/11/12 | 628 | | 10 shill | Phalaenopsis Lipperose | |
| | 629 | | 25 shill | Lycaste Aquila | |
| | 630 | | 30 shill | Vuylstekeara Cambria v. Plush | |
| | 631 | | 50 shill | Vuylstekeara Monica v. Burnham | |
| | 632 | | 90 shill | Odontocidium Crowborough v. Plush | |
| | 633 | | 100 shil | Oncidioda Crowborough | |
| | 634 | | 250 shil | Sophrolaeliocattleya Phena v. Satum | |
| | 635 | | 300 shil | Laeliocattleya Lykas | |
| | 636 | | 400 shil | Cymbidium Baldoyle v. Melbury | SS/ 1 stamp |
| | 637 | | 400 shil | Cymbidium Tapestry v. Long Beach | SS/ 1 stamp |
| 1990/12/27 | 680g | | 100 shil | Cattleya | "O" is for Owl, Opposum and Orchids [Stylized], Disney |

## THAILAND

| DATE ISSUE | SCOTT/ MICHEL | GIBBON NUMBER | FACE VALUE | SPECIES NAME | BRIEF DESCRIPTION |
| --- | --- | --- | --- | --- | --- |
| 1967/04/12 | 477 | | 20 satan | Vandopsis parishii | |
| | 478 | | 50 satan | Ascocentrum curvifolium | |
| | 479 | | 80 satan | Rhynchostylis retusa | |
| | 480 | | 1 baht | Rhynchostylis gigantea v. Sagarik | |
| | 481 | | 1.50 bah | Dendrobium falconeri | |
| | 482 | | 2 baht | Paphiopedilum callosum | |
| | 483 | | 3 baht | Dendrobium formosum v. giganteum | |
| | 484 | | 5 baht | Dendrobium primulinum | |
| 1974/12/05 | 714 | | 75 satan | Vanda coerulea | |
| | 715 | | 2.75 bah | Dendrobium aggregatum | |
| | 716 | | 3 baht | Dendrobium scabrilingue | |
| | 717 | | 4 baht | Aerides falcatum v. houlletianum | |
| | 717a | | SS | Vanda | SS/ 4 stamps, #714 thru #717 |
| 1975/08/12 | 745 | | 75 satan | Dendrobium cruentum | |
| | 746 | | 2 baht | Dendrobium parishii | |
| | 747 | | 2.75 bah | Vanda teres v. gigantea | |
| | 748 | | 5 baht | Vanda denisoniana | |
| | 748a | | SS | Dendrobium | SS/ 4 stamps, #745 thru #748 |
| 1978/01/18 | 840 | | 75 satan | Dendrobium heterocarpum | |
| | 841 | | 1 baht | Dendrobium pulchellum | |
| | 842 | | 1.50 bah | Doritis pulcherrima v. buyssoniana | |
| | 843 | | 2 baht | Dendrobium hercoglossum | |
| | 844 | | 2.75 bah | Aerides odoratum | |
| | 845 | | 3 baht | Trichoglottis fasciata | |
| | 846 | | 5 baht | Dendrobium wardianum | |

| DATE ISSUE | SCOTT/ MICHEL | GIBBON NUMBER | FACE VALUE | SPECIES NAME | BRIEF DESCRIPTION |
|---|---|---|---|---|---|
| **THAILAND {Continued}** | | | | | |
| 1978/01/18 | 847 | | 6 baht | Dendrobium senile | |
| 1978/08/25 | 862 | | 3 baht | Dendrobium farmeri | Background of butterfly |
| 1985/05/01 | 1107 | | 2 baht | Vanda | Background upper right |
| 1986/11/07 | 1157 | | 2 baht | Vanda varavuth | |
| | 1157a | Bookle | 10 baht | Vanda varavuth | Booklet/ 1 pane of 5 stamps #1157 |
| | 1158 | | 3 baht | Ascocenda emma | |
| | 1159 | | 4 baht | Dendrobium sri | |
| | 1160 | | 5 baht | Dendrobium ekapol | |
| | 1160a | | SS | Vanda | SS/ 4 stamps, #1157 thru #1160 |
| 1989/06/28 | 1312 | | 6 baht | Dendrobium | Stylized/ Brooch design |
| **TIMOR** | | | | | |
| 1950 | 260 | | 1 avo | Vandopsis lissochiloides | |
| **TOGO** | | | | | |
| 1964/09/26 | 461 | | $0.50 | Odontoglossum grande | |
| 1965/12/25 | 547 | | 20 franc | Odontonia | |
| **TONGA** | | | | | |
| 1981/10/21 | 488 | | $3.00 | Odontoglossum | Bridal Bouquet Di's {Wedding} |
| 1982/04/14 | B1 | | $3.00 | Odontoglossum | #488 OP "Cyclone relief" |
| 1990/05/11 | | 1072 | $2.50 | Dendrobium | SS/ 1 stamp, Orchid right side |
| **TRANSKEI** | | | | | |
| 1984 | Telegrm T16t | | --- | Disa uniflora | |
| 1990/09/23 | 244 | | $0.35 | Disa crassicornis | Sheetlet/ 10 stamps |
| **TRENGGANU {Malaysia}** | | | | | |
| 1965/11/15 | 86 | | 1 sen | Vanda hookeriana | |
| | 87 | | 2 sen | Arundina graminifolia | #87a Black omitted |
| | 88 | | 5 sen | Paphiopedilum niveum | |
| | 89 | | 6 sen | Spathoglottis plicata | |
| | 90 | | 10 sen | Arachnis flos-aeris | #90a Black omitted |
| | 91 | | 15 sen | Rhynchostylis retusa | |
| | 92 | | 20 sen | Phalaenopsis violacea | #92a Magenta omitted |
| **TRINIDAD & TOBAGO** | | | | | |
| 1978/06/07 | 284 | | $0.12 | Paphinia cristata | |
| | 285 | | $0.30 | Caularthron bicornutum | |
| | 286 | | $0.40 | Miltassia species | |
| | 287 | | $0.50 | Oncidium ampliatum | |
| | 288 | | $2.50 | Oncidium papilio | |
| | 288a | | SS | Paphinia | SS/ 5 stamps, #284 thru #288 |
| **TUNISIA** | | | | | |
| 1980/11/17 | 772 | | 20 milli | Ophrys scolopax | |
| 1990/11/08 | | | 600 mill | Ophrys lutea | |
| **TURKEY** | | | | | |
| 1979/11/26 | 2125 | | 10 liras | Ophrys holosericea | |
| 1980/11/26 | 2157 | | 20 liras | Orchis anatolica | |
| **TURKS & CAICOS ISLANDS** | | | | | |
| 1982/07/21 | 532 | | $0.70 | Odontoglossum | Bridal Bouquet Di's {Birthday}  Sheetlet/ 5 stamps, 1 label |
| 1990/01/11 | 793 | | $0.20 | Encyclia gracilis | |
| | 797 | | $0.50 | Encyclia rufa | |
| **TUVALU** | | | | | |
| 1977/02/09 | 45 | | $0.50 | Cattleya | Bridal Bouquet QE2 {Silver Jubilee} |
| | 45a | | SS | Cattleya | SS/ 3 stamps, 1 is #45 |
| 1987/11/20 | 455 | | $0.60 | Cattleya | Bridal Bouquet QE2 {40th Wedding Anniversary} |
| **UGANDA** | | | | | |
| 1989/12/18 | 747 | | 10 shill | Aerangis kotschyana | |
| | 748 | | 15 shill | Angraecum infundibulare | |

| DATE ISSUE | SCOTT/ MICHEL | GIBBON NUMBER | FACE VALUE | SPECIES NAME | BRIEF DESCRIPTION |
|---|---|---|---|---|---|

## UGANDA {Continued}

| DATE ISSUE | SCOTT/ MICHEL | GIBBON NUMBER | FACE VALUE | SPECIES NAME | BRIEF DESCRIPTION |
|---|---|---|---|---|---|
| 1989/12/18 | 749 | | 45 shill | Cyrtorchis chailluana | |
| | 750 | | 50 shill | Aerangis rhodosticta | |
| | 751 | | 100 shil | Eulophia speciosa | |
| | 752 | | 200 shil | Calanthe sylvatica | |
| | 753 | | 250 shil | Vanilla imperialis | |
| | 754a | | 350 shil | Polystachya vulcanica | |
| | 755 | | 500 shil | Ansellia africana | SS/ 1 stamp |
| | 756 | | 500 shil | Ancistrochilus rothschildianus | SS/ 1 stamp |
| 1990/07/30 | 782 | | 10 shill | Aerangis kotschyana | #747 OP "Expo 90" >SILVER< |
| | 783 | | 50 shill | Aerangis rhodosticta | #750 OP "Expo 90" >SILVER< |
| | 784 | | 200 shil | Calanthe sylvatica | #752 OP "Expo 90" >SILVER< |
| | 785 | | 250 shil | Vanilla imperialis | #753 OP "Expo 90" >SILVER< |
| | 786 | | 500 shil | Ansellia africana | #755 OP "Expo 90" >SILVER< International Garden & Greenery |
| 1990/11/01 | 840 | | 15 shill | Angraecum infundibulare | #748 OP "Expo 90" >SILVER< |
| | 841 | | 45 shill | Cyrtorchis chailluana | #749 OP "Expo 90" >SILVER< |
| | 842 | | 100 shil | Eulophia speciosa | #751 OP "Expo 90" >SILVER< |
| | 843 | | 350 shil | Polystachya vulcanica | #754 OP "Expo 90" >SILVER< |
| | 844 | | 500 shil | Ancistrochilus rothschildianus | #756 OP "Expo 90" >SILVER< International Garden & Greenery |

## UMM AL QIWAIN

| DATE ISSUE | SCOTT/ MICHEL | GIBBON NUMBER | FACE VALUE | SPECIES NAME | BRIEF DESCRIPTION |
|---|---|---|---|---|---|
| 1972 | NS | --- | 1 riyal | Dendrobium | Background of birds >3D< |
| | NS | --- | 1 riyal | Dendrobium nobile & Cattieya | >3D< |
| 1973 | NS | --- | 1 riyal | Cypripedium calceolus | MS/ 1 stamp, >Imperf Pink< and >Imperf White< |
| | NS | --- | 1 riyal | Cypripedium calceolus | MS/ 1 stamp, >Perf Blue< and >Perf Pink< |
| | NS | --- | MS | Cypripedium calceolus | MS/ 16 stamps, 1 an Orchid >Perf Dull< and >Perf Shiny< paper |
| | NS | --- | MS | Cypripedium calceolus | MS/ 16 stamps, 1 is an Orchid >Imperf White< and >Imperf Pink< |
| | NS | --- | SS | Cypripedium calceolus | SS/ 16 stamps, 1 an Orchid >Perf Dull< and >Perf Shiny< paper |
| | NS | --- | SS | Cypripedium calceolus | SS/ 16 stamps, 1 is an Orchid >Imperf White< and >Imperf Pink< |

## UNITED NATIONS {Geneva}

| DATE ISSUE | SCOTT/ MICHEL | GIBBON NUMBER | FACE VALUE | SPECIES NAME | BRIEF DESCRIPTION |
|---|---|---|---|---|---|
| 1991/03/15 | 197 | | 90 centi | Anacamptis pyramidalis | Lower left in field |

## UNITED STATES

| DATE ISSUE | SCOTT/ MICHEL | GIBBON NUMBER | FACE VALUE | SPECIES NAME | BRIEF DESCRIPTION |
|---|---|---|---|---|---|
| 1890 | Post | UX14 | $0.01 | Vanilla | Advertising Postcard/ Empire Extract & Chemical Co. |
| 1904/08/29 | Enve | U385/W | $0.02 | Vanilla | Advertising Envelope/ Durkee's {#U385-389 colored paper} |
| 1906/08/22 | Enve | U385/W | $0.02 | Vanilla | Advertising Envelope/ Golden Gate {#U385-389 colored paper} |
| 1910/02/20 | Enve | U411 | $0.02 | Vanilla | Advertising Envelope/ Durkee's {#U411-415 colored paper} |
| 1914 | Enve | U429 | $0.02 | Vanilla | Advertising Envelope/ Durkee's {#U429-435 colored paper} |
| | Post | UX24 | $0.01 | Vanilla | Advertising Postcard/ #S33 "Guarding the Treasure Box" Allento |
| | Post | UX24 | $0.01 | Vanilla | Advertising Postcard/ #S33 "Who's the Lucky Man" Allentown Ad |
| 1969/08/23 | 1377 | | $0.06 | Cypripedium reginae | #1379a Block 4 stamps, 1 is #1377 |
| 1976/02/23 | 1664 | | $0.13 | Cypripedium reginae | #1682a Sheet, 50 stamps, 1 is #1664 >Minnesota Flag< |
| 1981/06/26 | 1924 | | $0.18 | Cypripedium calceolus v. pubescens | #1924a Block 4 stamps, 1 is #1924 |
| 1982/03/14 | 1975 | | $0.20 | Cypripedium reginae | >Perf 11< and #1975a >Perf 10.5x11< Minnesota State Flower |
| 1983 | Booklet | WH75 | $1.20 | Cypripedium calceolus v. pubescens | Booklet/ #1924a back cover >Blue and Red< |
| 1984/03/05 | 2076 | | $0.20 | Arethusa bulbosa | |
| | 2077 | | $0.20 | Cypripedium calceolus v. pubescens | |
| | 2078 | | $0.20 | Cleistes divaricata | |
| | 2079 | | $0.20 | Calypso bulbosa | #2079a Block 4 stamps, #2076 thru #2079 |
| 1984/05/01 | L.Sheet | --- | Prepaid | Arethusa | Folded Postcard/ #2076 thru #2079 on outside panel |

## UPPER VOLTA

| DATE ISSUE | SCOTT/ MICHEL | GIBBON NUMBER | FACE VALUE | SPECIES NAME | BRIEF DESCRIPTION |
|---|---|---|---|---|---|
| 1977/08/23 | 433 | | 400 fran | Eulophia cucullata | |
| 1983/06/01 | C276 | | 450 fran | Odontoglossum | Bridal Bouquet Di's {Wedding} |

## URUGUAY

| DATE ISSUE | SCOTT/ MICHEL | GIBBON NUMBER | FACE VALUE | SPECIES NAME | BRIEF DESCRIPTION |
|---|---|---|---|---|---|
| 1976/01/19 | C416 | | $0.50 | Oncidium bifolium | |

## VANUATU

| DATE ISSUE | SCOTT/ MICHEL | GIBBON NUMBER | FACE VALUE | SPECIES NAME | BRIEF DESCRIPTION |
|---|---|---|---|---|---|
| 1981/07/22 | 308 | | 15 vatus | Dendrobium spectabile | Charles Wedding Wreath |
| 1982/06/15 | 323 | | 1 vatu | Flickingeria comata | |
| | 324 | | 2 vatus | Calanthe triplicata | |
| | 325 | | 10 vatus | Dendrobium sladei | |
| | 325a | Bookle | 2.3 vatu | Dendrobium | Booklet/ 3 panes of #327/4, #326/6 and #325/6 stamps |

## VANUATU {Continued}

| DATE ISSUE | SCOTT/ MICHEL | GIBBON NUMBER | FACE VALUE | SPECIES NAME | BRIEF DESCRIPTION |
|---|---|---|---|---|---|
| 1982/06/15 | 326 | | 15 vatus | Dendrobium mohlianum | |
| | 327 | | 20 vatus | Dendrobium macrophyllum | |
| | 328 | | 25 vatus | Dendrobium purpureum | |
| | 329 | | 30 vatus | Robiquetia mimus | |
| | 330 | | 35 vatus | Dendrobium mooreanum | |
| | 331 | | 45 vatus | Spathoglottis plicata | |
| | 332 | | 50 vatus | Dendrobium seemannii | |
| | 333 | | 75 vatus | Dendrobium conanthum | |
| | 334 | | 100 vatu | Dendrobium macranthum | |
| | 335 | | 200 vatu | Coelogyne lamellata | |
| | 336 | | 500 vatu | Bulbophyllum longiscapum | |
| 1984/01/09 | 365 | | 25 vatus | Orchid plants | Background of mushroom |
| 1985/01/22 | 383 | | 5 vatus | Flickingeria comata | #323 Surcharged |
| 1987/05/12 | B1 | | 20 vatus | Calanthe triplicata | #324 SC & OP "Hurricane Relief Fund" |
| 1989/10/18 | 512 | | 100 vatu | Calanthe triplicata | #324 SC & OP with Melbourne Stamp Show logo |

## VENDA

| DATE ISSUE | SCOTT/ MICHEL | GIBBON NUMBER | FACE VALUE | SPECIES NAME | BRIEF DESCRIPTION |
|---|---|---|---|---|---|
| 1981/09/11 | M46 | | $0.05 | Cynorkis kassnerana | |
| | M47 | | $0.15 | Eulophia fridericii | |
| | M48 | | $0.20 | Bonatea densiflora | |
| | M49 | | $0.25 | Mystacidium brayboniae | |
| | MB50 | | SS | Cynorkis | SS/ 4 stamps, #M46 thru #M49 |
| 1984 | Telegrm T16v | | --- | Disa uniflora | |

## VENEZUELA

| DATE ISSUE | SCOTT/ MICHEL | GIBBON NUMBER | FACE VALUE | SPECIES NAME | BRIEF DESCRIPTION |
|---|---|---|---|---|---|
| 1953/12/01 | 590 | | $0.05 | Cattleya violacea | Green |
| | 591 | | $0.10 | Cattleya violacea | Red |
| | 592 | | $0.15 | Cattleya violacea | Brown |
| | 593 | | $0.20 | Cattleya violacea | Ultramarine |
| | 594 | | $0.40 | Cattleya violacea | Red orange |
| | 595 | | $0.45 | Cattleya violacea | Rose violet |
| | 596 | | 3 boliva | Cattleya violacea | Blue grey |
| | C500 | | $0.05 | Cattleya violacea | Blue green |
| | C501 | | $0.10 | Cattleya violacea | #C501a "1" short, 82nd position of sheet )Carmine( |
| | C502 | | $0.15 | Cattleya violacea | Dark brown |
| | C503 | | $0.25 | Cattleya violacea | Sepia |
| | C504 | | $0.30 | Cattleya violacea | Deep blue |
| | C505 | | $0.50 | Cattleya violacea | Henna brown |
| | C506 | | $0.60 | Cattleya violacea | Olive brown |
| | C507 | | 1 boliva | Cattleya violacea | Purple |
| | C508 | | 2 boliva | Cattleya violacea | Violet grey |
| 1955 | Post | HG23 | $0.10 | Cattleya | Postcard/ Picture side has single orchid {Type #5} |
| 1962/05/30 | 804 | | $0.05 | Oncidium papilio | |
| | 805 | | $0.10 | Caularthron bilamellatum | |
| | 806 | | $0.20 | Stanhopea wardii | |
| | 807 | | $0.25 | Catasetum pileatum | |
| | 808 | | $0.30 | Masdevallia tovarensis | |
| | 809 | | $0.35 | Epidendrum stamfordianum | |
| | 810 | | $0.50 | Encyclia atropurpurea | |
| | 811 | | 3 boliva | Oncidium falcipetalum | |
| | C794 | | $0.05 | Oncidium volvox | |
| | C795 | | $0.20 | Cycnoches chlorochilon | |
| | C796 | | $0.25 | Cattleya gaskelliana v. alba | |
| | C797 | | $0.30 | Epidendrum difforme | |
| | C798 | | $0.40 | Catasetum callosum | |
| | C799 | | $0.50 | Oncidium bicolor | |
| | C800 | | 1 boliva | Brassavola nodosa | |
| | C801 | | 1.05 bol | Epidendrum lividum | |
| | C802 | | 1.50 bol | Schomburgkia undulata | |
| | C803 | | 2 boliva | Oncidium zebrinum | |
| 1965/08/06 | C885 | | $0.25 | Epidendrum lividum | #C801 SC & OP "Rezellado Valor Rs.25" |
| | C886 | | $0.25 | Schomburgkia undulata | #C802 SC & OP "Rezellado Valor Rs.25" |
| | C887 | | $0.25 | Oncidium zebrinum | #C803 SC & OP "Rezellado Valor Rs.25" |

## VENEZUELA {Continued}

| DATE ISSUE | SCOTT/ MICHEL | GIBBON NUMBER | FACE VALUE | SPECIES NAME | BRIEF DESCRIPTION |
|---|---|---|---|---|---|
| 1965/08/27 | 872 | | $0.25 | Oncidium falcipetalum | #811 SC & OP "Rezellado Valor Rs.25" |
| 1970/07/29 | C1049 | | $0.20 | Epidendrum elongatum | |
| 1971/08/25 | C1055 | | $0.20 | Cattleya percivaliana | Sheetlet/ 5 stamps, 1 label |
| | C1056 | | $0.25 | Cattleya gaskelliana | Sheetlet/ 5 stamps, 1 label |
| | C1057 | | $0.75 | Cattleya mossiae | Sheetlet/ 5 stamps, 1 label |
| | C1058 | | $0.90 | Cattleya violacea v. superba | Sheetlet/ 5 stamps, 1 label |
| | C1059 | | 1 boliva | Cattleya lawrenceana | Sheetlet/ 5 stamps, 1 label |
| 1988/06/17 | 1416c | | 11.50 bo | Cattleya | Sheetlet/ 2 strips of 5 stamps, 2 are #1416c |

## VIET NAM

| DATE ISSUE | SCOTT/ MICHEL | GIBBON NUMBER | FACE VALUE | SPECIES NAME | BRIEF DESCRIPTION |
|---|---|---|---|---|---|
| 1976/12/20 | M917A | 126a | 6 xu | Dendrobium primulinum v. album | #N848 RP, "Vietnam 1976" added on bottom )Pale orange( |
| | M918 | 126b | 12 xu | Dendrobium primulinum v. album | #N849 RP, "Vietnam 1976" added on bottom )Blue green( |
| | M918a | 126c | 5 xu | Dendrobium primulinum v. album | #N848 RP, "Vietnam 1976" added on bottom )Ochre( |
| | M918b | 126d | 10 xu | Dendrobium primulinum v. album | #N849 RP, "Vietnam 1976" added on bottom )Dark green( |
| 1979/08/10 | M1054 | 288 | 12 xu | Dendrobium heterocarpum | |
| | M1055 | 289 | 12 xu | Cymbidium hybrid | |
| | M1056 | 290 | 20 xu | Rhynchostylis gigantea | |
| | M1057 | 291 | 30 xu | Dendrobium nobile | |
| | M1058 | 292 | 40 xu | Aerides falcatum | |
| | M1059 | 293 | 50 xu | Paphiopedilum callosum | |
| | M1060 | 294 | 60 xu | Vanda teres | |
| | M1061 | 295 | 1 dong | Dendrobium phalaenopsis | |
| 1983/07/30 | M1355 | 602 | 40 xu | Phalaenopsis amabilis | Background of moth |
| | M1360 | 607 | 1 dong | Rhynchostylis gigantea | Background of butterfly |
| 1984/03/28 | M1425 | 680 | 50 xu | Brassocattleya hybrid | |
| | M1426 | 681 | 50 xu | Cymbidium species | |
| | M1427 | 682 | 1 dong | Cattleya Dianx v. alba | |
| | M1428 | 683 | 2 dong | Dendrobium williamsoni | |
| | M1429 | 684 | 3 dong | Cymbidium hybrid | |
| | M1430 | 685 | 5 dong | Dendrobium Phoenix Winged | |
| | M1431 | 686 | 8 dong | Vanda Yellow Queen | |
| 1989/04/30 | --- | | 200 dong | Paphiopedilum siamenese | |

## WALLIS & FUTUNA ISLANDS

| DATE ISSUE | SCOTT/ MICHEL | GIBBON NUMBER | FACE VALUE | SPECIES NAME | BRIEF DESCRIPTION |
|---|---|---|---|---|---|
| 1982/05/24 | 283 | | 34 franc | Acanthephippium vitiense | |
| | 284 | | 68 franc | Acanthephippium vitiense | |
| | 285 | | 70 franc | Spathoglottis pacifica | Sheetlet/ 4 stamps and 5 strips of #283, #284 and #285 |
| 1990/05/17 | 392 | | 78 franc | Vanda species | |

## WEST IRIAN

| DATE ISSUE | SCOTT/ MICHEL | GIBBON NUMBER | FACE VALUE | SPECIES NAME | BRIEF DESCRIPTION |
|---|---|---|---|---|---|
| 1968/08/17 | 41 | | 15 sen | Dendrobium lancifolium | |

## ZAIRE

| DATE ISSUE | SCOTT/ MICHEL | GIBBON NUMBER | FACE VALUE | SPECIES NAME | BRIEF DESCRIPTION |
|---|---|---|---|---|---|
| 1984/05/28 | 1148 | | 3 zaire | Disa erubescens | |

## ZAMBIA

| DATE ISSUE | SCOTT/ MICHEL | GIBBON NUMBER | FACE VALUE | SPECIES NAME | BRIEF DESCRIPTION |
|---|---|---|---|---|---|
| 1983/05/26 | 280 | | 12 ngwee | Eulophia cucullata | |
| 1983/06/26 | 283a | | SS | Eulophia cucullata | SS/ 4 stamps, 1 is #280 |

## ZIL ELOGINE SELSEL

| DATE ISSUE | SCOTT/ MICHEL | GIBBON NUMBER | FACE VALUE | SPECIES NAME | BRIEF DESCRIPTION |
|---|---|---|---|---|---|
| 1980/07/04 | M397 | | $0.20 | Vanilla humblotii | |
| 1981 | M397ii | | $0.20 | Vanilla humblotii | #M397 RP, with "1981" added in selvage |
| 1986/11/12 | 8611 | | 3 rupees | Phaius tetragonus | |

IVORY COAST MC532 & MD532; EQUATORIAL GUINEA M426; ISLE OF MAN 306a; COOK ISLANDS 681A; BURUNDI 167; CENTRAL AFRICA 69; TONGA 488; OMAN G364; LUXEMBOURG B305; DOMINICA REPUBLIC RA55; SOUTH KASAI K13; BOLIVIA 704 & 704A; SOUTHERN RHODESIA 101; CENTRAL AFRICA 8203a; GUATEMALA C559; CUBA 611; and NEVIS 8441.

## ACACALLIS
cyanea - Brazil 1438; Guyana 1990 New Issue $30

## ACAMPE
pachyglossa - Comoro Islands J11; Malawi 332

## ACANTHEPHIPPIUM
vitiense - Fiji 312; Wallis & Futuna Islands 283 & 284

## ACERAS
anthropophora - Germany B623

## ACIANTHUS
atepalus - New Caledonia 503

## AERANGIS
articulata - Guyana 403, 409, 550, G1853, G1990, G2265, G2463 & G2465
curnowiana - Malagasy 915
kotschyana - Malawi 338 & 578; Rwanda 782; Uganda 747 & 782
luteo-alba - Ghana 1224
luteo-alba v. rhodosticta - Malawi 580
rhodosticta - Uganda 750 & 783
stylosa - Malagasy 737

## AERANTHES
grandiflorus - Malagasy 735

## AERIDACHNIS
Apple Blossum - Fiji 442
Bogor v. Apple Blossum Pink - Indonesia 945

## AERIDES
crassifolium - Monaco 1441
falcatum - Vietnam M1058
falcatum v. houlletianum - Thailand 717
odoratum - Laos 468; Thailand 844
savageanum - Guyana 612c, 613d, 614a 615b, 706a, 707b, 7C8d, 709c & 677

## AGROSTOPHYLLYM
occidentale - Seychelles 720

## AMESIELLA
philippinesis - Philippines 1811

## ANACAMPTIS
pyramidalis - Germany DDR 1731; Luxembourg B304; UN-Geneva 197

## ANCISTROCHILUS
rothachildianus - Ghana 4c New Issue; Gambia 923; Uganda 756 & 844

## ANGRAECUM
- Guyana B34, B36, B37; Hungary 2855; Manama 1972 Unlisted 2R
brongniartianum - Seychelles 282
conchiferum - Malawi 258
distichum - Gambia 924
eburneum - Comoro Islands C28 & Malawi 579
eburneum v. longicalcar - Malagasy 738
eburneum v. superbum - Malagasy 740; Seychelles 698
humblotii - Guyana 05, 633 & 1989 Unlisted OP
infundibulare - Uganda 748 & 840
leonis - Malagasy 614
magdalenae - Malagasy 736
mauritianum - Mauritius 640
ramosum - Malagasy 613
sesquipedale - Equatorial Guinea M429, Guyana 454, G2096 & G2472; Malagasy 346,
    - 612 & 739; Romania 3535h; Sierra Leone 919
sororium - Malagasy 913

## ANGULOA
- Ecuador C713
uniflora - Ecuador C709 & C712

## ANOECTOCHILUS
setaceus - Sri Lanka 725

## ANSELLIA
africana - Gambia 999; Ghana 404, 790 & 793b; Rhodesia 214, 231 & 247; Uganda 755 & 786
gigantea - Belgian Congo 274; Botswana 224; Congo 331; Hungary 2852; Katanga M32:
    - Lesotho 773 & 759; Malawi 116 & 330; Mozambique 797; Ruanda-Urundi 125;
    - Rwanda 785; St. Thomas & Prince 8212c & MB4; South Kasai K13; S. Rhodesia 101
gigantea v. nilotica - Burundi 143, 149, 4 SS unlisted, C19, 161, 167, C29, MB17; MB18; MB19 & MB20

## APOROSTYLIS
bifolia - New Zealand 986e

## ARACHNIS
- Malaysia 4 & 5
Catherine - Cuba 1786
clarkei - Guyana 565, 679 & G2578
flos-aeris - Ivory Coast G519; Johore 173; Kedah 110; Kelantan 95; Malacca 71;
    - Malaysia Post P1 & P2; Negri Sembilan 80; Pahang 87; Penang 71; Perak 143;
    - Perlis 44; Sabah 21; Sarawak 232; Selangor 125; Trengganu 90
flos-aeris v. insignis - Indonesia 978 & 978a
hybrid - Seychelles 662
Maggie Oei - Barbados 402; Singapore 62
moschifera - Ceylon 301 & 303
species - Malaysia 274; Sarawak 94 through 108

## ARANDA
- Malaysia 4 & 5; Singapore 486b
Christine - Singapore 247
Elizabeth Douglas-Home - Singapore 249
Majula - Singapore 248
Noorah Alsagoff - Singapore 250

## ARETHUSA
- United States 1984 Lettersheet
bulbosa - United States 2076

## ARPOPHYLLUM
jamaicense - Jamaica 376; Great Britian FB30

## ARUNDINA
graminifolia - Fiji 254 & 274; Johore 170; Kedah 107; Kelantan 92; Malacca 68;
     - Negri Sembilan 77; Pahang 84; Penang 68: Perak 140; Perlis 41;
     - Sabah 18; Sarawak 229; Selangor 122; Trengganu 87
speciosa - South Molucass 1954 & 1979 Unlisted

## ASCOCENDA
emma - Thailand 1158
Laikeun - Singapore Postcard 1990
Red Gem - Barbados 408

## ASCOCENTRUM
curvifolium - Thailand 478
miniatum - Laos 217

## ASPASIA
lunata - Romania 3536k
variegata - Guyana 1990 New Issue $10

## BARKERIA
cyclotella - Guyana 1990 New Issue $9.75
iindleyana - Costa Rica C622
skinneri - Guatemala C659

## BIFRENARIA
speciosa - Great Britian FB29

## BLETIA
- Belize 528g & 561g
catenulata - Peru 603
patula - Barbados 406 & B2
purpurata - British Honduras 210, 306 & 307; Cuba 2328; Saint Vincent 1369
roezlii - Nicaragua RA73, 842, 1965 Unlisted, 850, 866 & 907

## BOLLEA
violacea - Suriname 523

## BOLUSIELLA
imbricata - Ghana 1991

## BONATEA
densiflora - Venda M48
steudneri - Rwanda 784

## BRACHYPEZA
archytas - Christmas Islands 183

## BRASSAVOLA
acaulis - Cuba 3164
cucullata - Dominica 1193; Montserrat 557; Nevis 633
digbyana - Belize 717; British Honduras 226, 306 & 307; Costa Rica C620 & C726;
     - Honduras C510, C511, C519, C519a & C640
nodosa - British Honduras 256; Montserrat 661; Nicaragua 1210, M2651 & M2742;
     - Saint Thomas & Prince 8211, 8212a, 8212b, MB1, MB2 & MB3; Venezuela C800
perrinii - Romania 3536a

## BRASSIA
- Jamaica 594 & 594a
arcuigera - Costa Rica 332
caudata - Guyana 1990 New Issue $10
gireoudiana - Grenada 1800
lanceana - Suriname 429
maculata - British Honduras 258; Jamaica 378
maculata v. guttata - Saint Vincent 1365

## BRASSOCATTLEYA
hybrid - Vietnam M1425
Olympia v. alba - Rwanda 381
Sindrossiana - Cuba 1677
Thailie - Grenadines 9020; New Zealand Formula 1988

## BRASSOLAELIOCATTLEYA
Horizon v. Flight - Cuba 2882
Nugget - Barbados 409
St. Helier - Jersey 346

## BROUGHTONIA
- Jamaica 378a
domingensis - Dominican Republic 788 & C350
sanguinea - Jamaica 375, 502a & 709

# BULBOPHYLLUM

barbigerum - Ghana 1990 New Issue 60p; Sierra Leone 1078
blumei - Solomon Islands 633
dennisii - Solomon Islands 631
distans - Sierra Leone 1083
falcatum - Sierra Leone 1079
intertextum - Seychelles 719
lepidum - Gambia 918
lobbii - Romania 3535d
longifolium - Mauitius 641
longiscapum - Vanuatu 336
micronesiacum - Palau 240
species - Fiji 308

# CALANTHE

- South Africa 556a
belle - Guyana E2 & 672
burfordiens - Guyana E2 & 672
discolor - Japan Postcard 1987
izuinsularis - Japan 1730
langei - New Caledonia 544; Solomon Islands 632
nataiensis - Malawi 329; South Africa 553
sylvatica - Uganda 752 & 784
triplicata - Fiji 307; New Caledonia 408; Samoa 752; Vanuatu 324, B1 & 512
vestita - Russia Envelope 1977
victor v. regina - Guyana E2 & 672

# CALEANA

major - Australia 999

# CALOPOGON

- Scotland {Grunay} 1982 Unlisted 1L
pulchellus - Saint Pierre & Miquelon 361

# CALYPSO

bulbosa - Sweden 484, 485, 486, 486a, 1763 & 1763a; United States 2079

# CALYPTROCHILUM

christyanum - Sierra Leone 1082

# CATASETUM

- Columbia C491a; Guyana 504a
atratum - Equatorial Guinea M428
callosum - Venezuela C798
discolor - Guyana 1991 New Issue $17.80; Suriname 663
fimbriatum - Laos 644
macrocarpum - Colombia C491; Guyana 1990 New Issues $8.90 & $12.65
pileatum - Guyana 469, 504, G1932, G1938, G1947, G1948, G1988, G2014, G2057, G2380 &
       - G2433; Venezuela 807
saccatum - Bolivia C329, MB41 & MB45

# CATTLEYA

- Ajman M429A & M430A; Antigua 925 & 1068; Barbados 454, 469 & 547; Barbuda 8636 & 8820;
- Belgium Postcards 1985 {3 types}; Belize 385, M534, 528, 528i, 561, 561i; Bolivia MB38;
- Bulgaria Envelopes {2 types} 1990; Burundi C140 & C142a; Colombia C690; Cook Islands
- 336, 337 & 338; Cuba Postcards 1977, 1981 1982 {2 types}, 1983 & 1984; Dominica 950 &
- 1064; Ecuador 1006; French Polynesia C120; Fiji 442; Fujeria M1334; Gambia 729 & 731;
- Grenada 1428 & 1577; Grenadines 8802; Guyana 504b & 676a; Hungary Postcard 1988; Japan
- Postcard HG94c; Nanumea 8702; Nicaragua C805 & C968; Paraguay M2531, M3375 & MB3373;
- Philippines B6, B7 & 872; Romania Envelope 1968 & Postcard 1969; Russia Aerograme 1976,
- Postcards 1965, 1971, 1979 & 1984, Envelope 1986; Saint Thomas & Prince 1989 New Issue
- 20d; Saint Vincent 483, 488, 489 & 494; Samoa 465 & 465a; Seychelles 592 & 625; Sierra
- Leone 953; Sri Lanka Aeorgrames 1979 & 1981 {2 types}; Tanzania 680g; Tuvalu 45, 45a &
- 455; Venezuela 1416c & Postcard HG23
aclandiae - Germany DDR; Kampuchea G929; Scotland {Staffa} 1982 Unlisted 40p
amethystoglossa - Brazil 1711; Guyana 583 & 657
anceps - Brazil 1860
arnoldiana - Guyana 595 & 08
ballantineana - Guyana 438, 471, G2109, G1987, G2013, G2054, G2375, G2376 & G2447
bicolor - Brazil 477
bowringiana - Belize 716; British Honduras 155 & 227; Guatemala C656; Guyana 555, 557,
       - G2102, G2426 & 1990 New Issue Se-tenant
chocoensis - Anguilla 73; Colombia 548
Countess of Derby - Cuba 1185
deckeri - Guyana 1990 New Issue $10; Nevis 626
Dianx v. alba - Vietnam M1427
dowiana - Costa Rica C449 & C632; Equarotial Guinea M432; Grenada 1801
dowiana v. aurea - Albania 1150; Belize 661; Colombia 550, 584 & C489; Cuba 1192;
       - Guyana 410, 518, G1942, G1943, G2030 & G2646; Laos 643
dowiana v. chrysotoxa - Guyana 466, 527, G2059 & G2517
eldorado v. crocata - Guayan 408, 536, G1991, G1992, G2065, G2401 & G2416
fabria - Germany DDR
gaskelliana - Venezuela C1056
gaskelliana v. alba - Barbados 396; Venezuela C796
gigas v. Regina Burfordinse - Cuba 1187
gigas v. warscewiczii - Colombia 697, C317, C318 & C342; Honduras C136
granulosa - Saint Thomas & Prince 1989 New Issue 20d
grandulosa v. schofieldiana - Guyana O14, 619, 1989 Unlisted SC & OP
guatemalensis - Guatemala Envelope 1978
guttata - Brazil 2122
guttata v. leopoldii - Guayan 386, 505, G1955, G1958, G2042, G2372 & G2373
Gytrics Eva - Hungary Postcard 1989
hardyana - Cuba 2881, Guyana 612a, 613b, 614c, 614d, 706c, 707d, 708b, 709a, 665 & 699

## CATTLEYA {Continued}

harrisoniana - Belgium Postcards 1990 {3 types} & 1334
hybrid - Niue 331, 413E, 429 & 013
intermedia - Russia Envelope 1969
intermedia v. punctatissima - Guyana 551, 558, G2418 & 1990 New Issue Se-tenant
iricolor - Ecuador 1005
labiata - Argentina 680; Brazil 616 & 696; Cuba 977; Guyana 608, 681, 1989 Unlisted $6.75
        - & $6.40 SC & OP; Haiti C171, C175, C176a, CO4, CO5a, CB32, CB32a, CB33 & CB34a;
        - Kampuchea G931; Laos 232; Poland 1354; Russia Aerogrames 1967 & 1971, Envelope
        - 1977; Rwanda 386; Saint Vincent 1368
labiata v. gaskelliana - Guyana 406, G1975, G2398 & G2399
labiata v. lueddemanniana - Guyana 490, 652, G2481 & G2431
labiata v. macfarlanei - Cuba 1183
labiata v. trianae - Colombia 551 & 582
labiata v. warneri - Guyana 407, 533, G1191a, G2041, G2400 & G2467
lawrenceana - Guyana 373 & G1935; Venezuela C1059
loddigesii - North Korea M2481
lueddemanniana - Laos 639; Nicaragua 1211, M2662 & M2752
lueddemanniana v. alba - Guyana 617, G2219, G2219a, G2220, G2222, G2222a & G2223
luteola - Bolivia C327, MB42 & MB46
maxima - Ecuador 1003
mendelii v. Duchess of Montrose - Cuba 1189
mendelii v. Duke of Malborough - Guyana 452, 514, G2009, G2050, G2259 & G2532
mendelii v. majestica - Cuba 1181
mendelii v. measuresiana - Guyana 503, 653, G2369, G2370 & 1990 New Issue Se-tenant
mendelii v. Quorndon House - Guyana 607 & 684
mossiae - Cuba 3170; Russia Envelopes 1974, 1979 & 1981, Postcard 1975; Venezuela C1057
mossiae v. reineckiana - Guyana 564, 678 & G2577
nobilior - Bolivia 558
O'Brieniana - Guyana 624A & 666
pachecoi - Guatemala C652
parthenia - Guyana 624C, 693 & G2584
percivaliana - Guyana 398, G2026 & G2394; Venezuela C1055
Principessa Grace - Monaco 1709
rex - Guyana 603 & 695
rochellensis - Belize 657; Guyana 468, 508, G1960, G2045, G2497 & G2518
schroederae v. alba - Guyana 473, 643, G2413, 1988 Unlisted SC & OP & 1990 New Issue Se-tenant
skinneri - Costa Rica 184, C448, C623 & 420; Cuba 1620; Nicaragua RA71, 1965 Unlisted, 848, 864 & 905
skinneri v. alba - Costa Rica C801
species - Ecuador 1256
speciosissima - Cuba 1180
superba - Scotland {Staffa} 1982 Unlisted 40p
trianae - Burundi 412, 419 & C172; Colombia C468, 791, 862 & 863; Cuba 3154;
        - Grenada 1798; Honduras C143; Laos 796f; Romania 3535b
trianae v. alba - Guyana 389, 515, G1957, G2010, G2051 & G2382; San Marino 397
trianae v. amesiana - Cuba 1182
trianae v. ernesti - Guyana 455, 543, G1658, G2099, G2130, G2131 & G2525
trianae v. schroederiana - Belize 653; Guyana 421, G2116 & G2476
victoria-regina - Guyana 560 & 688
violacea - Guyana 138, 440, G1341, G2512 & 1990 New Issue $10; Venezuela 590 through
        - 596 & C500 through C508
violacea v. superba - Venezuela C1058
warscewiczii - Belize 655; Guyana 375, G1951 & G2429; Paraguay MB45, MB65 & MB66
warscewiczii v. gigas - Hungary 1707; Poland 1349

## CATTLEYAOPSIS

lindeni - Bahamas 636; Cuba 611 & 2331
rosea - Dominican Republic RA71

## CAULARTHRON

bicornutum - Barbados 410; Guyana 1990 New Issue $10; Trinidad & Tobago 285
bilamellatum - Salvador C374; Venezuela 805

## CEPHALANTHERA

- Japan 1990 Booklet New Issue
kurdica - Iran G2515
longifolia - Aland 44
rubra - Denmark 921 & 921a; Germany Berlin 9NB150; Germany DDR 880; Luxembourg B310

## CHLORAEA

chrysantha - Chile 795a
gaudichaudi - Falkland Islands 1991 New Issue 31p
species - Saint Lucia 241 & 243

## CHONDRORHYNCHA

aromatica - Costa Rica C443; Guyana 384, 511, GE4, G1930, G1954, G1962, G1983, G1986,
        - G2020, G2048, G2361 & G2364
chestertoni - Rwanda 383
discolor - Costa Rica C630, C716, C719 & C727

## CHYSIS

bractescens - Belize 656 & 719; Guyana 428, G1536, G2087 & G2133; Romania 3536f;
        - Russia Envelope 1988

## CIRRHOPETALUM

umbellatum - Fiji 305 & 305a; Maiawi 328

## CLEISTES

divaricata - Unites States 2078
revoluta - Brazil 1972c

## COCHLEANTHES

discolor - Cuba 3155; Romania 3536g

## COCHLIODA

vulcanica - Ecuador 933

## CODONORCHIS

lessonii - Falkland Islands 169, 200, 213 & 1991 New Issue 26p

## COELOGLOSSUM

viride - Oman State G363

## COELOGYNE
- Guyana 1990 New Issue $13.90
cristata v. maxima - Guayna 431, 537, G1685a, G1685b, 31685c, G1685d, G2085, G2093,
- G2119, G2234a, G2234b, G2334c, G2234d, G2519 & 1990 New Issue $6.40
lamelata - Vanuatu 335
lycastoides - New Caledonia 543
ochracea - Bhutan 221
pandurata - Guyana 585, 680 & G2582; Indonesia 980
sanderae - Guyana 676, 1989 3 Unlisted SC & OP
swaniana - Guyana 594, O9, 1989 Unlisted SC & OP

## COMPARETTIA
falcata - Dominica 1195; Saint Vincent 1364; Suriname 665
speciosa - Ecudaor 1004

## COMPERIA
comperiana - Iran G2517

## CORYANTHES
- Cuba 3170a; Guyana 1990 New Issue $15.30
leucocorys - Cuba 3166
speciosa - British Honduras 3166

## CORYBAS
macranthus - New Zealand 986b

## CORYMBORCHIS
- Palau 241a
veratrifolia - Christmas Islands 294; Palau 237

## CRYPTARRHENA
lunata - Guyana 1990 New Issue $10

## CRYPTOPUS
elatus - Mauritius 638

## CYCNOCHES
chlorochilon - China Taiwan 1191; Guyana 584 & 658; Suriname 744; Venezuela C795
egertonianum - Nigaragua RA72, 1965 Unlisted, 849, 865 & 906
warscewiczii - British Honduras 257

## CYMBIDIELLA
humblotii - Malagasy 912

## CYMBIDIUM
- Barbuda 8627 & 8628; China Postcard 1981; Gabon C110, C111a & C111b; Grenada 1681a;
- Hong Kong 267; Hungary Postcards 1986, 1989 & 1990 {2 types}; Niutao 8537 through 8544,
- 8544A, 8545 & 8546; North Korea MB194, MB195 & MB196

Baldoyle v. Melbury - Tanzania 636
Elliot Rogers v. Red Beauty - Saint Vincent {Grenadines} 9034
ensifolium - China Taiwan 1381; Japan 346
ensifolium v. Dafengwei - China 2187
faberi v. Dayipin - China 2185
faberi v. honglianban - China 2188
giganteum - Bhutan 880
goeringii - Japan 218, 220, 346, Postcards 1973, 1987 & 1989; Manchukuo 111, 116, 118,
- 122, 123, 124, 126, Postcards HG49a, HG49b, HG50a, HG50b, HG50b, HG51, HG52, HG53, HG54 & HG55
goeringii v. Lungzi - China 2184
Hamsey - Burundi 414, 421 & C174
hybrid - Maderia 70, 72; Rwanda 385; St. Vincent {Grenadines} 9032; Vietnam M1055 & M1429
lowianum - Guyana 605, 682 & G2585
mastersii - Guyana 437, G2091, G2136, G2257 & G2446
Mavourneen v. Jester - Jersey 446
Ormoulu - Grenadines 9027; New Zealand 1988 Formula
Pontac - Jersey 442
pumilum - New Zealnd 1988 Envelope
sinense v. margicoloratum - China 2186
species - China Taiwan 1100 & 1101; Japan 1991 Booklets{ 3 types}; Russia Postcards 1976
- & 1979; Vietnam M1426
speciosa - Great Britian FB30
Tapestry v. Long Beach - Tanzania 637
Vieux Rose - Grenadines 9029
winnianum - Guyana O3, 673 & 658a

## CYNORKIS
- Venda MB50
kassnerana - Rwanda 1012; Venda MB50

## CYPRIPEDILUM
- Occussi-Ambeno 1978 Unlisted SS
acaule - Canada 424 & Aerogrames A43, LS14, LS26 & A55; Saint Pierre & Miquelon 360;
- Saint Vincent {Grenadines} 9037
calceolus - Aland 56; Bulgaria 1111 & 3144; Comoro State MB76; Czechoslovakia 1082;
- Denmark 923; Equatorial Guinea M426; Germany 858; Germany DDR 327 & 1734;
- Great Britian FB28; Hungary 3087; Oman State 1971 Unlisted; Poland 785;
- Romania 2336 & 3465; Saint Vincent {Grenadines} 8519 & 9037; Sweden 484, 485,
- 486, 486a, 1419b; Switzerland B128; Umm Al Qiwain 1973 {6 types} all Unlisted
calceolus v. pubescens - United States 1924, Booklet WH75 & 2077
Clunatec - Czechoskovakia 1895
irapeanum - Guatemala C654
japonicum - Japan Postcard 1987
macranthos - Kampuchea M775
macranthum - North Korea M460; Romania 2250
passerinum - Canada 711, 711a, 786 BK77, BK78 & BK80
reginae - United States 1377, 1664 & 1975

## CYRTOPODIUM
andersoni - Dominica 1189
punctatum - Guyana 1990 New Issue $10; Saint Vincent 1367; Salvador C378

FALKLAND ISLANDS 200; GABON 178; SAINT KITTS 395; NANUMAGA 8516; PALAU 145; PAPUA 652; TURKEY 2125; BARBUDA 8820; ANTIGUA 1068; HONDURAS C136; MALDIVES ISLANDS 1062; FUJERIA M857; GAMBIA 689A; URUGUAY C146; MEXICO C633; MALAYSIA 4; WEST IRIAN 41; TIMOR 260; SUMMER ISLES 1979 Unlisted; JERSEY 63; NICARAGUA 1214; TUNISIA 772; MONACO 1047; RUSSIA 4114; MOCAMBIQUE 594; BAHAMAS 637; and AUSTRALIA 438.

## CYRTORCHIS

arcuata - Central Africa 828a; Malawi 337 & 581 & 581a; Sierra Leone 1086
chailluana - Uganda 749 & 841
grandulosa - Malawi 337
praetermissa - Malawi 341; Rwanda 1010

## DACTYLORCHIS

foliosa - Maderia 77 & 80a
latifolia - Germany DDR 1098

## DACTYLORHIZA

- Liechtenstein Postcard 1987
fuchsii - Norway 970
incarnata - Germany DDR 1730
maculata - Faroes 170; Guernsey 70; Iceland 394; Luxembourg B317; Poland 1988;
    - Russia 4115; Saint Kilda 1969 & 1970 Unlisted; Summer Isles 1979 Unlisted;
purpurella - Denmark 561; Postcard 1974
romana - Bulgaria 3140; Hungary 3093
romana v. georgia - Iran G2516
sambucina - Aland 40; Germany B626; Germany DDR 1732; Sweden 1419d

## DENDROBIUM

- Cuba Postcards 1982 & 1984; Fiji 371; French Polynesia 388 & 402; Indonesia
- 1110; Japan Postcards HG94c & 1988; Kampuchea M554; Maldives 1096 & 1095;
- Oman State 1973 Unlisted 10b; Papua 303; Philippines 853a; Russia Envelope
- 1988; Saint Lucia 826, 827, 828. 831 & 833; Scotland {Eynhallow} 2L 1982;
- Sri Lanka Postcard 1983; Thailand 748a & 1312; Tonga 1990 New Issue $2.50;
- Umm Al Qiwain 1972 Unlisted 3D; Vanuatu 325a
abang - Indonesia 1349
aggregatum - Barbados 403; Laos 216 & 469; North Vietnam M862; Thailand 715
Alpha - Germany DDR 1062
anocha - Singapore 1991 New Issue $2
anosmum - Papua 403; Philippines 853; Saint Vincent {Grenadines} 9039
antennatum - New Guinea B20
aphyllum - Bhutan 884
biflorum - Samoa 637
bigibbum - Australia 438, Envelopes 38 & 49; China Taiwar 2520; Maldives 1062
bracteosum - Papua 402
brymerianum - Guyana 390, 532, G1939, G1949, G1989a, G2040 & G2384
cassiope - Guyana 486, 668 & 1989 Unlisted 3 OP
cattilare - Fiji 596
conanthum - Papua 290; Solomon Islands 598; Vanuatu 333
cruentum - Thailand 745
crystallinum - North Vietnam M427
cunninghamii - New Zealand 986c
cuthbertsonii - British Solomon Islands 243; Papua 654; Solomon Islands 307 & 450
devonianum - North Vietnam M857
discolor - Indonesia 1108
draconis - Laos 467
ekapol - Thailand 1160
falconeri - Russia Envelope 1974; Thailand 481
farmeri - Laos 472; North Vietnam M861; Thailand 862

finetianum - New Caldeonia 426
formosum - Guyana 498, 639, G1998, G2389 & 1990 New Issue Se-tenant
formosum v. giganteum - Thailand 483
fractiflexum - New Caledonia 482C
goldfinchii - Solomon Islands 601
gordonii - Fiji 316
gouldii - Guyana 599, O13, 1989 Unlisted $3.50 OP; Solomon Islands 600
hercoglossum - Thailand 843
heterocarpum - Guyana 381 & G2357; Thailand 840; Vietnam M1054
hybrid - Cuba 1780 & 1785
insigne - Indonesia 1107; Papua 405
johnsoniae - Guyana 604 & O11; Papua 653
lancifolium - West Irian 41
lasianthera - Indonesia 1109
lawesii - Papua 288
leechanum - Guyana 464, 519, G2031, G2403, G2496 & 1989 Unlisted $10.50
lineale - Papua 652
loddigesii - Bbutan 887
macarthiae - Ceylon 309 & 342
macranthum - Vanuatu 334; Fiji 442;
macrophyllum - Br. Solomon Islands 136 & 157; Indonesia 1037, 1038 & 1038a; Vanuatu 327
margaritaceum - Bhutan 893
melanodiscus - Guyana 487, 645, G2411, G2412, G2590a through G2590d & 1990 New Issue
    - Se-tenant
mohlianum - Fiji 595; New Hebrides 174 & 193; Samoa 754; Vanuatu 326
moniliforme - Japan Postcard 1987
mooreanum - Vanuatu 330
moschatum - Laos 471; North Vietnam M425
muricatum v. munificum - New Caledonia 482B
musiciforum - Papua 302
nindii - Australia 998
nobile - Bhutan M216, MB14 & 873; Great Britian Booklet FB27; North Vietnam M428; Romania
    - 3535k; South Vietnam 262 & 492; Vietnam M1057; Umm Al Qiwain 1972 Unlisted 3D
nobile v. sanderiana - Guyana 425, G2118 & G2442
none - Indonesia 1348
oppositifolium - New Caledonia 482A
ostrinoglossum - Papua 287
Pakarena - Indonesia 944
palawense - Palau 145 & 145A
parishii - Bhutan 223; Thailand 746
patellaris - North Vietnam M430
phalaenopsis - China Taiwan 1192; Cuba 2839 & Aerogrames {2 types} 1987; Czechoslovakia
        - 1496; Guyana 478, 649 & G2427; Indonesia B148, Formulas SD36 & SD40; Japan
        - Postcards 1985 & 1988; Niue 428 & O12; North Korea MB194, MB195, MB196,
        - M2442, M2485, Unlisted 1986 & 1989; St.Thomas & Prince 1989 New Issue 20d
        - St. Vincent {Grenadines} 9032; Seychelles 664; Syria 948; Vietnam M1061
phalaenopsis v. amabilis - Indonesia B108
phalaenopsis v. statterianum - Guyana 494, 636, G2365 & 1990 New Issue Se-tenant
Phoenix Winged - Vietnam M1430
platygastrium - Fiji 320
prasinum - Fiji 184, 328 & 329
primulinum - Bhutan 229; Thailand 484
primulinum v. album - North Vietnam M841 & M842; Vietnam M917A, M918, M918a & M918b
pseudofrigidum - Papua 289

## DENDROBIUM {Continued}

pulchellum - Thailand 841
purpureum - Vanuatu 328
Rose Marie - Barbados 398
sanderae - Philippines 852
scabrilingue - Thailand 716
secundum - Laos 470
seemannii - Vanuatu 332
senile - Thailand 847
smillieae - Papua 404
species - Seychelles 661
spectabile - British Solomon Islands 137, 158 & 159; Indonesia 1012 & 1012a; Vanuatu 308
sri - Thailand 1159
superbiens - Guyana 462, 534, G2104, G1985, G2063, G2414 & G2515
teretifolium - New Hebrides 171 & 190
tokai - Fiji 313
tortile - North Vietnam M859
vaupelianum - Samoa 638
venus - Guyana 486, 668, 1989 Unlisted 3 OP
veratrifolium - British Solomon Islands 129 & 150
vexillaris - Papua 651
wardianum - Guyana 392, 509, G1979, G1980, G1996, G2138, G2139, G2002, G2005, G2017,
    - G2022, G2387 & 1990 Unlisted OP; Thailand 846
williamsoni - Vietnam M1428

## DENDROPHYLAX

fawcettii - Cayman Islands 287 & 538
funalis - Saint Vincent 1362

## DIAPHANANTHE

fragrantissima - Rwanda 256
kamerunensis - Ghana 1991 New Issue 2c
pellucida - Sierra Leone 1085
rutila - Ghana 1991 New Issue 6c

## DICHEA

muricata - Guyana 1990 New Issue $10

## DIMERANDRA

emarginata - Saint Vincent 1362

## DIMORPHORCHIS

lowii - Guyana 383, 522, G1952, G1976, G2034, G2034a & G2360

## DIOTHONEA

imbricata - Saint Thomas & Prince 1989 New issue 50d

## DIPLOCAULOBIUM

ou-hinnae - New Caledonia 502

## DIPODIUM

freycinetanum - Papua 239

## DISA

crassicornis - Lesotho 501; Transkei 244
erubescens - Rwanda 1089; Zaire 1148
hamatopetala - Malawi 117 & 336
incarnata - Malagasy 706
ornithantha - Malawi 115 & 340
stairsii - Rwanada 781
uniflora - Cuba 2886; Guyana 497, 549, G2386, G2419 & 1990 Unlisted Se-tenant;
    - Lesotho 763; Poland 1353; South Africa 516, 556, Aerogrames K25, K33, K36a
    - through K36f, K37, K43, K46, K47, K48 & 11 unlisted Aerogrames
welwitchii - Malawi 257

## DISPERIS

capensis - Lesotho 762
fanniniae - South Africa 555
tripetaloides - Seychelles 696

## DOMINGOA

nodosa - Dominican Republic RA37

## DORITIS

pulcherrima - Bhutan 879; North Vietnam M860; Saint Vincent {Grenadines} 8939
pulcherrima v. buyssoniana - Thailand 842

## EARINA

autumnalis - New Zealand 705

## ELLEANTHUS

capitatus - Dominican Republic RA49 & C352

## ELYTHRANTHERA

emarginata - Australia 997

## ENCYCLIA

- Bahamas 639a
alatum - Nicaragua 1194
atropurpurea - Romania 3535j; Russia Envelope 1973; Venezuela 810
atropurpurea v. randii - Guyana 602 & 698
citrina - Guyana 434, 539, G1570 through G1570d, G2086, G2094, G2106a through
    - G2106d, G2121, G2449 & G2521; Romania 35361
cochleata - Belize M610; British Honduras 255; Cuba 2330; Dominica 1187;
    - Dominican Republic C349; Salvador 1135; Scotland {Staffa} 1982
    - Unlisted 25p; Saint Vincent 1366
cordigera - Guatemala C657; Saint Vincent 1366
fragrans - Suriname 431
fucata - Cuba 2332 & 2662
gracilis - Turks & Caicos Islands 793

## ENCYCLIA {Continued}

hodgeana - Bahamas 638
lleidae - Bahamas 639
lucayana - Bahamas 637
microcharis - Salvador 1138
phoenicea - Cuba 2333
plicata - Cayman Islands 537
rufa - Turks & Caicos Islands 797
spondiadum - Costa Rica C616
truncata - Dominican Republic C351
vagans - Salvador C377
vitellina - Guyana 402 & G1972; Salvador C377

## EPHEMERANTHA

comata - British Solomon Islands 242; New Hebrides 172 & 191; Russia Postcard 1969;
   - Solomon Islands 306 & 450

## EPIDENDRUM

   - Cuba 3160a; Dominica 700; Ecuador C510a; Fujeria M785
anceps - Suriname 745
brittonianum - British Virgin Islands 588
ciliare - Barbados 350, 352a, 405, Aerogrames K6 & K7; Dominica 1188; Montserrat 556;
   - Nevis 8441, 08502, 8441a & 627; Saint Kitts 241;
   - Saint Vincent 803; Suriname 743
cubincola - Cuba 2631
difforme - Montserrat 555; Saint Kitts 395; Venezuela C797
elongatum - Saint Vincent 1363; Venezuela C1049
fragrans - Cuba 3157; Guyana 1991 New Issue $8.90; Nev's 628
ibaguense - Antigua 1286; Barbados 399; Barbuda 9033; Guyana 1991 New Issue $8.90;
   - Nevis 629; Suriname 430; Salvador C376; St. Vincent {Grenadines} 9034 & 9040
imatophyllum - Guatemala C658
latifolium - Nevis 630
lividum - Venezuela C801 & C885
mirabile - Costa Rica C621
nocturnum - Antigua 1292; Barbuda 9039; Guyana 1991 New Issue $15.30
peraltensis - Costa Rica 333
polyanthum - Belize 721
porpax - Suriname 668
prismatocarpum - Guyana 451, 526, G2058 & G2453
radicans - Russia Envelope 1973
rigidum - Guyana 1990 New Issue $10
secundum - Antigua 1287; Barbuda 9034; Ecuador C508; Saint Vincent 805
stamfordianum - Belize 549; Venezuela 809
stenopetalum - Suriname 428
strobiliferum - Nevis 632
truncatum - Haiti C355
vespa - Suriname 746

## EPIGENEINUM

lyonii - Philippines 1809

## EPIPACTIS

   - Norway 971a
atrorubens - Hungary 3092; Norway 971
helleborine - Oman State G360
palustris - Bulgaria 3141; Germany Berlin 9NB218; Luxembourg B305; Oman State G364;
   - Sweden 1419c
veratrifolia - Cyprus 568

## EPISTEPHIUM

parviflorum - Guyana 1991 New issue $100

## ERIA

pannea - North Vietnam M863

## ERIAXIS

rigida - New Caledonia C125

## EULOPHIA

abyssinica - Rwanda 783
alta - Central Africa 71
angolensis - Botswana 464; Rwanda 786
cucullata - Belgian Congo 283; Burundi 413, 420 & C173; Central Africa 67 & 830;
   - Congo 339; Ghana 923 & 926; Malawi 256; Rwanda 779; Sierra Leone 690, 691,
   - 692, 693 & 1087; Upper Volta 433; Zambia 280 & 283a
erthoplata - Central Africa 828 & 828a
fridericii - Venda M47
gigantea - Guyana 598 & 697
guineensis - Gambia 358, 689A, 927 & 1991 New Issue 20p; Sierra Leone 1084
hereroensis - Botswana 465
horsfallii - Central Africa 68; Gabon 178
petersii - Botswana 466
quartiniana - Malawi 333
speciosa - Botswana 466; Mozambique 594; South Africa 554; Uganda 751 & 842
streptopetala - Rwanda 780
tricristata - Malawi 335

## EULOPHIELLA

elizabethae - Malagasy C180
roempleriana - Malagasy 345 & 707

## EURYCHONE

galeandrae - Belgian Congo 268; Katanga M28; Ruanda-Urundi 119

## FLICKINGERIA

comata - Vanuatu 323 & 383

## GALENANDRA

devoniana - Guyana 1990 New Issue $10

## GASTORCHIS
humblotii - Guyana 395, 496, G1965, G2062 & G2393; Malagasy 344
tuberculosa - Guyana 480, 656 & G2428; Malagasy 708

## GAVILLEA
australis - Falkland Islands 1991 New issue 12p
littoralis - Falkland Islands 1991 New issue 62p
macroptera - Falkland Islands 179

## GLOMERA
montana - Samoa 639

## GONGORA
armeniaca - Costa Rica C627
claviodora - Costa Rica C614
portentosa - Peru 553
quinquenervis - Guyana 141, 141A, GF4, GF4a, GO13, G896a, G889, G889a G1083, G1241,
          - G1358, G1358a, G1359, G1359a & G1359; Monsterrat 660

## GOODYERA
macrophylla - Maderia 82 & 85a
repens - Hungary 2851

## GOVENIA
utriculata - Cuba 3151

## GRAMMANGIS
ellisii - Malagasy C181
fallax - Malagasy 911
spectabilis - Malagasy C182

## GRAMMATOPHYLLUM
speciosum - Singapore 64; Solomon Islands 634

## GYMNADENIA
conopsea - Oman State G361 & G366

## HABENARIA
- Malawi 258a
macrandra - Sierra Leone 1080
pauciflora - Dominica 1190
praestans - Rwanda 156
radiata - Japan Postcard 1984
rhodocheila - North Vietnam M858
splendens - Malawi 255
susannae - Hong Kong 344

## HELCIA
sanguinolenta - Ecuador C711

## HERSCHELIA
graminifolia - Lesotho 758

## HEXISEA
bidentata - Costa Rica C629, C715, C718; Nicaragua RA66, 1965 Unlisted, 843, 855, 859 901
bilamellata - Russia Envelope 1974

## HIMANTOGLOSSUM
hircinum - Germany DDR 1729; Hungary 3089

## HOLOTHRIX
- Malawi 117a
longiflora - Malawi 114

## HUNTLEYA
- Bolivia MB39
meleagris - Bolivia 560; Guyana 609, 692 & G2583

## HUTTRONAEA
pulchra - Lesotho 757

## IONOPSIS
- Suriname 562
utricularioides - Antigua 1291; Barbuda 9038; Guyana 1990 New issue $190;
             - Saint Vincent 804 & 1370; Suriname 460

## IPSEA
speciosa - Sri Lanka 497 & 498a

## JUMELLEA
recta - Mauritius 639

## KEGELIELLA
atropilosa - Nicaragua C844a

## LACAENA
- Guyana 1990 New issue $12.90

## LAELIA
- Brazil 968; Bulgaria Envelope 1990; Cuba 1193a & 3165a; Fujeria M857;
- Sharjah 1972 Unlisted
albida - Guyana 414, 493, G1937, G1937a, G2056, G2378, G2379 & G2435
anceps - Cuba 1193 & 3161; Grenada 1797; Kampuchea G933; Saint Vincent {Grenadines} 8524
anceps v. alba - Cuba 3162
anceps v. barkeriana - Guyana 443
anceps v. percivaliana - Guyana 659, 417 & G2439
anceps v. sanderiana - Guyana 424, G2117 & G2441

## LAELIA {Continued}

anceps v. schroderiana - Guayan 481, 495, G2385, G2424 & 1990 New Issue Se-tenant
anceps v. stella - Guyana 443
autumnalis v. alba - Guyana 562, 689 & G2432
autumnalis v. xanthotropis - Guyana 397, G1968 & G2027
cinnabarina - Brazil 1712
cripsa - Romania 3535i
euspatha - Belize 647; Guyana 377, G1933 & G1950
gouldiana - Belize 660; Equatorial Guinea M427; Guyana 382, G2243 & G2359a; Rwanda 388
grandis - Cuba 3152; Guyana 474, 647, 1989 Unlisted 4 SC & OP
harpophylla - Guyana 447, 541, G2123, G2126 & G2523
jongheana - Guyana 1990 New Issue $50
lobata - Brazil 2121
praestans - Guyana 491, 640, G1999, G2390, 1989 Unlisted 3 SC & OP, 1990 New Issue Se-tenant
pumila - Kampuchea G934
purpurata - Brazil 652 & 1792a; Guyana 559, 654 & G2576; Russia Envelope 1988;
        - Thomas & Prince 1991 New Issue SS/500d
purpurata v. werkhauserii - Brazil 1203
rubescens - Grenada 1803
species - Brabuda 8625; Nicaragua 1214, M2667 & M2757
tenebrosa - Brazil 1714

## LAELIOCATTLEYA

baehrensiana - Guyana 621, 671 & 1989 Unlisted 4 SC & OP
callistoglossa - Equatorial Guinea MB436; Rwanda 382
elegans - Belize 658; Guyana 374 & G1949; Hungary 1711
elegans v. bleheimensis - Guyana 492, 641, G2000, G2391 & 1990 New Issue Se-teant
Hon. Mrs. Astor - Guyana 592 & 702
Hybrid - Laos C79; Russia 3598
Katona Gyorgyi - Hungary Postcard 1989
Lykas - Tanzania 635
Maggie Raphaela v. alba - Germany DDR 1057
Mme. Chiang Kai-Shek - China Taiwan 1190
phoebe - Guyana E4 & 674
Prinicpie Negro - Panama MB70 & MB71
prism v. paiette - Cuba 2886
species - Laos 796a

## LAELIOPSIS

dominguensis - Haiti 636

## LIMODORUM

abortivum - Germany 3143

## LIPARIS

guineensis - Gambia 925
loeselii - Oman State G362

## LISTERA

cordata - Germany Berlin 9NB216
ovata - Oman State G365

## LUISIA

teretifolia - Samoa 753

## LYCASTE

Aquila - Tanzania 629
Auburn Ditchling - Jersey 444 & Aerograme A23
Auburn Seaford - Jersey 444
cochleata - British Honduras 228
cruenta - Costa Rica C625; Romania 3535e; Salvador C380
deppei - Czechoslovakia 1492
macrophylia - Nicaragua RA69, 1965 Unlisted, 846, 857, 862 & 904
reichenbachii - Peru C377
skinneri - Poland 1348; Salvador 794; Guyana 444
skinneri v. alba - Costa Rica C617 & C723; Guatemala C189, C190, C354, C418, C419, C420,
                - C559, C572, C571, C573, C661 & C794; Guyana 444 & 1990 New Issue $100;
                - Nicaragua C626
skinneri v. armeniaca - Guyana 502, 552, G1946, G2420, 1989 Unlisted SC & OP, 1990 New Issue Se-tenant

## LYPERANTHUS

gigas - New Caledonia 409

## MALAXIS

setipes - Palau 238
seychellarum - Seychelles 722

## MASDEVALLIA

amabilis - Peru C378
caudata - Guyana 433, 538, G1684, G2092, G2107, G2110, G2120, G2233, G2233a, G2448, G2520
caudata v. xanthocorys - Guyana 433, 538, G1684, G2092, G2107, G2110, G2120. G2233,
                - G2233a, G2448 & G2520
chimaera - Colombia 580
chimaera v. backhousiana - Belize 649; Guyana 400, G1969 & G2028
chimaera v. mooreana - Guyana 624 & 694
coccinea - Colombia C490; Saint Vincent {Grenadines} 9036
coccinea v. splendens - Guyana O1, 663, 1989 Unlisted SC & OP
courtauldiana - Guyana 611 & 686
ephippium - Costa Rica C615
geleniana - Guyana 611 & 686
measuresiana - Guyana 611 & 686
nycterina - Colombia 546 & 583
tovarensis - Venezuela 808

## MAXILLARIA

alba - Dominica 1191
albertii - Costa Rica C654
atrata - Salvador 1136
conferta - Antigua 1288; Barbuda 9035; Nevis 631
eburnea - Saint Thomas & Prince 1989 New Issue 50d
parkeri - Guyana 1991 New Issue $12.80
sanderiana - Equatorial Guinea MB437; Guyana 432, 540, G2108, G2111, G2122, G2522, 1990
                - Unlisted 2 SC & OP; Laos 640
setigera - Guyana 1990 New Issue $11.40

## MAXILLARIA {Continued}

species - Costa Rica 334; Grenada 666
striata - Ecuador C509
tenuifolia - British Honduras 209; Nicaragua RA70, 1965 Unlisted; 847 & 863; Salvador 1131
triloris - Bolivia C330, MB40 & MB44; Colombia 807

## MEIRACYLLIUM

trinasutum - Salvador 1133

## MENADENIUM

labiosum - Guyana 691 & 664

## MICROCOELIA

macrorhynchium - Central Africa 72 & 78

## MILTASSIA

hybrid - Burundi 416 & C169
species - Trinidad & Tobago 286

## MILTONIA

- Belgium B498 through B502; Paraguay M3455
blueana - Guyana 500, 642, G2001, G2392 & 1990 New Issue Se-tenant
Candida - Saint Vincent {Grenadines} 9033
endresii - Costa Rica C444
hybrid - Burundi 417 & C170; Great Britian FB27; Paraguay M3692
Melissa Baker - New Zealand 1988 Formula
spectabilis - Czechoslovakia 1490
spectabilis v. moreliana - Guyana 593 & 700

## MILTONIOPSIS

phalaenopsis - Guyana 610 & 670
roezii - Belize 600A; Costa Rica C619 & C725; Guyana 426, 521, G2033, G2045 & G2444
vexillaria - Colombia 547, 585 & C232; Cuba 3159; Guyana 489, 650 & G2485; Laos 641

## MORMODES

buccinator - Costa Rica C613
rolfeanum - Colombia C572

## MORMOLYCA

peruviana - Peru 555
ringens - Romania 3535f

## MYSTACIDIUM

brayboniae - Venda M49

## NEOFINETIA

falcata - Japan 1731; South Korea 1152

## NEOTINEA

intacta - Isle of Man 306a

## NEOTTIA

nidus-avis - Oman State G358

## NIGRITELLA

- Liechtenstein Postcard 1987
nigra - Sweden 1528
rubra v. miniata - Romania 2334

## OBERONIA

titania - Norfolk Island 337

## OCTOMERIA

erosilabia - Guyana 1990 New Issue $10
graminifolia - Antigua 1293; Barbuda 9040
surinamensis - Suriname 464

## ODONTIODA

Eric Young - Jersey 443
Hambuhren - Genadines 9022
Itaque - Colombia C635
Mt. Bingham - Jersey 347

## ODONTOCIDIUM

Crowgborough v. Plush - Tanzania 632
Tigersum - Grenadines 9021

## ODONTOGLOSSUM

- Aitutaki 262a, 263a, 263b, 268a, 269a & 270a; Ajman M431A; Antigua 664, 673, 799, 800,
- Barbados 587; Barbuda 8215 & 8218; Bhutan 333, 362, 458 & 479; Cayman Islands 488;
- Central Africa C253, C253a, MB191, C274, 8203, 8203a, 648 & 648a; Chad 515b;
- Colombia 900j; Cook Islands 677A, 678A, 681A, 682A, 834, 836 & 983; Dominica 775 & 784;
- Falkland Dependencies iL74; Falkland Islands 350; Fujeria M1333; Guinea 937; Guyana
- B35; Japan Postcard 1982; Lesotho 374; Manama 1972 Unlisted 1R; Mauritius 550; Monaco
- 1047; North Korea M2175, M2176, 1982 Unlisted 2 OP, GN2229 & MB131; Paraguay M3459,
- M3462, MB3461 & MB3466; Saint Helena 374; Saint Lucia 593; Sierra Leone 1256; Swaziland
- 408; Tonga 488 & B1; Turks & Caicos 532; Upper Volta C276
blandum - Guyana 459, 512, G1864, G1865, G1931, G1961, G2019, G2047, G2344, G2527 & G2529
cervantesii v. decorum - Guyana 677, 612b, 613a, 614d, 615c, 706d, 707c, 708a, 709b & 685
chiriquense - Costa Rica C450; Guyana E3 & 667
cirrhosum - Ecuador 936
constictum - Guyana 467, 525, G2037, G2407, G2345 & G2484
coradinei - Guyana 472, G2383, 1988 Unlisted value & 1990 New Issue Se-tenant
crispum - Colombia 549 & 581; Guyana 420 & G2112
crispum v. hrubyanum - Guyana 430, G1537, G2088 & G2134
crispum v. kinlesideanum - Guyana 445, 544, G2124, G2128 & G2526
crispium v. mundyanum - Guyana 483, 651 & G2475
cristatum - Peru 554
edwardii - Guyana 448, G2137, G2258 & G2450

## ODONTOGLOSSUM {Continued}

excellens - Guyana 587 & 660
grande - Brazil 2124, Ghana 59 & 224; Guyana 460, 530, G1944, G2038, G2514 & G2528;
    - Poland 1346; Russia Envelopes 1974 & 1988; Togo 461
hallii - Ecuador 934
hallii v. xanthoglossum - Guyana 418 & G2114
harryanum - Guyana 393, 548, G1964, G1966, G1994, G2003, G2007, G2015, G2024, 1990 Unlisted SC & OP
hebraicum - Belize 652; Guyana 422, G2115 & G2440
hebraicum v. aspersum - 458, 523, G2100, G2035, G2406, G2343 & G2473
humeanum - 465, 516, G2011, G2052, G2260 & G2516
insleayi v. splendens - Guyana 396 & G1967
leroyanum - Guyana 586 & 661
luteo-purpureum - Colombia C361, C364, C367, C422 & C425; Guyana 457, G2098, G2342 & G2479; Laos 638
luteo-purpureum v. prionopetalum - Guyana 411, 507, G2044 & G2421
Moselle - Colombia C365
naevium - Guyana 485, 648, 1989 Unlisted 2 SC & OP
pescatorei - Guyana O6, 634 & 1989 Unlisted OP
ramosissimum - Guyana 556, 655 & G2581
reichenheimii - Guyana 387, 529, G2061 & G2374
rossii - Cuba 3160; Grenada 1799; Guyana 453, G1539a through G1539d, G2095 & G2105a
    - through 2105d; Russia Envelope 1981; Singapore 115 & 115a
Royal Sovereign - Kampuchea G930
schlieperianum - Costa Rica C447
St. Brelade v. Montmillais - Jersey 445
suberuciforme - Nicaragua C844a
triumphans - Guyana 385, 546, G1847, GE2, GE2a, G1953, G1956, G2055, G2055a, GE11, G2264,
    - G2362 & G2377
wattianum - Guyana 484, 646, G2102, G2409, G2410 & 1990 New Issue Se-tenant
wilckeanum v. rothschildianum - Guyana 501, 637, G2368 & 1990 New Issue Se-tenant

## ODONTONIA

- Togo 547
hybrid - Poland 1581
Sappho - Grenadines 9028

## OECEOCLADES

maculata - Gambia 921

## OEONIA

oncidiiflora - Malagasy 914

## ONCIDIODA

Crowborough - Tanzania 633

## ONCIDIUM

- Guatemala Postcard 1897; Guyana B33; Montserrat 557a; Romania 3535;
- Singapore 1990 Aerogram A45
altissimum - Antigua 1289; Barbuda 9036; Saint Vincent 806
ampliatum - Barbados 401; Trinidad & Tobago 287
ampliatum v. majus - Guyana 380 & G2358
ascendens - Nicaragua RA75, 1965 Unlisted, 852 & 868
bicolor - Venezuela C799

bifolium - Argentina 1348, 1443 & 1571; Uruguay C416
calochilum - Dominican Republic RA75; Haiti 638
carthagenense - Guyana 1990 New Issue $10
cebolleta - Nicaragua RA75, 1965 Unlisted, 852 & 868; Russia Envelope 1973
concolor - Guyana 429, G1538, G2089 & G2135
desertorum - Haiti C356
falcipetalum - Venezuela 811 & 872
flexuosum - Brazil 1792b
guibertianum - Cuba 612 & 633
haitiense - Haiti 637
incurvum - Peru C381
isthmi - Costa Rica C801
jonesianum - Guyana 456, G2097 & G2129
jonesianum v. phaeanthum - Guyana 456, G2097 & G2129
kramerianum - Costa Rica C631, C717, C720 & C728; Guyana O7, 632 & 1989 Unlisted OP
lanceanum - Dominica 1194; Grenada 1804; Guyana 139, G809, G023, G864, G977, G1009,
    - G1242, G1342, G1343 through G1348, 405, G2077, G2078, G2080, GB32, G1974,
    - G2273 & G2397; Montserrat 662; Romania 3535a; Suriname 427
leiboldii - Cuba 2329
loxense - Guyana 588, 680a & G2579
macranthum - Cuba 1190; Ecuador 602, 627, 670, 670a & 670b; Guyana 394, 547, G1981,
    - G1982, G1995, G2004, G2008, G2016, G2025, 1990 Unlisted SC & OP
nubigenum - Saint Thomas & Prince 8715
obryzatum - Costa Rica C626
oliganthum - Salvador C375
papilio - Dominica 339 & 340a; Suriname 667; Trinidad & Tobago 288; Venezuela 804
prionochilum - British Virgin Islands 401, 406 & 406a
pulchellum - Jamaica 377
pusillum - Dominica 1186; Suriname 462
sanderae - Peru 557
splendidium - Belize 654a; Grenada 1796; Guatemala C655; Guyana 449, 506, G1959, G2043 &
    - G2451; Romania 3535l
superbiens - Guyana 601 & 683
tigrinum - Guyana 415, 528, G2060 & G2436
tuerckheimii - Dominican Republic RA55
turialbae - Costa Rica 335
urophyllum - Montserrat 554
variegatum - Cayman Islands 290; Dominican Republic RA80; Montserrat 658
volvox - Venezuela C794
zebrinum - Venezuela C803 & C887

## OPHRYS

apifera - Belgium B1060; Kampuchea G932; Luxembourg B307
argolica - Cyprus 567
bertolonii - San Marino 1219
cornuta - Bulgaria 3142
fusca - Morocco 130
holosericea - Great Britian 1991 Booklet; Hungary 1393, 1397 & 2222; Liechtenstein 467;
    - Luxembourg B311; Turkey 2125
insectifera - Germany Berlin 9NB217; Luxembourg B303
kotschyi - Cyprus 565
lutea - Tunisia 1990 New Issue 600m
scolopax - Tunisia 772
scolopax v. cornuta - Hungary 3090

## OPHRYS {Continued}

speculum - Morocco 129
sphegodes - Luxembourg B316
tenthredinifera - Morocco 131

## ORCHIS

albanica - Albania 2285
anatolica - Turkey 2157
coriophora - Germany Berlin 9NB219; Germany DDR
graminifolia - Japan Postcards 1982 & 1987
italica - Hungary 3093
laxiflora - Guernsey 332; Israel 414; Jersey 63 & B13; Scotland {Grunay} Unlisted 10p
mascula - Iran G2518; Sweden 1419a
militaris - Germany DDR 1197
morio - Jugoslavia 476
paparisti - Albania 2284
papilionacea - Bulgaria 3145
punctulata - Cyprus 566
purpurea - Denmark 922; Hungary 3088
simia - Jugoslavia 1956
spectabilis - Saint Vincent {Grenadines} 9038; Scotland {Staffa} Unlisted 75p
tridentata - Gibraltar 340 & 340a
ustulata - Germany B624

## PAPHINIA

cristata - Guyana 140, G887, G1352, G1357, G1357b & 1990 New issue $26.70; Trinidad & Tobago 284
rugosa - Guyana E1 & 664

## PAPHIOPEDILUM

- Cuba 1188a; Czechoslavkia 905; Guyana 635a; Indonesia 1047b; Sharjah 1972 Unlisted 1R;
Albertianum - Germany DDR 1058
appletonianum - South Vietnam 491
argus - Guyana 463, 531, G2039, G2466 & G2480
Aureum - Germany Berlin 9N434
bellatulum - Bhutan 878
boxalli v. atratum - Guyana 476, 644, G2408 & 1990 New Issue Se-tenant
Bucolique - Cuba 1682
callosum - Thailand 482; Vietnam M1059
calypso - Guyana 600 & 696
castleanum - Guyana 479, 545, G2371, G2417 & 1990 New issue Se-tenant
Champollion - Cuba 1681
concolor - North Vietnam M864
Deirosi - Grenadines 9023
Doraeus - Cuba 1678
Euryiochus - Cuba 1179
exul - Cuba 1679; Laos 231
exul v. O'Brien - Cuba 1781
eyermannianum - Guyana 482, 653, G2097 & G2129

FC Puddle - Barbados 404
Geelong - Grenadines 9025
glaucophyllum - Cuba 1623
haynaldianum - Bhutan 886
hirsutissimum v. album - New Zealand 1988 Formula
hookerae v. volonteanum - Cuba 1186
hybrid - Bolivia 782; Hungary 1709, Postcards 1984, 1985, 1987 & 1988; Laos 796b, 796d &
   - 796e; Malagasy 495 & 498; Poland 1347 & 1351; Rwanda 384
hybridium v. youngianum - Guyana O15, 623 & 1989 Unlisted SC & OP
insigne - Belgium 484; Bhutan 877; Romania 1781
Io - Guyana 376 & G1936
lathamianum v. inversum - Guyana 488, 553, G2423, G2482 & 1990 New issue Se-tenant
laucheanum - Guyana 482, 653, G2477 & G2580
lawrenceanum v. hyeanum - Guyana O4, 662, 1989 Unlisted SC & OP
leeanum v. giganteum - Guyana 612d, 613c, 614b, 615a, 706b, 707a, 708c & 709d
lemoinierianum - Guyana 412, 517, G1978, G2012, G2053 & G2422
lowii - Indonesia 1045
Maudiae - Czechoslovakia 2322; Romania 3536b
maynardii - Guyana 596, O10 & 1989 Unlisted OP
Morganiae v. Burfordiense - Cuba 1184; Guyana 590, 659, 1989 Unlisted SC & OP
Mowgli - Cuba 1625
niveum - Bhutan 892; Guyana 442; Johore 171; Kedah 108; Kelantan 93; Malacca 69;
   - Negri Sembilan 78; Pahang 85; Penang 69; Perak 141; Perlis 42; Sabah 19;
   - Sarawak 230; Selangor 123; Trengganu 88
oenanthum v. superbum - Guyana 436 & G2445
philippinense - Philippines 1810 & 1941
pollettianum - Guyana 596, O10 & 1989 Unlisted OP
praestans - Equortial Guinea M433; Indonesia B149
Prince Rainer III - Monaco 1707
purpuratum - Hong Kong 343
Rosy Dawn - Cuba 1680
rothschildianum - Bhutan 875; Guyana 378 & G2356
sanderianum - Guyana 427 & G2084
selligerum v. majus - Guyana 388, 520, G2032, G2381 & G2404
siamenese - Vietnam 1989 Unlisted
Slipper - Saint Vincent {Grenadines} 9031
Solum - Cuba 1626
species - Nicaragua C964; Russia Postcard 1976
stonei v. cannartae - Cuba 1188
stonei v. platytaenium - Cuba 1191
Sullanum - Cuba 1683
tautzianum - Guyana 413, 513, G1598, GE1, G1693, G2021, G2049, G2221, G2221a, G2434, G2437 & G2530
venustum - Cuba 1622

## PENTHEA

filicornis - Lesotho 761

## PERISTERIA

- Guyana 1990 New issue $225
elata - Costa Rica C618 & C724; Panama C143, C227, C357, C357a & 523
cerina - Cuba 3165

## PESCATORIA

klabochorum - Guyana 591 & 701

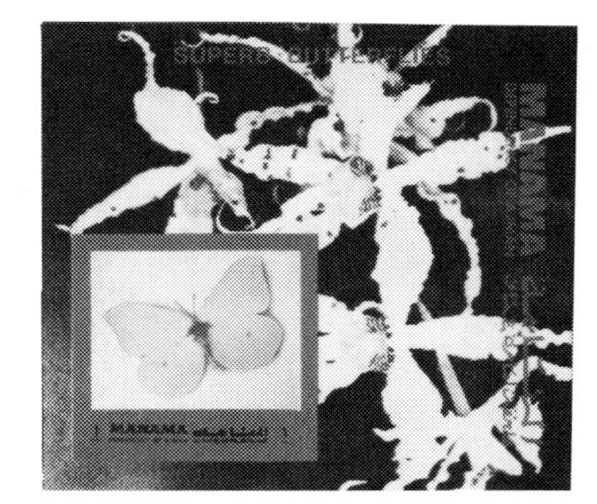

CZECHOSLOVAKIA 1082; SAN MARINO 397; COSTA RICA C621 & C623; BOLIVIA MB38; COLOMBIA C425; SRI LANKA 497; HUNGARY 2852; MALAGASY 840a; SAINT THOMAS & PRINCE 8212a; and MANAMA 1972 Unlisted.

## PHAIUS

amabilis - Guyana O2, 631, 1989 Unlisted SC & OP
cooksonii - Guyana 499, 638, G2366, G2367 & 1990 New Issue Se-tenant
daenikeri - New Caledonia 425
flavus - Samoa 751
marthae - Guyana O2, 631, 1989 Unlisted SC & OP
sinensis - China Taiwan 1092 & 1095a
tankervilleae - Ceylon 314, 314a & 351; Fiji 310; Macau 375; South Molucass Unlisted 1954
       - & 1979; Sri Lanka 631 & 631a
tankervilleae v. assamica - Guyana O17, 620, 1989 Unlisted SC & OP
tetragonus - Zil Eloigne Sesel 8611

## PHALAENOPSIS

- Antigua 867 & 866A; Barbuda 8560 & 8559A; Dominica 906; Guyana B34 & B35;
- Hungary Postcards 1986 & (2 types) 1990; Indonesia 475; Manama M800; Monaco 1085;
- Niue 329, 330, 332, 333, 334, O14, C16, O19 & 594; Solomon Islands 478, 480a & B5
amabilis - Bhutan 885; Guyana 419 & G2113; Indonesia B147; North Boreno 286;
      - North Korea M2484; Romania 3536h; Sabah 7; Vietnam M1355
aphrodite - China Taiwan 1189; Japan 1840; Philippines 851
cornu-cervi - Bhutan 891
Elisa v. Chang Lou 9036
equestris - Bhutan 889
gigantea - Indonesia 1047 & 1047a
hybrid - Saint Vincent (Grenadines) 9040
intermedia v. portei - Guyana 597, O12 & 1989 Unlisted SC & OP
leuchorrhoda - Guyana 450, 524, G1977, G2036, G2036a, G2452, G2474 & G2478
Lipperose - Tanzania 628
Lippstick v. Malibu - Belgium 1188
lueddemmanniana - Romania 3536e
margil v. Moses - Cuba 2883
mariae - Bhutan 881
Princesse Grace - Monaco 1190 & 1706
sanderiana - Guyana 597, O12, 1989 Unlisted SC & OP; Papua 314
schilleriana - Bhutan 876; Cuba 1783; Russia Aerograme 1971
schilleriana v. Sunset Glow - Barbados 407 & 406B
species - Niue 305, 306, 417 & O1
speciosa - Guyana 379 & G1934
Sri Rejeki - Indonesia 1036
stuartiana - Guyana 446, 542, G1657, G1993, G2125, G2127 & G2524
violacea - Bhutan 872; Cuba 2885; Indonesia 1011; Johore 175; Kedah 112; Kelantan 97;
      - Malacca 73; Negri Sembilan 82; Panang 89; Penang 73; Perka 145; Perlis 46;
      - Sabah 23; Sarawak 234; Selangor 127; Trengganu 92

## PHRAGMIPEDIUM

- Colombia C805; Seychelles 527a
caudatum v. lindenii - Ecuador 930
grande - Guyana 616 & 705
niticissimum - Guyana 475, 554, G2402, G2425 & 1990 New Issue Se-tenant
schlimii - Romania 3535g
weidlichianum - Guyana 589 & 669

## PHREATIA

crassiuscula - Norfolk Islands 325

## PLATANHERA

bifolia - Poland 1067; Sweden 782, 786a & 786b
micrantha - Azores 327 & 328a
species - Russia Envelope 1969

## PLATYCORYNE

crocea - Burundi 411, 418 & C171

## PLECTRELMINTHUS

caudatus - Gambia 926; Guyana 423, G2132, G2256 & G2443; Liberia 352

## PLEIONE

hookeriana - Bhutan M133, M137, M362 & 434
pricei - Romania 3536i

## PLEUROTHALLIS

diffusa - Guyana 1990 New Issue $10
johnsoni - Costa Rica C656
schiedei - Salvador C379

## PODANGIS

dactyloceras - Ghana 1991 New Issue 3c

## POLYSTACHYA

affinis - Central Africa 70; Gambia 922
concreta - Seychelles 699
cucullata - Ivory Coast 187
dendrobiiflora - Malawi 339
galeata - Ghana 1991 New Issues 80p
kermesiana - Rwanda 692 & 808
luteola - Dominica 1085
pubescens - Lesotho 760
vulcanica - Uganda 754 & 843

## PONTHIEVA

maculata - Salvador 1132

## PORROGLOSSUM

peruvianum - Peru C380

## POTINARA

Medea - Japan Postcard 1982

## PROMEMAE

xanthina - Guyana E1 & 664

## PTEROSTYLIS
banksii - New Zealand 986d, Envelopes 1988 & 1989

## RANGERIS
musicola - Ghana 1991 New issue 5c

## RENANTHERA
monachica - Bhutan 870
storiei - Barbados 397; Ivory Coast MD532 & 497

## RHYNCHOSTYLIS
coelestis - Guyana 470, G2363, 1988 Unlisted value, G2430, 1990 Unlisted Se-tenant
gigantea - Belize 654; Guyana 391, 510, G1619a through G1619d, G1940, G1941, G1989,
  - G1997, G2006, G2018, G2023, G2232a through G2232d, G2388 & G2531a through
  - G2531d; Laos 230; South Vietnam 490; Vietnam M1056 & M1360
gigantea v. Sagarik - Thailand 480
retusa - Johore 174; Kedah 111; Kelantan 96; Malacca 72; Malaysia Envelope 1964;
  - Negri Sembilan 81; Pahang 88; Penang 72; Perak 144; Perlis 45; Sabah 22;
  - Sarawak 233; Selangor 126; Thailand 479; Trengganu 91

## RHYNCOVANDA
hybrid - Singapore 319

## ROBIQUETIA
mimus - Vanuatus 329

## RODRIGUEZIA
- Guyana 1990 New Issue $22.95
candida - Suriname 520
decorata - Suriname 666
lanceolata - Antigua 1294; Barbuda 9041; Nevis 634
secunda - Suriname 461

## ROSSIOGLOSSUM
grande - Saint Vincent (Grenadines) 9035

## SACCOLABIUM
archytas - Christmas Islands 276
archytas v. ridley - Christmas Islands 77 & 275

## SATYRIM
princeps - Lesotho 756

## SCHOMBURGKIA
- Barbados 400a
humboldtii - Barbados 400
sanderiana - Guyana 016, 622 & 1989 Unlisted OP
thomsoniana - Cayman Islands 155, 288, 471 & 536
thomsoniana v. minor - Cayman Islands 535

---

tibicinis - British Honduras 208; Nicaragua RA67, 1965 Unlisted, 844, 856, 860 & 902
undulata - Venezuela C802 & C886

## SCUTICARIA
- Ecuador C714
hadwernii - Guyana 1990 New Issues $17.80, $12.80 & 1991 New Issue $20
salesiana - Ecuador C710
steelii - Guyana 142, GF5, G811a, G839, G919, G1090, G1247, G1247a, G1248, G1252, G1253,
  - G1513 & G1608; Suriname 522

## SELENIPEDIUM
palmifolium - Dominica 1192; Grenadines 8427 & 8430

## SIEVEKINGIA
suavis - Costa Rica C628

## SIGMATOSTALIX
peruviana - Peru C379

## SOBENNIKOFFIA
robusta - Malagasy 910

## SOBRALIA
- Scotland (Eynhallow) Unlisted 2L
amabilis - Costa Rica Aerogrames 1980 & 1983
macrantha - Belize 718; Bolivia 462; British Honduras 211; Germany DDR 1061; Grenada 1802;
  - Nicaragua 1219, Postcard 1984, M2656 & M2746; Paraguay 699 through 703; Romania 3536j
macrantha v. splendens - Costa Rica C624
macrophylla - Poland 1352
panamensis - Panama C354 & C354a
pleiantha - Nicaragua RA74, 1965 Unlisted, 851, 867 & 908
sessilis - France 1192; Suriname 463
species - Ecuador 1254; Laos 796c
xantholeuca - Guatemala C653; Guyana 401 & G1971; Salvador 1137

## SOPHROLAELIOCATTLEYA
Phena v. Satum - Tanzania 634
Riffe Burlingame - Belgium 1189

## SOPHRONITIS
cernua - Romania 3535c
coccinea - Romania 3536c; Russia Aerograme 1973
grandiflora - Colombia C611; Scotland (Staffa) 1982 Unlisted 2L
species - Guyana 329, G1390, G1646, G1897 & G2247

## SPATHOGLOTTIS
aurea v. The Gold - Barbados 404C
kimballiana - Guyana 563 & 690
pacifica - Wallis & Fununa islands 285
petri - New Hebrides 173 & 192

## SPATHOGLOTTIS {Continued}

plicata - British Solomon Islands 241; Johore 172; Kedah 109; Kelantan 94; Malacca 70;
    - Maldives 1238 & 1446; Negri Sembilan 79; Pahang 86; Penang 70; Perak 142;
    - Perlis 43; Sabah 20; Samoa 640; Sarwak 231; Selangor 124; Solomon Islands
    - 305, 450 & 599; South Molucass 1954 Unlisted 7.5k; Trengganu 89; Vanuatu 331
pubescens - Hong Kong 342

## SPIRANTHES

lanceolata - Antigua 1290; Barbuda 9037
orchiodes - Guyana 1990 New Issue $10
species - Oman State G359
speciosa - Guatemala C660; Salvador C381

## STANHOPEA

- Bolivia MB38
cirrhata - Costa Rica C445
ecornuta - Costa Rica 337; Nicaragua RA68, 1965 Unlisted, 845, 861 & 903
grandiflora - Bolivia C328, 704 & MB148; Suriname 521
shuttleworthii - Belize 647a; Guyana 441
tigrina - Kampuchea G935; Romania 1780
tigrina v. wardii - Colombia C365, C370 & C423
wardii - Venezuela 806

## STENIA

pallida - Guyana 1990 New Issue $10

## STENOGLOTTIS

longifolia - Lesotho 764

## TAENIOPHYLLUM

species - Indonesia 1010

## TETRAMICRA

canaliculata - Anguilla 282, 404, 410 & 414
elegans - Haiti C354

## THELYMITRA

aristata - Australia 196; Maldives 1063
pauciflora - Burundi 415 & C168
pulchella - New Zealand 986a
venosa - Nanumaga 8516; New Zealand 705
veriegata - Australia 1000
villosa - Hutt River 1979 Unlisted 15c

## THUNIA

alba - Bhutan 222
bracteata - North Korea M2483
brymeriana - Guyana 561, 687 & G2483

## TRICHOCENTRUM

pulchrum - Peru 556

## TRICHOGLOTTIS

fasciata - Laos 218; Thailand 845

## TRICHOPILIA

marginata - Costa Rica 336
suavis - Costa Rica C446
suavis v. alba - Belize 651; Guyana 399, G1970 & G2029

## TRIDACTYLE

bicaudata - Central Africa 69; Malawi 331
tridactylites - Gambia 919

## VANDA

- Manama 1972 Unlisted 1.5R; Philippines 360, C35 & C51; Ross Dependencies L19;
- Samoa 344; Singapore 335; Sri Lanka 725a; Thailand 717a, 1107 & 1160a
alpina - Bhutan 888
Bank of Ceylon - Sri Lanka 923
coerulea - Belgium 1187; Bhutan 229 & 871; Guyana 404, G1973, G2395 & G2396; Nanumaga
    - 8512; Monaco 1441; Russia 3924, 3929, Envelopes 1972 & 1973; Seychelles 663; Thailand 714
coeruiescens - Bhutan 882
cristata - Bhutan 890
denisoniana - Thailand 748
genta v. Pride O'Lanka - Indonesia 946
Gilbert Tribulet - Cuba 1784
hookeriana - Guyana 461, 535, G2103, G1984, G2064, G2415 & G2454; Johore 169; Kedah 106;
    - Kelantan 91; Malacca 67; Negri Sembilan 76; Pahang 83; Penang 67; Perak 139;
    - Perlis 40; Sabah 17; Sarawak 228; Selangor 121; Trengganu 86
hybrid - Cuba 1621; Singapore 320, 321 & 322
Josephine - Ivory Coast 496
Josephine Black - Barbados 411
limbata - Indonesia 1046
memorian v. Soysa Ernest - Sri Lanka 722
Miss Joaquim - Niue 131; Singapore 65, Aerogrmes A13, A14, A14, A15, A36, A37, A38, A39 & 1991 New Issue
Miss Joaquim v. Rose Marie - Cuba 1782
pumila - Russia Envelope 1971
Putri-serang - Indonesia 979
sanderiana - Guyana 439, G2513; Philippines 850, 931, 932, 933, 1188, 2036; Poland 1350
species - French Polynesia 300; Jamaica 500 & B3; Wallis & Futuna Islands 392
Tan Chay Yan - Singapore 63
teres - Cook Islands 266; Equatorial Guinea M430; Guyana 416 & G2438; Laos C89 & 796;
    - New Caledonia C136; North Vietnam M426; Penrhyn 216, 218, 220, 222, 343 & 344; Vietnam M1060
teres v. alba - Malaysia 4 & 5
teres v. gigantea - Thailand 747
teres v. hookeriana - Palau 241
tessellata v. rufescens - Sri Lanka 724
tricolor - Cuba 1624 & Postcard 1978; Great Britian FB29; Indonesia B146; Laos 796g;
    - Saint Thomas & Prince 1989 New Issue 100d
tricolor v. suavis - Bolivia 460
varavuth - Thailand 1157 & 1157a
Yellow Queen - Vietnam M1431

## VANDOPSIS

gigantea - North Vietnam M429
lissochiloides - Bhutan 874; Romania 3536d; Timor 260
parishii - Bhutan 883; Thailand 477
parishii v. mariottianum - Guyana 606 & 704

## VANILLA

- Belgium Postcards 1940 {2 types}, 1954 {4 types}; Denmark Booklet 1953; France
- Lettercards 1888 {2 types}, Booklets 1920, 1921 & 1922; Germany Lettercard 1920;
- Seychelles 283a; Switzerland Postcards 1880 & 1881; United States Postcard 1890;
- Envelopes 1904, 1906, 1910 & 1914, Postcards 1914 {2 types}
barbella - Russia Envelope 1979
Beans Drying - Dominica 129, 139 & 149
claviculata - Cayman Islands 289
humblotii - Seychelles 391, 391A & 391a; Zil Eloigne Sesel M397 & M397ii
imperialis - Gambia 920; Uganda 753 & 785
indora - Guyana 1991 New issue $7.65
mexicana - Antigua 1285; Barbuda 9032
phalaenopsis - Seychelles 281 & 697
planifolia - Belize 720; British Indian Ocean Terr. 2; Comoro Islands 80 & J16; Comoro
         - State MB69; Grenada 665; Guadeloupe 54 through 62, B1, B2, Lettercards 1906
         - {2 types}, Postcards 1906 {2 types}; Madagascar 299 & 299a; Malagasy 348 &
         - 840a; Mexico C633; Montserrat 659; Nicaragua M2590; Reunion J6 through J25,
         - 224 through 247; Seychelles 199 & 721
planifolia v. jackson - Saint Vincent 1371
polylepsis - Malawi 327
species - Colombia RA37
tahitiensis - French Polynesia 530 & 531
vine - Colombia 555, 567 & 610

## VUYLSTEKEARA

Cambria v. Plush - Tanzania 630
Monica v. Burnham - Tanzania 631
Rutilant - Colombia C635
Yokara - Grenadines 9024

## WILSONARA

Tigerwood - Grenadines 9026

## WORDS

- China Taiwan 1881, 2686 & Aerograme 1978; Switzerland Postcards 1929 & 1932

## ZYGOPTEALUM

- Bolivia MB39; Guyana 1990 New issue $190
bolivianum - Bolivia 559
citrinum - Brazil 1713; Guyana 618 & 703
intermedium - Guyana 435 & G2090

# NOTES